THE ROLE OF NAVAL FORCES
IN
21st-CENTURY OPERATIONS

Other Notable Naval Titles From Brassey's

Crossed Currents: Navy Women in a Century of Change, 3rd Edition
  —Jean Ebbert and Marie-Beth Hall

CVX: A Smart Carrier for the New Era
  —Jacquelyn K. Davis

Forged in War: The Naval-Industrial Complex and American Submarine Construction, 1940–1961
  —Gary E. Weir

Hunters in the Shallows: A History of the PT Boat
  —Curtis L. Nelson

Revolt of the Admirals: The Fight for Naval Aviation, 1945–50
  —Jeffrey G. Barlow

Theodore Roosevelt and the Great White Fleet: American Sea Power Comes of Age
  —Kenneth Wimmel

War in the Boats: My WWII Submarine Battles
  —William J. Ruhe

THE ROLE OF NAVAL FORCES
IN
21st-CENTURY OPERATIONS

Edited by
Richard H. Shultz Jr.
Robert L. Pfaltzgraff Jr.

BRASSEY'S
WASHINGTON, D.C.

Library of Congress Cataloging-in-Publication Data

The role of naval forces in 21st-century operations / edited by Richard H.
Shultz, Jr., Robert L. Pfaltzgraff, Jr.— 1st ed.
    p. cm.
  Includes bibliographical references and index.
  ISBN 1-57488-256-2 (alk. paper)
    1. United States. Navy—Forecasting. 2. Navies—Forecasting.
3. Operational art (Military science) 4. Unified operations (Military
science) 5. Combined operations (Military science) I. Shultz, Richard
H., 1947- II. Pfaltzgraff, Robert L.

VA50.R745 2000
359'.00973'0112—dc21   99–086769

ISBN 1-57488-256-2   (alk.paper)

Printed in Canada on acid-free paper that meets the American
National Standards Institute Z39-48 Standard.

Brassey's
22841 Quicksilver Drive
Dulles, Virginia 20166

First Edition

10 9 8 7 6 5 4 3 2 1

Part II
Dimensions of the Twenty-First-Century Security Environment

Part III
New Missions—New Strategies

CONTENTS

Part IV
Modernization/Innovation/Societal Challenges

PREFACE

The international security environment of the 1990s has been marked by great uncertainty and dramatic changes. These developments have, in turn, had a major impact on how we think about and understand the most basic security and defense concepts and issues. Many of the international security principles that were conceptualized during the cold war no longer hold true in this new and evolving environment. For example, what will instability, conflict, and war look like in the twenty-first century? During the cold war, the dimensions of conflict were clearer. What about today and in the future? In the foreword that follows, the 31st commandant of the Marine Corps, General Charles C. Krulak, now retired, proposes that "warfare is changing," and that it is doing so in some rather striking ways. Several of the authors in this volume explore this fundamental question and find much to agree with in the commandant's assertion.

If warfare is changing, how does this affect the doctrine and force structure of the U.S. military? Krulak argues that it will mean "Our response has got to change." What are the implications of this for the Navy and Marine Corps? How will it affect their existing roles and missions? Will they have to undergo significant change? How will it change doctrine and force structure? These and related fundamental questions are likewise addressed by several of the authors of this volume.

On November 19 and 20, 1997, the International Security Studies Program of The Fletcher School of Law and Diplomacy, in association with the Institute for Foreign Policy Analysis, the Office of the Commandant of the United States Marine Corps, and the Office of the Chief of Naval Operations convened a major conference entitled "The Role of Naval Forces in Twenty-First-Century Operations." This meeting brought together a large group of participants drawn from the military and civilian policy communities, primarily from the United States but also from abroad. Planned with the active support, interest, and participation of the senior leadership of the Navy and the Marine Corps, this conference was based on the need to address as fully as possible the major sources and dimensions of future conflict with the realization that the growing complexity and changing nature of conflict presents significant challenges for naval forces in the twenty-first century.

This volume, which provides key papers delivered at the conference, examines four major themes: symmetrical and asymmetrical warfare in the twenty-first century; the dimensions of the twenty-first-century security environment; new missions and strategies for naval forces; and modernization, innovation, and societal challenges. Within and outside the Navy and Marine Corps, there is a need to address a number of critical issues arising from each of these thematic areas. Based on conference papers, as well as the discussions that followed such presentations, the chapters contained in this volume examine in detail many of these issues, and this book has been published to provide for the broader dissemination of these issues.

The preparation of this volume and the conference of which it is a product were made possible only as a result of extensive support from each of the cosponsoring organizations. All phases of planning for the conference had the active support and direct engagement of the senior leadership of the Navy and the Marine Corps. Throughout the conference planning process, constructive contributions were made by Colonel Bob Work and Lieutenant Colonel Vic Dutil of General Krulak's staff and by Commander Frank Pandolfe from the staff of the chief of Naval Operations. Dr. Jacquelyn K. Davis, executive vice president of the Institute for Foreign Policy Analysis, made indispensable contributions to the conference conceptualization and the overall planning process. The extensive correspondence and other communications, without which the conference could not have been convened, were handled with great efficiency by Roberta Breen of the International Security Studies Program and Polly Jordan of the Institute for Foreign Policy Analysis. Lieutenant Colonel Stephen Wright, U.S. Air Force National Defense Fellow assigned to the International Security Studies Program for the 1997–98 academic year, contributed greatly to planning that helped ensure the high quality of the meeting, providing ample evidence of the reality of "jointness" among our military services. In the conference itself and for assistance in the editorial process leading to publication of this volume, Rhoda Margesson, research and program coordinator of the International Security Studies Program, and Daniele Riggio, of The Fletcher School, together with Polly Jordan, of the Institute for Foreign Policy Analysis, played indispensable roles. Last but not least, special thanks are owed to Freda Kilgallen, program administrator, who in this conference, as in other programmatic activities of the International Security Studies Program, provided outstanding support and continuing evidence that logistics are at least as important as strategy in conferences no less than in military operations.

Richard H. Shultz Jr.
Robert L. Pfaltzgraff Jr.

FOREWORD

NE CRAS: NOT LIKE YESTERDAY

Charles C. Krulak

In A.D. 9, a Roman proconsul by the name of Quinctilius Varus took three legions and crossed the Germanic border to bring recalcitrant tribes under Roman control. The legions marched in three columns; at the head of those three columns was the Roman Eagle, the signature of the power of Rome. This was the second time in three years that Varus had crossed the same border to put down these same barbarian tribes. Three years before, he had decimated them and sent twenty thousand men, women, and children back to Rome as slaves. And he thought that this outing would be no different.

On a hot August morning, the two warring factions collided at the battle of the Teutoburg Forest, which is where the city of Minden is currently located. At the end of the day, as nightfall approached, Varus was fighting a desperate rearguard action and trying to save what remained of his legions. He had lost, in less than twelve hours, all three eagles. And, as he was walking and fighting his way back across the Germanic border, he had his head down and he could be heard to mutter: "Ne Cras, Ne Cras," or "Not like yesterday, not like yesterday."

And in our vernacular it was not like yesterday, because the Germans had learned from the past. Three years earlier, they had seen and experienced the technology of Rome and what that technology could do. You say, What technology? The technology of the heavy cavalry and the archers. And so, the barbarians lured the heavy cavalry into the marshes and into the swamps, where their shock power, mobility, and agility were negated. They pulled the archers into the woods, where the trees and the limbs and the leaves negated the flight of the arrow. And, what was left was the light infantry, which, without the cavalry's supporting arms, was destroyed. And, the fact of the matter is that three days later Varus's head was found on a German war pike surrounded by those three eagles.

The point here is that, hemmed in by the forest and marshes, the column was exterminated almost to a man by the very enemy it had always slaughtered like cattle and whose life or death had depended solely on the wrath or the pity of the Romans. And on hearing the news, Augustus Caesar, who was over seventy at the time, did what Marines cannot abide. He stopped cutting his hair and let his beard grow. And he could be heard around the palace, bashing his head against the doorframe, saying: "Quinctilius Varus, give me back my legions. Give me back my legions."

Varus believed that nothing would change, that past successes would rule the future. Our view of warfare is also colored by past successes. Specifically, the largest success we ever had, which was World War II, was fought in a methodical and industrial manner, stressing clear lines of authority and action against a well-defined opponent. Strategic, operational, and tactical levels of war were clear and separate. Most of us, when we think about World War II and about these points, immediately jump to the Pacific campaign, which is the only campaign that we, as a nation, controlled.

The levels of war were discrete; Roosevelt had control of the strategic level. Admiral Chester Nimitz and General Douglas MacArthur worked largely at the operational level sequentially. That operational level was neatly tied to the strategic and the tactical levels. At the tactical level, there is no question that there were set-piece battles and a symmetrical enemy. There was no real linkage. What that young Marine sailor, soldier, or airman did on the ground, under the sea, or in the air, really did not have much of a strategic impact. It was tactical. This was massive combat power, attrition warfare, in an industrial age at its very best.

One of the reasons we embrace the Desert Storm model, instead, for example, of the Vietnam model, is because that model is so comfortable. It looks like the last good war. Clear aims, well-defined means, well-defined threat, attrition warfare, coalitions, massed armies, massed corps. It looks like nothing was different. Or maybe there was a difference. In Desert Storm there was. And that difference is a result of technology, which altered the battlefield dimensions in time and in space.

And what happened, and what is happening, is that the levels of war are beginning to merge. Operational depth expands. Deep, close, and rear battles became seamless. You had the CINC, and he was running the show. He had the capability to strike at any time on his timetable. And he had the kind of knowledge that he needed to fight the continuous battle. It was a multidimensional envelopment. From the standpoint of Saddam Hussein, all the levels were operating at one time—strategic, operational, and tactical—he was having to deal with them all at one time. And not only was he dealing with all at one time, but he also was having his mind fooled with through the destruction of his ability to command and control.

And, in his view, it was multidimensional attack that he was facing. And, in fact, maneuver began to become something of importance to us. In this view, it was important; but it still was attrition warfare. How it got there was through this idea of maneuver.

Perhaps we believe we have a new strategic legacy: post–Desert Storm. If you take a look at weapons range and lethality, some people argue that they are three times that of World War II. Proliferation of real-time C4I squared. I can remember getting a radio transmission from Walt Boomer, who said: "As long as this war lasts, I want to talk to all my commanders and I want to talk to them at these particular times, every four hours." And, sure enough, we got on the radio every four hours and all the Marine commanding generals talked to each other. I could not talk across a rice paddy dike in Vietnam. And here I am today, having this discussion with Marines and units hundreds of miles away. There were some very interesting things happening at that time, including the potential use of weapons of mass destruction. The bottom line is, they have used it before—they being an enemy. There is a growing realization that the levels of war are merging. I do not think there is any question this is one of the legacies. There is also a sense that it will not happen this way again because of the overwhelming U.S. success in the Gulf War. Yet today we are talking about some sandlot strongman pulling Uncle Sam's beard and inviting us to a rematch of Desert Storm. Nothing that we are doing translates to it will not happen again. Our doctrine, most of our training, and our weapons procurement, are all oriented toward our legacy.

What is going to happen in the future? The character of warfare is changing. Consider a number of images. First, a ship on fire. Now it could be on fire because it hit a mine; it could be on fire because it has been sabotaged. It could be on fire because it was hit by an antiship missile, or the fire could signify piracy. But, it is all going to happen. A tank is an example of major theater war. In noncombatant evacuation situations, gas masks reveal that the threat is other than just bullets. Information warfare can be very, very dangerous. Another area of concern is the environment. The environment is going to play an important role in the future. It will be used as a weapon against us. And yet we are not even thinking about that possibility. One of the main issues that we need to grasp is—where does the military play in all of these contingency plans? It is a big mistake to think the military can simply put a line in the sand and define its responsibilities in one area and not in another.

Our current view is no longer adequate for many reasons. First and foremost, it does not consider the shift in economic power, and this is of primary importance because we will go to war to maintain our economic health. Former Secretary of State Warren Christopher said that our economic health is in Asia, our hearts are in Europe. And yet, the fact of the matter is that by the year 2020, our trade with Asia may double that with Europe.

Consider the demographics. Sixty percent of the world's population will be found in Asia. A total of 70 percent of the world's population will be found in cities within 300 miles of the ocean. This population will be found in urban slums and cities, all within 300 miles of a coastline. There will be no boundaries. It will be transnational. People will be flocking to cities that have absolutely no infrastructure to solve their problems and to make them healthy.

The rise of nonstate actors is not the main crisis that we have to worry about. It is chaos. It contrasts sharply with the good old days of crisis, where there were state actors and one could pick up the phone and talk to somebody. In the world I am describing there is no one that is going to answer the phone. This will be asymmetric warfare, driven by the CNN effect. The days when one could put 40,000 short tons of ammunition on the pier at the port of Al Jubayl are over. Now, your ammunition will be blown up.

The enemy is going to think of ways to negate your technological advantage and, at the same time, bolster its capabilities. When combined with all the high tech and weapons of mass destruction, this presents a real problem. One thing that is not going to change is geography, which means that the role of naval forces in the future is going to be critical. Why? Because of freedom of movement without the worry of basing rights and access.

Why is all of this important? Because there are a lot of people in cities. Why? We must look to Varus. His are the forces of the twentieth century. Hemmed in by forest and marshes, the column was exterminated almost to a man by the very enemy who had always been slaughtered liked cattle. This is the new force of the twenty-first century—the Urban Warrior. It is not where you want to fight that counts; it is where you have to fight that you need to understand. Take a look at CNN since Desert Storm. When was the last time you saw any kind of conflict happening anywhere but a city? Or the urban slum. This is dangerous, and it is the new battlefield.

What are we doing about it? Before we start developing systems and before we develop our requirements, we have to understand more about the fights we may find ourselves in. Before we build the future Marine, male or female, we need to know what we are building that Marine for. And what we have got to be worried about is what I call the three-block war. The three-block war is very simple. At one time a young Marine, male or female, can be wrapping a child in swaddling clothes, feeding it, and comforting it, and it is called humanitarian assistance. A short while later, that same Marine can have his arms spread apart. He is armed and it is called peacekeeping. Then, in the next moment, that same Marine is in one hell of a fight against a very tenacious and ferocious warrior who is armed to the teeth with extremely lethal weapons, and that is called combat. The point is, this all happens in the same day, within three city blocks.

How do you build that Marine? Transformation is what we are calling it; it is building a Marine to fight the three-block war. There is no other reason. If the spin-off is that we have men and women of character and we send them back at the end of their enlistment better for having been Marines, that is what we want. But, the bottom line is to fight and win the three-block war.

Warfare is changing. Our response has got to change. I see a multidimensional chess board that requires us to concentrate not just on the capital pieces, but also on the pawns. And, the pawns here exist on two levels. The pawns are obviously the sandlot strongman, whom we do not specifically know, but who must be watched. The capital pieces are China, Iran, and Iraq. With these, we have to stop worrying about things and platforms and start thinking about the mind and the modernization of the thought processes that develop the pawns and that develop the concepts driving the requirements. We are not doing that.

This is the key. The requirement to finally take all the elements of national power and focus them is going to be critical by the year 2015. Critical. If we do not do that, if we cannot do that, we are going to be in trouble. We cannot design inflexibility across the spectrum, and we must stop building single-mission, single-capable anythings. The days of spending precious Department of Defense dollars on something that can only do one thing have got to come to an end. Simply put, that means, whether you are talking about a rifle that has an over and under, lethal above / nonlethal below, we have got to stop just buying a single mission anything. It has got to operate across the spectrum of warfare. It has got to fight three-block wars. It has got to be as helpful and humanitarian as it can be in the lethality of midintensity conflict.

Conceptually, we must merge the levels of war and action. We need to understand that three years, ten years, fifteen years from now, the soldier, sailor, airman, and Marine is going to have in his or her hand the ability to rain death and destruction like we have never seen before. It will make that infantry person the equivalent of a regimental commander. In World War II, the equivalent of a division commander. That individual can, in fact, have an impact at the strategic level. The soldier can have a strategic impact. This important point leads us back to how we train. What are we doing to train tactics, techniques, procedures, and doctrine to meet future challenges?

We must reevaluate our strategic fundamentals, our economy, and our way of life. Where do those all fit in insofar as warfare is concerned? And the military? Although difficult territory, the result of this reevaluation suggests literally rebuilding our strategy-making process and rebuilding the whole way we look at national security in order to capitalize fully on all of our national strengths and on the character of our nation. We must combine the elements of national power and support. Long ago, Abraham Lincoln said our situation must be seen anew. So must we think anew and act anew. Today, the days of thinking anew need to be reinforced with action.

The first issue we ought to look at is jointness. Although everybody is talking about jointness, we must get beyond talk. There is a new threat out there, in which U.S. assets and allies can be attacked. It requires far more than just the response of a military service. We are operating with the National Security Act of 1947. By 2015 that act will be approximately seventy years old. Imagine going in to World War II with a national security architecture that was seventy years old. In other words, an act that came out five years after the Civil War! Goldwater / Nichols did a great job of closing some of the gaps between the services. But that is not even beginning to touch what is going to have to happen as we move into the twenty-first century.

Second, we have to go beyond interagency. The first requirement is for the government to adapt its organization to current national security reality. The interagency process will continue to experience shortcomings until all contributors to national security are prepared to play their role. There are two important elements here. Expertise from outside the federal government is needed to provide a combined effect for national power. Whether it is power projection or national defense, the point is, combined effect.

What are some of those capabilities? The talents of the best and the brightest from industry, science and technology, academics, communications, banking, humanitarian organizations, Green Peace, other environmental organizations. You name it. They all have strengths that we need to tap into formally for their expertise, knowledge, and information to build national resources and strength. For want of a better term, it means developing a virtual staff at the national level. A virtual staff that links national and some kind of regional commander together with the capability to tap into all elements of national power. At the Council on Foreign Relations I had a long talk after the meeting with the president and CEO of IBM, who endorsed this view. We put money and people into rooms so that they can try to determine how to defend against certain viruses and certain attacks on your systems, while at the same time, on a daily basis, private businesses like IBM put hundreds of people to work on that issue supported by millions of dollars. We can go to the Fed, walk into any room, and find it is filled with people with green eyeshades, working one issue and one issue only and, that is, defense of our banking system via computer. Why can we not tap into that? Formally?

This action would be the scaffolding that would allow us to really take a look at the future and really do the type of planning and operation we need to do. That is, by bringing all elements of national power onto the battlefield. We are doing it now on a very miniature scale with something called the Chemical/Biological Incident Response Force. And only two years ago everybody thought that such a force was crazy when we said we were going to do that.

Forget about whether you believe that this kind of capability is of any value. That is not the issue. The issue is, we are dealing with that problem through a virtual reach-back staff, led by a Nobel laureate. Nobel laureates want to be involved because they want to play. In this case, it is through a Nobel laureate that we are also tied into multiple laboratories, medical schools, and hospitals. And, when an incident goes down, whether we are training or whether it is for real, our reach-back staff is with us. And, in fact, they do a great deal of the diagnostic work and recommended treatment. Their determinations are good and clear, that you can get a mucus sample to some hospital that is tied into to us very quickly, and furthermore, we can get a reply back quickly. It can be done.

I realize what I am saying has all kinds of great words in it about the ability to think beyond and think anew. The point here is we have got to do it. We have got to get out of our box. The fact of the matter is that the old models, means, and relationships are breaking down. We do need a new model to frame and focus our thinking. This model would close, or nearly close, the interagency gaps. It would further refine jointness. What is required is a new national security act. Along with this is the need for naval forces. This thing has to happen. This has got to be tied to where we are going, or we are in real trouble. We cannot go into the twenty-first century with a national security apparatus that is more than fifty years old.

Picture a Haitian who is fourteen years old and who is wearing Air Jordans. In his hands is an AK-47. This is a worrying prospect, because now that individual can be very nasty. Picture a tribesman. He has a skull in his hand. In the hand is also a brand new weapons system. And behind him is an armored vehicle. He is not just a tribesman. He is an equipped tribesman. Another example is a child wearing a nuclear/biological/chemical suit. You probably saw pictures of this during the Iran-Iraq war. People, children, running around, playing in a playground, wearing a chem/bio suit. Does that worry us? And should it worry us? Finally, the environment. The power of the environmental groups. We do not even touch them. As a matter of fact, we want to stay away from them instead of embracing them.

In conclusion, Brutus at Phillipi reminds me of us. Our legions are brimful, our cause is right, and the enemy increases every day. We are at the height, but we are ready to decline. On such a full sea, we are now afloat. We must take the current when it serves or lose our ventures. We are not in a strategic pause. We are in a strategic inflection point. We have seen this in the inter-war years. We either take advantage of it, or we lose it forever. We have got to take advantage of it. We have got to understand the situations that will confront us in the future. Caesar Augustus got so upset about the Teutoburg Forest that he went there. The German chieftain left every single Roman soldier exactly where they fell. He took some of them and tacked them to the trees. The battle took place in the Teutoburg Forest and they did not bury them. They did not grab the weapons systems. They left everything where it fell. Then, the German chieftain built a road that went right through the forest, so that all of the German tribes could see that the might of Rome could, in fact, be beaten.

Caesar looked at that and withdrew the legions back to Rome. Three hundred years later, the Roman Empire collapsed, and that collapse can be traced back to this battle. As he walked out of the forest, Caesar said, "Ne Cras, Ne Cras." This, in Latin, can either be a lament—not like yesterday—or a prophecy, a warning for tomorrow. We can look at Ne Cras, where we are right now, as either not like yesterday or as a warning for tomorrow.

PART I

SYMMETRICAL AND ASYMMETRICAL WARFARE CHALLENGES

INTRODUCTION

In his foreword, General Charles C. Krulak, then commandant of the Marine Corps, raises fundamental questions about the nature of future conflict and the challenges it is likely to pose for U.S. interests abroad. Within that context, the commandant's discussion of Rome in A.D. 9 makes a powerful point: In the years ahead, the United States should not expect to fight either the last war or the war it would like to fight. The Romans made both mistakes. They believed nothing had changed and that their "way of war" was unbeatable. They were wrong. Things had changed and the Legion paid a terrible price for Rome's arrogance. Their enemy adopted an asymmetrical strategy to defeat them at Teutoburg Forest.

Is the United States military in danger of falling into the same trap of complacency? Two factors could lull it in that direction: one, the overwhelming success of the Gulf War; two, a growing conviction that adherence to the precepts of the revolution in military affairs (RMA) and information warfare (IW) will allow the Pentagon to dominate all future battlefields and enemies. In other words, the United States will be unbeatable. Will this be the case?

The search for answers to this question lies at the center of General Krulak's charge to the authors of this volume. Which proposition is correct—nothing has changed as Rome assumed, or "Ne Cras" ("not like yesterday") as Rome was to learn? Part one begins by exploring this fundamental issue. It is Krulak's view that "Our doctrine, most of our training, and our weapons procurement are all oriented toward our legacy" of Desert Storm, but that "the character of war is changing." Is this the case? The authors in this section find much to agree with in General Krulak's foreword and seek to describe the evolving nature of conflict and how it will affect U.S. doctrine, training, and procurement.

Professor Robert L. Pfaltzgraff Jr., president, Institute for Foreign Policy Analysis, and Shelby Cullom Davis Professor of International Security Studies at The Fletcher School of Law and Diplomacy and Lieutenant Colonel Stephen E. Wright, National Defense Fellow at The Fletcher School during the academic year 1997–98, describe a future spectrum of conflict in which they believe adversaries will challenge the United States in asymmetrical ways. They define asymmetric as actor based rather than capabilities based. Actors can selectively choose capabilities and develop niche advantages in which to challenge stronger powers. The authors identify three types of actors—state, substate, and nonstate—who could challenge the United States asymmetrically in future conflicts. Their framework replaces the old paradigm of state-to-state conflict with a new one.

Pfaltzgraff and Wright next examine three key points on their spectrum, beginning with regional conflict at the state level. In their estimation, the United States must still be concerned with major regional contingencies. The second point on the spectrum is area conflict, such as the turmoil in sub-Saharan Africa. The final point on the spectrum deals with substate and nonstate actors. According to the authors, these last two types of actors lead to an increase in the military or paramilitary attempts to overthrow governments and will contribute to state disintegration, especially for those regimes lacking the ability to maintain legitimacy. As is evident, this is a very different conflict environment from that of the cold war.

Pfaltzgraff and Wright add a further dimension to their revised spectrum by introducing the concepts of linear and nonlinear conflict. The former describes the military-to-military conflict paradigm under which the world has operated for most of its history. The latter encompasses other lethal and nonlethal means used to achieve an actor's goals. In cyberwar, this could entail a host of hacker operations, as well as satellite scrambling, jamming, or destruction. The authors conclude with an examination of strategies that potential asymmetrical adversaries of the United States might adopt in the future. A key operational element of these may be the brutality of the operations themselves, as asymmetric foes gain access to highly lethal weapon systems.

The next two chapters examine possible future conflict across the spectrum, as developed by Pfaltzgraff and Wright. David Ochmanek, senior defense analyst at RAND Corporation, observes that large-scale aggression is almost never regarded as likely until it occurs. Yet the threat and use of force by states have been endemic in the international system. He believes this will remain so well into the next century.

While the next war involving U.S. interests cannot be predicted, Ochmanek identifies the states against which the United States must be prepared to wage war. The confluence of the following three characteristics will define those adversaries: First, states whose objectives are antithetical to those of the United States; second, states whose objectives impinge on important U.S. interests; and third, states that possess sufficient military capabilities to threaten their neighbors. States meeting all three criteria today include Iraq and North Korea. States meeting only two of the three criteria include China, Russia, and Iran.

According to Ochmanek, the infrequency of large-scale interstate warfare should not be seen as indicative of the importance such warfare should have in U.S. defense planning. Indeed, the likelihood of large-scale interstate warfare depends in great measure on what the United States does and says. Wars that this country is prepared to fight rarely happen. If the United States were to lose the capacity or the will to defend its international interests, we would be inviting military challenges. Prudence therefore demands that the U.S. field forces be capable of winning major regional conflicts. We must have sufficient aggregate capability to defeat, in concert with allies, threats to U.S. interests in more than one region at a time.

In the remainder of his chapter, Ochmanek outlines likely future regional military challenges to U.S. interests. He then identifies the capabilities that will allow the United States to defeat enemy aggression quickly and effectively.

Professor Richard H. Shultz Jr., director of the International Security Studies Program at The Fletcher School, concurs with much of what General Krulak suggests. However, he believes the U.S. defense establishment has only begun to awaken to the instability that increasingly powerful and violent substate and transstate actors will be able to inflict in the years ahead. This understanding, he believes, is reflected in the U.S. military doctrine of operations other than war (OOTW).

However, defining conflict today as OOTW may not portray the true nature of these situations in the most accurate light. While new doctrine is crucial, it is also important that it accurately identify the context in which U.S. forces are to be deployed. Doctrine must reflect the threats and challenges in which the United States is likely to be engaged. Shultz asserts that the United States must avoid getting caught in 2010 in the position of being most prepared for the least-likely contingencies and least prepared for the most-likely challenges.

Today, there are only a few specialists, "strategic iconoclasts," Shultz calls them, who have attempted to describe these most-likely conflicts as they will actually occur. What they present suggests that the "faces of battle" will be very different from both Desert Storm and the images of warfare conjured up by RMA and IW theorists.

Shultz argues that many of the conflicts and internecine struggles taking place today and in the years ahead will differ in important ways from the Western understanding of the causes, conduct, and termination of war. The U.S. defense community needs to get in touch with these differences because they have consequences that are measured in blood and treasure. It must come to understand "the otherness of others."

How can such knowledge be gained? Shultz proposes the need to develop an analytic framework that identifies and illuminates the various elements of these new forms of conflict in a systematic manner. Such a framework would focus on the ways in which internal wars are actually fought, the strategies and tactics employed, combatant training and behavior, and the impact of internal war on the locations in which they take place. Such an understanding of the post–cold war "faces of battle" is essential. The concluding part of his study outlines one approach to developing such a framework that has a valuable contribution to make to the understanding of policymakers and military planners as they contemplate intervening in internal wars through U.S. power projection.

Who are these substate and transstate actors that will fight in asymmetrical ways? What is known about them? Ralph Peters, former Army Intelligence officer and novelist, believes a profile has begun to emerge, and "with increasingly rare, anachronistic exceptions, these enemies will not be so foolish as to attempt to compete with [the United States]" on its terms. Peters addresses three questions about these nonstate actors.

First, who are they? He believes they will range "from drug lords to war-lords, and from charismatic nationalists to religious fanatics." Their common trait, according to Peters, will be "that they will not present suitable targets for the military we have constructed."

Second, why will they fight? Peters argues for "belief systems, blood ties, clan and tribe, nationalism exclusively defined, personal gain, revenge . . . and for the ineradicable joys of subjugating, destroying, and killing." Their most powerful weapon "will be hatred." What Peters foresees in the future has already taken place in Bosnia, Rwanda, Somalia, Chechnya, and several other places. Powerful emotions, encouraged and manipulated by ruthless elites, have been among the hallmarks of these conflicts.

Finally, how will these new actors fight? In asymmetrical ways that range "from back street confrontation, to a pogrom, to an ethnic cleansing campaign and civil war, to attempted extermination and regional destabilization—roughly the pattern seen in the former Yugoslavia, in the multiple murder fests in the Caucasus and Transcaucasus, in the Indian neighborhood. The alternative pattern is state- or leadership-sponsored genocide, as in much of Africa . . . in regional efforts against the Kurds, in Chinese efforts against minorities, in Indonesia." According to the author, these are the "faces of battle" that the international community will be forced to respond to in the future.

In his essay, Senator John F. Kerry (D-Mass.) discusses the growing international security threat of one type of nonstate actor—organized criminal syndicates. He believes they are an important part of a new paradigm of conflict and war that is broader and more complicated than that which characterized most of this century. Kerry outlines how criminal organizations can undermine state structures, causing instability and ungovernability. He is particularly concerned with these developments in postcommunist Russia.

Having outlined the various activities of organized criminal syndicates, activities that encompass racketeering, fraud, and drug distribution; trafficking in weapons, radioactive material, prostitution, and illegal aliens; and extortion, embezzlement, and purchase of banks, Senator Kerry turns to examine how the United States has responded to these new security challenges. In his judgment, there is significantly more to do. He concludes with several interesting options, including significantly increasing our interdiction capabilities, shooting down the aircraft of drug smugglers, and employing special operations covertly to undermine criminal enterprises engaged in other countries.

Colonel Charles J. Dunlap Jr., who served as Staff Judge Advocate (SJA) at the U.S. Strategic Command and is currently SJA for the 9th Air Force/United States Central Command Air Forces (USCENTAF), notes that the concept of asymmetrical warfare is a much-discussed issue today. However, he believes the Western mind-set does not allow for a full understanding of this concept. In broad terms, it means warfare that seeks to avoid an opponent's strengths; it is an approach that focuses on whatever may be the comparative advantages of one belligerent against the opponent's weaknesses. For most potential adversaries, attacking the United States asymmetrically is the only military strategy they might reasonably consider for the foreseeable future.

Dunlap posits that, within the Pentagon, asymmetrical warfare is usually thought of in technological terms. However, he argues it is much more complicated than that. It is also more than simply a violent form of a Westernized notion of politics. The technological orientation of the Western mind-set, along with the assumed universality of its values, distorts the U.S. analysis of asymmetrical warfare. Dunlap proposes that the real asymmetrical challenge for the West lies in how an enemy will attack the West's resolve and will. The answer makes Americans uncomfortable because it raises the possibility that fundamental values will be the targets that future adversaries will exploit asymmetrically.

While the mind-set in the United States sees the moral and ethical standards of its troops as keys to military strength, adversaries willing to abandon Westernized legal and ethical regimes may well consider them vulnerable asymmetries. Opponents will seek to present Western militaries with moral and ethical conundrums. Consider that the Serbs were able to discourage high-tech NATO air attacks by the simple expedient of chaining UN soldiers to potential targets. As the Western public becomes more sensitive to casualties on both sides, enemies may consider the situation an asymmetrical one and exploit it in ways the Western mind-set considers unthinkable. Dunlap concludes that the West must look at war from the culturally distinct perspective of enemies, who will seek to turn against us the very values we are seeking to project.

In the closing essay of this section, Professor Alberto Coll, dean of the Naval War College, argues that the changing nature of the spectrum of conflict as outlined here suggests that two dimensions of operations other than war— peacetime engagement and chaos management—will be essential components of U.S. policy and strategy in the years ahead. As states become increasingly fragile and disintegrate into protracted internal wars, chaos management, to include humanitarian intervention, peacekeeping, and peace enforcement, will continue to grow in importance. Coll concludes by examining the demands such political-military operations will place on the Navy and Marine Corps and identifies capabilities needed to respond effectively. These include investing more in language training and regional specialization, expanding the skills needed to perform various civil affairs missions, and developing closer ties between the Naval services and the private sector, so that the military can draw on private-sector support and skills as needed.

THE SPECTRUM OF CONFLICT: SYMMETRICAL OR ASYMMETRICAL CHALLENGE?

Robert L. Pfaltzgraff Jr.
Stephen E. Wright

While conventional symmetric challenges will persist, the future holds increased likelihood of adversaries conducting asymmetrical strategies and operations. Closely related is the question of whether the spectrum of conflict has changed, and if so, why? We argue that it has changed, that the strategic environment has indeed altered and so should our view of the spectrum of conflict. We offer several new definitions to help clarify current arguments and examine how future asymmetrical strategies and operations could affect naval operational concepts. Why *must* we consider these issues? Simply stated, the lethality, affordability, and ubiquity of the types of technologies available to future adversaries compels us to examine future conflict as if we had just lost a war, rather than having won one.

To examine the emerging spectrum of conflict, it is necessary not only to consider the types of contingencies for which military power is likely to be used, but also to ask what weapons technologies and systems are being acquired by would-be users and how they will affect the ability of the United States to operate militarily in contingencies requiring naval forces. Even a cursory review of current writings on defense issues yields information about a broad range of capabilities that are becoming available to states and actors other than states in various parts of the world. These capabilities and their use will form the basis for confronting adversaries such as the United States in the years ahead. They encompass technologies to produce weapons of mass destruction and their delivery systems, as well as other capabilities such as advanced aircraft, submarines, and the information-age technologies embodied in computers and microchips. On a single day, for example, the October 1997 *Current News Early Bird* carried articles on missile and submarine proliferation, as well as on breaches in security at nuclear facilities. The brief summaries below are illustrative of the types of technologies that are becoming more widely available, with potentially important challenges for the early twenty-first century. In particular, they could challenge the ability of the United States to project military power and to maintain overseas presence in littoral regions of importance to national security:

➤ North Korea is building missiles that could strike U.S. forces in Asia and eventually Alaska, according to two former North Korean officials in testimony before a Senate subcommittee. These include two versions of the Nodong missile with ranges up to 620 miles, as well as the Taepodong, with a range up to 3,100 miles, capable of striking parts of Alaska. At the same time, North Korea has earned up to $1 billion a year from missile sales to such countries as Iran, Syria, Egypt, and Libya. The ability of North Korea to strike, or to threaten to strike, U.S. forces or the United States itself would present formidable problems in managing a future Korean Peninsula crisis contingency.

➤ The end of the cold war has triggered a submarine arms race among third world nations. Countries, some of which are hostile to the United States and its principal allies, are said to be buying, building, and arming submarines as rapidly as their economic circumstances will allow. Among those states acquiring submarines are China, Japan, and North Korea, as well as Libya, Algeria, and Syria. According to an unclassified report of the Office of Naval Intelligence, "the worldwide submarine challenges that the United States and its allies face today are more diverse and more complex than at any time during the Cold War. They run the gamut from the highly sophisticated and predictable to the unsophisticated and irrational."[1] The ability of the United States to operate in littoral areas and, in particular, to utilize sea lift assets could be diminished.

➤ In Russia on 29 September 1997, Vice President Al Gore expressed concern over security at Russia's nuclear facilities, while *USA Today* reported that a recent confidential Pentagon review obtained by the newspaper found inadequate safeguards throughout the network of weapons facilities run by the Department of Energy (DOE). The article went on to state that DOE officials acknowledge many of the problems, while pointing out that nuclear stocks remain well protected and that the deficiencies are being addressed. In early November 1997, Congress acted to establish an oversight panel to investigate reports of security lapses at the facilities where nuclear weapons are stored. Although the United States is no longer building nuclear weapons, it is now dismantling and storing components from weapons eliminated as a result of arms control agreements. The proliferation of nuclear warheads to adversaries, in combination with delivery systems, could create for the United States major problems for littoral operations.

Other studies and publications point to the increasing availability of other technologies that create a basis for asymmetrical operations against the United States. For example, the President's Commission on Critical Infrastructure Protection, established by President Bill Clinton in 1996, concludes that the classical resources needed to mount a terrorist attack (explosives) are well known.

However, the rapid expansion in the global computer-literate population and the accelerating use of computers in global networks will create a situation in which hundreds of millions of people will have the skills needed to attack our critically important information infrastructure. According to the study, the resources needed to conduct a cyberattack are already widely available at a time when our energy and communications infrastructures are growing in complexity and operating closer to capacity. This could provide cascading effects that might be triggered by an initial minor disruption. Whether or not this would lead to a digital Pearl Harbor, the prospect exists that key components of the U.S. infrastructure will be vulnerable to disruption and therefore will become the potential objects of asymmetrical strategies.

Other literature about technologies that will be central to military operations in the early twenty-first century focuses on space. As we move into the next millennium, we will witness an increasing commercialization of space, together with its growing importance for military operations. At the same time, the military use of civilian space-based assets, including communications and reconnaissance satellites, will rise dramatically. Space-based systems will be highly vulnerable to electromagnetic pulse (EMP) effects if, for example, a nuclear device were to be detonated at an altitude of about 300 kilometers above a theater of military operations such as the Persian Gulf or the Korean Peninsula. In a future major regional conflict, space assets are likely to be attacked early and perhaps repeatedly. Such systems would probably not be replaceable as rapidly as necessary. Their disruption, or even threats to them, would have important commercial and economic as well as political and military implications. It is well known that the U.S. success in Operation Desert Storm rested to a large measure on superior information made possible by space-based assets that were not assumed to be highly vulnerable to disruption. In the first decade of the new century, greater numbers of states will have their own imagery capabilities. As a result, the reconnaissance gap favoring the United States is likely to narrow. At the same time, the potential for interfering with U.S. systems, including attacks on them, will increase.

These examples could easily be supplemented by a seemingly endless list and description of proliferating capabilities across a broad spectrum. As we project into the second decade of the twenty-first century, the United States will probably not face a peer competitor capable of symmetrically challenging the United States with equivalent military forces. Instead, we are in the midst of a proliferation of asymmetrical capabilities that, individually or collectively, will be available to an unprecedented number of actors. Even if a peer competitor were to emerge, the types of capabilities that it would possess would not likely be designed to match those of the United States. Instead, the dynamics of the ongoing technological revolution, together with the vulnerabilities of postindustrial societies, are such that an optimal strategy for competitors, strong or weak, would include the use of asymmetrical means both to deter U.S. military action and, if conflict began, to shape the escalatory ladder to their advantage. However, it is also conceivable that a new peer adversary may, in fact, arise from an economic competitor that leaps over U.S. military technology by developing a whole new generation of weapons that render advanced U.S. forces obsolete, thus fundamentally changing the tools of war. This new revolution in military affairs (RMA) could occur without the adversary ever investing in a U.S.-style peer technology military force. Yet such a peer force, because it relied on revolutionary new technologies, could provide the means for asymmetrical warfare against the United States. Perhaps new types of biological weapons for which there are no known antidotes fall within this category, developed by a Saddam Hussein-type actor prepared to use them or to threaten their employment, to counter American RMA-based forces.

The term *asymmetrical warfare* that has recently entered the strategic lexicon actually describes an old concept. As long as 2,500 years ago, the ancient Chinese strategist, Sun Tzu, wrote: "To refrain from intercepting an enemy whose banners are in perfect order, to refrain from attacking an army drawn up a calm and confident array—this is the art of studying circumstances. It is a military axiom not to advance uphill against the enemy, nor to oppose him when he comes downhill."[2]

Basic to military strategy is the maxim that an enemy should be attacked at its point of vulnerability, not where it is strongest. Even military forces that possess basic equivalence but also differing types of force structures, as the United States and the Soviet Union did during the cold war, usually attempt to circumvent the strengths of the adversary. Thus, the United States developed what was termed a countervailing strategy. It chose not to match the Soviet Union tank for tank or missile for missile, but instead to counter tanks with innovative tactics based on such systems as helicopters or to make the huge Soviet investment in heavy ICBMs obsolete by conducting research designed ultimately to produce a defense against missiles. To the extent that the Strategic Defense Initiative helped to account for the demise of the Soviet Union, the United States succeeded brilliantly in fulfilling another of Sun Tzu's strategic axioms. He stated that: "To fight and conquer in all your battles is not supreme excellence; supreme excellence consists in breaking the enemy's resistance without fighting."[3] Thus an asymmetrical strategy, followed to its logical conclusion, would achieve victory (the attainment of policy objectives) without armed hostilities. Further, in the event of such conflict, it would place the enemy at such a decisive disadvantage as to eliminate the will to resist and lead to capitulation or a compromise favorable to the practitioner of asymmetrical warfare.

In the current literature there are two basic definitions of asymmetrical strategies and operations. The first is capabilities based, in which the actor with the more lethal, technologically advanced weapons is said to have an asymmetrical advantage over an adversary. By this definition, the United States held an asymmetrical superiority over Iraq in the Gulf War. The second approach, and the one adopted here, is actor based. In this definition, it is the weaker party, whether it is a state, substate, or nonstate entity that acts asymmetrically against a stronger power. The more powerful actor employs its dominant military forces while the weaker actor uses asymmetrical strategies and operations. Asymmetrical warfare is the use of strategies and tactics, supported by appropriate capabilities, designed to defeat an enemy by attacking, or threatening credibly to attack and exploit its weakness and vulnerability. Here it is important to draw a distinction between weakness and vulnerability. Actors are vulnerable where they are weak. However, they may also be vulnerable at points that are indispensable to the maximization of their strengths. What is perceived by the superior power to be a strength may in fact become a weakness. Thus, for example, postindustrial societies rely on advanced technologies such as communications and other information assets as sources of strength. To the weaker enemy, such alleged strengths become areas of vulnerability, opportunities to attack and disable.

A weaker actor employs asymmetrical strategies and operations to deter, delay, or deny the military actions of the stronger actor in an attempt to impose unacceptable costs that exceed the gain or benefit of taking action by the more powerful actor. The traditional military definition of "defeat" is excluded here because the weaker actor does not attempt to defeat the stronger belligerent force on force. Instead, the weaker agent plans attacks designed to erode the will of the government of the more powerful actor or its population to continue the conflict by defeating its strategy rather than its military forces. A more powerful actor may also be affected in its use of military power by efforts to shape its collective mind-set in psychological operations. Thus the United States was not militarily defeated in Vietnam. Instead, the war was lost by a combination of political, military, and psychological strategies that engaged the United States, asymmetrically, at points of vulnerability. Vietnam was the first war in which events were portrayed daily in vivid color on millions of television screens on the nightly news, thus offering unprecedented opportunities for shaping the mind-set. While the war was fought thousands of miles from the United States, millions of Americans were electronic witnesses to the war, which could only be seen by that part of the Vietnamese population directly engaged locally in the battle of the day.

The psychological opportunities afforded by the media, illustrated by the Vietnam War, have only become more evident since the 1960s. The goal of such operations is either to prevent the United States from initiating the use of its military power or from employing such capabilities as effectively as necessary to achieve its political objectives. For this purpose, it is essential either to convince the American public, or influential segments of the public, that the cause for which U.S. military power should be used is immoral and unjust—or to lead the American people to believe that the casualties to be inflicted on civilian populations, or the casualties to be taken by U.S. forces, do not provide a justifiable basis for military action. In this respect, the Vietnam War was lost in the United States itself, with images conveyed on the nightly television news being more powerful than many divisions on the battlefield. Consciously and subliminally, the national mind-set can be shaped by the media and by actions taken by an enemy and portrayed in the media to delegitimize the strategies and political goals of the superior power. A society that is casualty averse and in search of quick solutions, while being unwilling to engage in open-ended, protracted military operations that do not show sufficient promise, appears to be especially vulnerable to asymmetrical political or psychological strategies of this kind.

The increasing attractiveness of asymmetrical strategies for early twenty-first-century warfare against the United States arises from the emerging combination of larger numbers and diverse points of vulnerability on the part of postindustrial societies. These societies, led by the United States, are faced with an increasing array of capabilities available to the weaker actor for use against the stronger party. This is set within a global strategic environment that is characterized, as widely noted, by an unprecedented array of state, substate, and nonstate actors. There appears to be little or nothing on the global horizon that is likely to change that overall setting in the next generation. There will be an accelerating proliferation of technology and information, hardware and software that will become increasingly available. Technology is being driven primarily by the civilian sector, with military systems spinning off from commercial development, thus enhancing the likelihood of ever-wider availability. With greater numbers and types of actors will probably come a continually shifting balance of power, with declining influence of the West, including the United States. Modernization, measured in large part by the spread of technology, will more than likely not mean Westernization, but instead an expansion of other societies and civilizations. Although the state will remain the key international political unit, it will be increasingly fragmented and subjected to a variety of centrifugal forces. As we move into the twenty-first century, we are likely to see expanding economic and other links across national borders and transnational regions joined directly with the global economy—Alaska with the Asia-Pacific Rim, the Canadian West with the U.S. Northwest. This process will form part of a trend toward decentralization and devolution from the central government to other levels. The breakup of states will produce and exacerbate problems of crime, ungovernability, and anarchy as the authority of central governments is eroded, with capabilities for asymmetrical warfare increasingly in the hands of a wider variety of groups.

The emerging global system is also being shaped by important socioeconomic and demographic trends. By 2020, at current rates of growth, the world's population is projected to increase from 5.7 billion to about 8.3 billion. We will be adding a population the size of Mexico (100 million) every year and every decade nearly another China. Most of this additional population will be born in the developing world, from the Pacific Rim to Africa, from Southwest Asia to South America. Within the next generation, about sixty countries will have at least 20 percent of their population in the fifteen-to-twenty-four-year age group. Although perhaps mitigated depending on rates of world economic growth, there will be larger numbers of young, unemployed, and volatile populations, possibly resorting to violence and susceptible to radicalization in order to achieve their socioeconomic and political goals. For the most part, they will live in megacities that themselves may face formidable problems of poverty, crime, disease, instability, and ungovernability. Most of this population will live within 300 miles of a coastline. This means that such littoral geographical areas will be the probable locus for much of the early twenty-first-century conflict, although cyberspace, and space itself, will introduce novel dimensions to a multifaceted strategic setting.

Without necessarily ascribing to any specific actor the status of friend or foe, it is possible to envisage several major changes as we move well into the early decades of the next century. In addition to China as a major actor, we may look forward to a Korea that will be engaged in a unification process and eventually emerging as an increasingly important Asia-Pacific actor. Japan may be acquiring military capabilities designed to counter or offset China. The core of a European security and defense identity, to the extent that there is or will be one, necessarily must encompass Germany, France, and possibly the United Kingdom. At the same time, the new security perimeter of Europe lies along two arcs extending from the Balkans into North Africa and from the Balkans into Central Asia. This arc encompasses, in the latter case, the oil and natural gas reserves of the Caspian Basin and, in the former, burgeoning populations and instability on the southern littoral of the Mediterranean.

We may anticipate increasing Asian-Pacific, including Chinese, demand for oil and natural gas, together with numerous conflict flashpoints in and around the Caspian region. By the early years of the next century, China alone will probably be importing oil at the level of at least 1.5 million barrels a day, most of it from the Persian Gulf and the Caspian Basin. The Caspian has reserves estimated to exceed 130 billion barrels of oil, worth as much as four trillion dollars at 1997 prices, together with comparable reserves of natural gas. In the early twenty-first century the geoeconomic and geostrategic map will be redrawn to encompass a vast energy-providing region extending from the Persian Gulf to the Caspian, thus providing the basis for a new security paradigm that integrates Persian Gulf security issues with the Caspian region. A distinguishing characteristic of this region's new configuration as an energy producer is its exclusive dependence, in the Caspian Basin portion, on pipelines for exports to world markets across countries divided by ongoing ethnic and other conflicts. Much of the Caspian oil and natural gas will be shipped from ports in the Black Sea, the Mediterranean, or the Persian Gulf to more distant world markets. As China's energy import needs have grown, its links with Iran have solidified. Iran is a major supplier of energy to China, while both Beijing and Moscow provide Iran with advanced technologies for civilian and military applications.

Within the overall context of asymmetrical strategies in this emerging security environment, the potential for state-to-state war will remain. However, a larger number of conflicts will continue to be fought by substate or nonstate actors, whose approaches to warfare differ dramatically from those of postindustrial states. At the substate and nonstate level, there will be greater numbers of diverse types of actors in possession of advanced technologies as the lead time for technology acquisition shortens. Such a process, together with the growing availability of cyberspace, will create a more level playing field in which substate and nonstate actors may threaten the United States with a broad array of asymmetrical means. At the same time, there will be greater difficulty in preventing proliferation, as national borders become more permeable and essentially lose their meaning as barriers to external penetration. In short, there will be growing asymmetries in how and why armed conflicts are waged.

Especially in situations in which their vital interests are not clearly defined, postindustrial societies will be casualty averse and reluctant to wage war. However, substate and nonstate actors and even certain states themselves will be embued with levels of fanaticism and willingness to accept casualties that will enhance their ability to exploit the vulnerabilities of postindustrial societies by asymmetrical means. For such entities, the use of nuclear and other weapons of mass destruction may be seen not as weapons of last resort, but instead as weapons of first resort, thus negating the concept of mutual-assured destruction that dominated Western strategic thought during the cold war. An adversary, seeking by such means to disable U.S. space-based assets, including communications and reconnaissance satellites in a future conflict, could detonate a high-altitude nuclear weapon. This tactic would not be part of a strategy of graduated escalation at a relatively late stage in the conflict. Instead, it would be used at the outbreak of war to deprive the United States and its coalition allies of the "situational awareness" deemed to be vitally important to the successful integration of RMA technologies. The ability of a state, such as Iraq or Iran, to target U.S or coalition forces with weapons of mass destruction systems, while also having the means to strike more distant targets in Europe or in the United States itself, will introduce new security issues and prospects for asymmetrical warfare.

The spectrum of conflict still includes the potential for nuclear warfare at the high end of the scale, as well as low intensity conflict at the opposite end. In the future, however, military operations to support a range of activities from humanitarian relief or recovery to peacekeeping or peace enforcement will most likely continue to occupy much of the military's operational time. While this spectrum sounds familiar, new twists may be set forth as we ponder what future armed conflict might look like. In this discussion, we will exclude global nuclear war and military operations other than war. Instead, the focus will be on a narrower spectrum of potential combat operations. Specifically, we emphasize regional conflict with two variations followed by potential substate and then nonstate conflicts.

The possibility of regional conflict remains high in three key regions. The first two, Southwest Asia (SWA) and the Korean Peninsula, are familiar. These two regions need no further discussion except to note that both remain potential flashpoints. The need to protect energy resources in SWA remains obvious, just as the United States must continue to maintain its forward presence in the Korean peninsula. The third, however, the Caspian Sea region, is less familiar. Regional states such as Iran will seek to expand their influence in the respective regions within which they are located, for example, Iran in the Caspian basin. Iran is poised to play a key role not only in the Persian Gulf, but also in the Caspian region, where it seeks to extend its influence in the development of Caspian energy resources. Its developing ties to China and other energy-deficient nations serve to ensure a market for its fossil-fuel resources. Thus, with a solid economic base, Iran stands ready to increase its influence astride both the Gulf and Caspian regions. The United States may face China, a country with superpower potential, Iran and its growing regional influence, and both Beijing and Teheran sharing an interest in diminishing the political and military posture of the United States in the Caspian Sea region, as well as in SWA. Russia, too, relies on this region as a source of economic gain, including hard currency. Thus the Caspian Sea region draws together major powers, regional powers, and a surfeit of small countries "caught" in the middle.

In addition to regional conflicts, it is useful to set forth another concept, termed area conflicts. Areas do not fit neatly into the geographical and regional context, currently used in DOD planning. Area conflict will be characterized by extreme violence, especially where noncombatants are concerned. Conflict in areas will most likely resemble guerrilla warfare, whether urban or countryside in location, and will be fought with irregular forces against people traditionally thought of as noncombatants. This new concept characterizes conflicts such as Bosnia. It includes transnational phenomena such as the criminal enterprise armies described in a later chapter in this volume by Lieutenant Colonel Ralph Peters. The term also encompasses transregional areas like Africa, a prime example of area conflict.

Robert Kaplan observed in the *Coming Anarchy* that Africa is confronted with an increasing ungovernability of nations formed in the aftermath of colonialism. The problems and conflict found in Africa illustrate many of the key factors leading to increasing ungovernability and state failure. Kaplan looked at African states and found rapidly rising birth rates and a movement of population from the countryside to burgeoning megacities along the coasts. Extensive crime and the rise of private armies tore away at what little control governments could provide. In some states, he found it difficult to tell the criminals from the government itself. The two things that the countries in West Africa shared were poverty and disease. Kaplan noted that two-thirds of the world's known cases of HIV-positive people lived in Africa. Further, he reported that deforestation and erosion of huge land areas were key motivators for the migration to cities, cities that are now becoming megacities. Once people had congregated in these new population centers, the creation of shantytowns, with their attendant filth and disease, only exacerbated difficult conditions. In the last years, we have watched this story be repeated in Somalia, Rwanda, and the Congo Republic. The waist of Africa forms the precipice of a human abyss of unimaginable deprivation and death. Unfortunately, these horrors are not solely equatorial Africa's. In the north, the death and destruction continues in places like Algeria, where at least seventy-five thousand civilians have been killed in the last six years.

The technology that will be available, both for information and for weapons, will only make the groups that fight area conflicts increasingly lethal and, in many cases, more lethal than even the governments that exist within the nations affected by these groups. We must face the challenges in the security considerations of area conflict and their transnational concerns, because they will be the source of much conflict in the future. Unfortunately, as Colonel Charles J. Dunlap Jr. pointed out, ineffectual nation-state governments will face "warrior societies" employing brutality-driven strategies that create situations that psychologically, militarily, and politically advanced societies, such as the United States, are poorly equipped to deal with, including attacks on noncombatants.[4]

A step down from area considerations on the spectrum of conflict is the substate level. Substate conflict ranges from the military coup to the insurgent faction seeking to establish a new regime. It includes groups seeking to force changes in the current government through extralegal processes such as revolutionary war. As governments break down under the pressures of megacities, population, environmental concerns, drugs, and disease, it may be a well-meaning military or paramilitary force or even a law enforcement entity that takes over a government in an effort to restore order. Cambodia is the latest in a long lineage of countries where political change occurs at the direction of the military. The military coup usurped power in country after country in South America during the cold war time frame. This form of power transition may again return to the forefront of political change methodologies as a result of fragmenting societies with ineffectual governments.

In the past, this type of conflict would be viewed as an internal conflict rarely requiring U.S. consideration or intervention. In the future, choices may not be simple or clear cut. With the increasing pervasiveness and lethality of modern weapons, these conflicts will, in many cases, spill over their own boundaries to engulf neighbors and even the major powers. Like the Rwandan tragedy, refugee migration and mass violence, brought to our living rooms each night via CNN, will demand a response.

Two additional substate examples may assert themselves in the future. Although we do not think about insurgencies too much of late, they may be lying in wait to strike out again, feeding on the unrest of a growing youth population caught in the slums, poverty, and disease of the megacity. The urban jungle will become the new recruiting ground for those seeking to transform societies through force. The final example of the potential substate conflict would be a group seeking specific political outcomes, although less in scope than an insurgency, but similarly characterized by brutal levels of violence. The Palestinian Intifada is one example of this type of conflict. A legacy of bombing market places, school buses, and street shootings attests to the brutality of this method. Another example would be religious radicals such as those who bombed the Khobar Towers in Saudi Arabia. Here an extremist group sought to force the government to alter its policy on cooperation with the United States. From the attackers' point of view, this operation was "win-win," as they destroyed an American-controlled facility, brutally killed

American personnel, and still made their point (and, to date, have been caught, albeit not under satisfactory terms for the United States). Indicative of a long-term result of this bombing may be seen in the refusal by Saudi Arabia to allow U.S. strikes on Iraq from bases within its borders.

A final point of consideration on the redefined continuum is that of nonstate conflict. Nonstate conflict results when nonstate actors fight between themselves or with state or substate entities. The most obvious example is organized crime discussed later in this chapter. With the increasing globalization of the business and financial worlds, the opportunity for abuse and subsequent conflict will exist in the future, if it does not exist already. Multinational corporations (MNCs) can easily be imagined that might destabilize a government or region to manipulate currency valuations. As MNCs merge into supercorporations, their impact at local, state, and regional levels could be overwhelming, especially in less-developed areas. The current instability in South Korea and South Asia illustrate the potential to destabilize nations and regions. While a rogue MNC may not have precipitated the current crisis, this case illustrates the magnitude of chaos that can result in world markets. Advancements in information technologies and a growing global reliance on the same will offer lucrative opportunities for unscrupulous business enterprises. Certainly one sees the need for business and financial regimes that provide transparent and standardized requirements for international business and finance.

As governments struggle with the ungovernable, organized crime has moved to fill power vacuums in many countries and regions, while globalizing its operations throughout much of the world. A classic example is Colombia, where drug cartels have long plagued the government. Colombia's 1997 political elections indicate that the cartels may have achieved the upper hand. Fewer than 30 percent of the Colombians turned out for the election. The poor showing can be linked to the fact that the cartel leaders ordered the execution of many of the candidates. In Russia, crime seems to be the most organized activity in the aftermath of the communist implosion. Crime rivals the government in access to and use of force and seems to have already established global links to drug cartels like those in Colombia. Kaplan's criminal armies, or if one prefers, Peters's criminal enterprise armies, attack not just the weak in third world countries, but they even challenge the West in some of the highest of high-stakes operations. Zachery Selden of the organization Business Executives for National Security noted that Russian hackers stole $400,000 from Citibank in 1994. He cited a Senate hearing that resulted in the revelation that certain U.S. corporations had lost $400 million to computer theft in 1995 alone. Organized crime is high tech and highly lethal. Drug revenues have resulted in cartels oftentimes having better combat capability than local and state governments do.

Less well organized, but nevertheless an important element of crime, are the gangs that roam the streets in cities around the globe. What once was a phenomenon limited to the few megacities in the world will increase proportionally to the expansion in megacities. As Kaplan points out, such gangs are endemic in large parts of Africa and elsewhere. With access to high-tech weaponry, computers, and cell phones, such gangs have the potential to link up with organized crime in new and detrimental ways. Technology may allow them to extend their influence, perhaps becoming the storm troopers of international organized crime.

A challenging and potentially violent world awaits tomorrow's security planners. Accurately characterizing this environment within the revised spectrum of conflict requires two new definitional concepts. These definitions not only accommodate how actions occur, but also account for the actors themselves. Modern warfare typically involved clearly defined nation-states, or definable territorial entities. Within this paradigm, two military approaches existed—direct and indirect. In future war, however, state-to-state conflict may not predominate. In fact, force-on-force battle may not be the preferred course of action. Recall that the revised spectrum of conflict contains three points (of four discussed) that involve conflict at other than the state level. Thus, we offer two new terms to encompass conflict between nation-states, substates, or nonstate antagonists, or any combination thereof. The new descriptive terms are "linear" and "nonlinear." Linear conflict is that which occurs between states, the historical pattern of modern warfare. This term incorporates the direct and indirect approaches and the potential for asymmetric strategies or operations within each. Nonlinear conflict encompasses state versus substate or nonstate actors and the combinations possible between substate and nonstate actors. This term also includes the possibility of a weak state actor, or even a substate actor using other actors as proxies for conflict against another actor at any of the levels discussed. For example, potential actors and actions could include terrorism sponsored by states like Libya, or nonstate actors such as Hamas. Nonlinear warfare relies almost exclusively on asymmetrical strategies and operations.

Future war will likely see more nonlinear than linear conflict. Industrialized, and especially postindustrialized, countries will seek to avoid or minimize conflict with one another. They will certainly want to avoid large-scale linear war. With globalized markets, international financial structures, and increasing numbers of multinational corporations, these countries understand that war will be bad for business (and just about everything else). The current instability in world markets results in large part from debt equity problems in Asian economies. The effect of these problems is felt in London, New York, and every other stock exchange around the world. Imagine a major war in Asia and the effect it would have on these markets. Third world state-to-state conflict may still occur, as well as major powers engaging less-developed states to ensure access to markets and resources. Increasingly, however, future war will be nonlinear. Unlike the major regional contingencies (Iraq and Korea) envisaged in the aftermath of the Gulf War, this new form of warfare has few, if any definable battle lines. The battle is fought in diverse environments. Several actions, in widely separated geographical and functional settings, may take place nearly simultaneously, or in sequences designed to exploit the vulnerabilities of the United States or its allies. These might include attacks on elements of population, a terrorist incident such as the bombing of the World Trade Center, or efforts to disrupt vital infrastructures. Indeed, the "front" may seem to be everywhere. In addition to having no definable battle lines, such warfare may blur the traditional distinction between war and peace. Will attacks on infrastructures like gas pipelines, electrical grids, telephone networks, and so forth, be considered acts of war? Will the classification of war, conflict, or criminal act differ depending on whether the actor was a state, substate, or nonstate entity? One thing is sure. These actors will seek to manipulate the omnipresent media, including not only global television, with its increasingly customized channels, but also the unprecedented opportunities provided by the Internet. Future war will be viewed in our living rooms, unfiltered and in real time. These factors will place tremendous pressures on official policymakers and crisis action managers.

Asymmetrical strategies and operations will be the preferred course of action for the foreseeable future of conflict. Without a peer competitor, the United States will face potential adversaries determined to affect U.S. actions in three basic ways. Their first objective would be to deter the United States (and its allies and coalition) from acting on any course of action. For example, the adversary might seek to intimidate a country that allied forces count on for deployed basing. This intimidation could come from threatened use of weapons of mass destruction or physical attack. An enemy might even exercise a terrorist option by destroying infrastructure, disrupting satellite systems, or using information warfare against one or more national computer systems. Second, if the United States had already begun a military response, then the enemy's strategy would seek to delay (or even deny) U.S. action as it deployed forces into an area of operations or region. For example, the destruction of embarkation and debarkation port facilities or denial of landing terrain through physical occupation might thwart U.S. action, especially if high casualty rates were anticipated in conducting an opposed landing. Third, if U.S. or coalition forces were already in the region, the enemy would take action to increase the cost of action of force termination. The rapid withdrawal of U.S. forces from Somalia after the attack on Task Force Ranger would be an example of denial operations to force the termination of U.S. action. With the blurring of battle lines, however, the enemy could target noncombatants either through direct attack on them or by attacks on those infrastructures that support them. The primary mechanism for achieving policy outcomes that deter, delay, or deny U.S. or coalition action will be the threat of, or act of, brutality. The threat or actual brutal event resulting in casualties, destruction, or gridlock of key and essential human services would be designed to achieve such a goal. Cyberspace will offer no relief from the potential for brutality and human casualties, because computer viruses and information system attacks may be used to shut down essential services, such as 911 response networks, hospital power supplies, or air traffic control systems. Indeed, it may be in the threats and actual operations behind the frontline of force-to-force conflict that asymmetrical strategies inflict their devastation and have their maximum effect. Table 1 provides a sample summary of adversary strategies and potential operations as they might be used against U.S. or coalition forces responding to a crisis.

Table 1.

Adversary Strategies/Operations by Phase of U.S./Coalition Crisis Response

U.S/Coalition Response Phase	Enemy Strategy	Enemy Operations/Actions
Predeployment	Deter Goal: raise the cost of action to U.S./coalition; prime focus at policy level (political will)	Threaten/attack regional coalition supporters Threaten use of weapons of mass destruction Initiate regime destabilization Economic blackmail—cyberattacks Attack critical infrastructure Directly threaten coalition members Terrorist attacks within coalition states Attack coalition citizens in region Exploit own people/systems and blame U.S./coalition—propagandize world opinion
Deploy/Arrival	Deter/Delay Goal: raise cost of action to U.S./coalition members/supporters; prime focus at political/policy and military strategic/operational levels	Continue/adopt courses of action above Attack points of arrival (ports, airports, land access points) Mines (sea and land) Chemical/biological attack—target people as well as area as well as area attack Emergency response capabilities Attack forces as they near region/points of embarkation Antiship tactics (mines, cruise missiles, antiship missiles, even ballistic missiles with chemical/biological warheads) Attack aircraft/air control facilities Attack infrastructures that support arriving forces (fuel, transportation, food)

TABLE 1: *continued*

		Provoke disproportionate military response from U.S./coalition forces Employ terrorist surrogates in target countries Target world opinion—even at expense of own people/infrastructures Use proxies to create contingency diversions in other regions
Arrival/Employ	Delay/Deny Goal: raise cost of action to U.S./coalition members/supporters; prime focus at political/ policy and military strategic/ operational/ tactical levels; as U.S./coalition moves toward employ-ment, enemy objective increasingly focuses on efforts to increase casualties	Continue/adopt courses of action above Increase infrastructure attacks, especially against information assets/supports Attack C4 patterns, if known/able Attack space systems to extent possible Increase attacks within U.S./coalition countries Destruction of critical infrastruc-tures or services may be more effective here than causing casualties Cause in-theater casualties to U.S. coalition forces to maximum extent possible
Employ	Deny Goal: expect drastic escalation of violence to effect political will via any means available; military considerations will be clearly secondary to the attack on political will	Casualties—casualties—casualties Expect adversary to attack its own people to affect world opinion; use own people as human shields Threat of nuclear detonation escalates

How then might a potential adversary use linear and nonlinear asymmetrical strategies and operations to deter, delay, or deny U.S. naval forces in future war? In linear conflict, war planners may more readily discern the adversary, but their challenges will be every bit as great as in nonlinear warfare.

Further, planners should note that many of the asymmetrical strategies or operations discussed below could be promulgated by state, substate, or nonstate actors (or combinations thereof). In fact, in many cases, the more high-tech the strategies or operations, the more likely it is that they would be executed by other than traditional state actors (as opposed to force-on-force options). States with the technology to attack in cyberspace or against infrastructure will not be able to generate the same level of plausible deniability as substate and, especially, nonstate actors. Planners may find themselves fluctuating between linear and nonlinear operations in minute-to-minute decision cycles, further exacerbating contingency response efforts. As mentioned earlier, the enemy might opt for the early use of a nuclear device to destroy communications, navigation, surveillance, and intelligence satellites. This direct-type attack could gridlock deployment time lines, deny information dominance, or disrupt employment timing, creating fears of drastically increased casualties. This factor alone might raise the cost of operations above what would be acceptable to the national command authority, the Congress, and the American people, an increasingly problematic issue the less vital the interest. An adversary could threaten to use weapons of mass destruction against a state in which the United States desires to deploy its forces. In essence, the enemy would hold such a state hostage, coercing them to disallow access to deploying U.S. or coalition forces. Weapons of mass destruction can also form the basis of linear operations against U.S. forces. The use of chemical agents during an otherwise unopposed landing operation could result in extensive casualties, again raising the cost of action. As discussed earlier, the ubiquitous nature of commercial technology puts real-time surveillance, tracking, and targeting of naval forces afloat into the hands of weaker actors who tap into SPOT-type imagery with incountry download capability. Couple this technology with that of cruise and ballistic missiles, Global Positioning System (GPS) accuracy for target footprint, and terminal guidance and the seriousness of the threats posed to naval operations can readily be seen.

The asymmetrical adversary potentially has two other very deadly linear options available. The first one is the mine. We might find thousands of mines strewn across potential landing areas for forces and logistics support. An adversary might even use mines to channel U.S. operations to a location deemed advantageous to the enemy for reasons unknown or not obvious to our planners. Certain strategic choke points could be mined to deny access (as in the Strait of Hormuz, the Suez Canal, and others). Will we have minesweepers in every naval surface group sent forward in the future? How long would it take to get minesweepers to an area of operations? Do minesweepers become high-value surface assets? How vulnerable is the naval task force during that delay? A second deadly option is the submarine. Diesel-powered, brown-water submarines pose unique challenges to naval forces designed to fight the blue-water subs of the cold war. An adversary could use its submarines as a counterforce option. But perhaps a more likely scenario would be to threaten shipping going to a potential host nation. Or perhaps submarines would target naval replenishment ships or prepositioning vessels. We may speculate that an enemy's submarine force would have a short life expectancy, but how many (or few) casualties would it take to cause the United States to pull out of an operation, or to have a potential host nation deny access? It only took eighteen killed in action in Somalia to reverse U.S. policy there.

While we can see the enemy in the examples above, information warfare in cyberspace provides us no such luxury, for, indeed, seeing one's enemy before, or as, he strikes may become more and more a luxury in future war. Imagine if we were trying to deploy forces from bases in the United States and cyberterrorists brought down computer networks at, say, Charleston Air Force Base, Fort Bragg, Camp Le June, and Norfolk Naval Station. The result would be disorder and confusion on a huge scale, because these four bases are the key marshaling and deployment centers for the Eastern seaboard. Special Agent Jim Christy of the President's Infrastructure Protection Task Force cited a General Accounting Office study that showed DOD computers being attacked 250,000 times per year, of which two-thirds are successful. In that same study, Agent Christy noted that the Defense Security Agency acknowledged that only 4 percent of all DOD intrusions are detected and, of those, only 25 percent are reported. The actual number of cyberattacks each year may be staggering. In the private sector, virtually no attacks are reported. Are these master criminals, highly trained by some clandestine organization? The 1994 breach of computer systems at Rome Laboratories in New York was traced back to a sixteen-year old hacker called "Datastream," who used nothing more than a 486sx computer and a modem. Not only did he breech Rome's system, he used the valid ID and login from Rome to break into the South Korean Atomic Research Institute. He was caught only because he bragged about his activities to fellow hackers over the Internet. One of the coauthors of this chapter personally witnessed the virtual halt of electronic information for a week at a military installation when hackers attacked the basewide information network, using electronic routings through foreign countries. The very information we count on to give us battle space dominance can be, and already has been, turned against us.

The truly frightening aspect in considering the linear attack options discussed above is to realize that nonlinear adversaries could prosecute most of these operations themselves. Mines, cruise missiles, GPS, and satellite imagery are all within the technological and monetary grasps of these entities. The manufacture of chemical and many biological weapons requires skills already resident in most illegal drug laboratories. As noted earlier, a handful of cyberwarriors could wreak havoc on systems, ashore or afloat, that rely on computer technologies. A satellite-phone system, laptop, and modem could put network-centric systems at risk anywhere on the Earth's surface. Hacker attacks on home-based computer systems or networks supporting logistical lines of communication could shut down, or at least drastically curtail forward operations. These threats already exist, and they will only increase in their abilities and potential for impact.

Of even greater concern is the potential for new and novel uses of the new lethal and nonlethal technologies in the hands of rogue states, nonstate, and substate actors. Certainly Colonel Dunlap and Lieutenant Colonel Peters provide nightmarish views of the future. We suggest it could be even worse. If the littorals contain the potential problem zones, it is the littorals that will be the problem zone for the Navy. With CNN providing a continuous intelligence feed, the prospect of SPOT or LANDSAT imagery, coupled with GPS accuracy, creates a new security dilemma for the carrier battle group. Operating in the littorals removes much of the "big ocean" safety net and places the group at risk. The fleet cannot simply "hide" over the horizon, because the enemy will be able to see well beyond its shore-based line of sight. The network-centric capabilities the Navy counts on for its edge in the future will provide the innovative enemy an opportunity to employ its hackers to disrupt or jam navigation signals and interfere with satellite data-transfer systems. The operations tempo maintained by naval battle and readiness groups will likely increase, spreading these resources even thinner. An enemy could easily conduct disruptive hacker operations, targeting shore-based support networks as well as systems afloat. Further, the attacks could come from anywhere on the globe, routed through scores of dummy sites promulgated by a state, substate, or nonstate actor.

In conclusion, the spectrum of conflict has increased its complexity with the advent of the revolution in information technologies. But has the fog of war decreased, or do we simply know more and understand less? If we count on new technologies to reduce the price in blood and treasure of future war, we are likely to be wrong. We have greatly increased our lethality, precision, speed of delivery, and ability to find, track, and target a conventional, linear enemy. However, we must also note that the enemy is adapting himself to this new technology and is opting for nonlinear, asymmetrical strategies and operations that point to a very dangerous future. The technological superiority on which we count may be more difficult to preserve as a result of the commercialization of advanced information and integration systems. We cannot contemplate degrading GPS or restricting U.S. commercial telecommunications satellites, let alone those owned by allies and potential adversaries, for any reason short of national survival. We face a future in which the United States will be at an unprecedented risk from asymmetrical strategies and operations employed with savagery and brutality. As we look to build the force structures, organizations, and doctrines for the twenty-first century, we must ensure that we will be able to deal with adversaries whose strategies will be increasingly asymmetrical. Indeed, future conflicts may extend across a spectrum encompassing both "Son of Desert Storm" and "Stepchild of Somalia and Chechnya".[5]

Notes

1. Tony Perry, "Hunting beyond Red October," *Los Angeles Times* (Washington, D.C., edition), October 21, 1997, p. 2.
2. Sun Tzu, *The Art of War*, edited and with a foreword by James Clavell (New York: Dell Publishing, 1983), p. 34.
3. Ibid, p. 15.
4. Charles J. Dunlap Jr., "How We Lost the High-Tech War of 2007," *Weekly Standard*, January 29, 1996, pp. 22–28.
5. Terms used by General Charles C. Krulak, former commandant, U.S. Marine Corps, "Draft Remarks for the Business Executives for National Security, 5 July 1996." Remarks prepared for a speech given in Washington, D.C. Text provided by General Krulak's staff group.

IMPLICATIONS FOR U.S. DEFENSE PLANNING

David Ochmanek

An invasion of South Korea is unlikely.
— CIA analysis, January 1950

Large-scale aggression by one state against another is almost never regarded as "likely" in the normal sense of the word until it actually occurs.[1] Yet the threat and use of force has been a prominent feature of the human experience since the dawn of history.

This chapter offers some thoughts on large-scale aggression and the role that preparing for it should play in U.S. defense planning. Specifically, the chapter addresses the questions of

➤ whether preparations to deter and defeat large-scale aggression should play the central role in U.S. defense planning;

➤ how U.S. defense planners can identify threats for which they must prepare;

➤ how future adversaries might employ the military capabilities available to them to threaten U.S. interests and allies; and

➤ what general types of U.S. military capabilities are called for to meet these emerging challenges.

Deterring and Defeating Large-Scale Aggression: Does It Matter?

U.S. forces have fought five major wars in the twentieth century—on average, one every twenty years. From the standpoint of an American defense planner at the end of the twentieth century, the prospect is for fewer large wars in the twenty-first century. The powerful, ideologically driven adversary that served as the West's antagonist during the cold war has disappeared and is not likely to return or be replaced. Even more important than this development is the fact that technology and modernization have changed forever the rules of the "state-power game." Many of the things that states used to fight over, such as land and control of natural resources, are no longer the keys to national wealth and power. Indeed, wars of conquest are likely to debilitate states that undertake them, rather than adding to their power and prestige. Such is the extent of these changes that wars between states that belong to the growing club of industrial market democracies can now safely be regarded as obsolete. Writing about "the coming war with Japan" might sell books, but it is poor strategic analysis.

That said, U.S. defense planners have powerful and enduring reasons for continuing to focus on major aggression as the chief determinant of force structure and posture.

Our Adversaries

The ongoing crisis with Iraq reminds us that the United States faces other states—some of them powerful regional actors—that are pursuing objectives antithetical to our own. To the extent that these states seek to harness military capabilities in pursuit of their objectives, they constitute threats of concern to defense planners.

The infrequency of large-scale interstate warfare should not in itself be seen as indicative of the importance it should have in U.S. defense planning. After all, the likelihood of future conflicts depends in large measure on what the United States does and says. Wars that this country is prepared (both physically and psychologically) to fight rarely happen. Hence the relative rarity of actual aggression against U.S. interests is, in part, a mark of the success of the U.S. defense strategy and posture.

Global Sheriff

Unlike the nineteenth century, when the United Kingdom maintained a military balance in and around Europe, patrolled the seas, and provided a general framework for orderly relations among states, today there is no acceptable alternative to the United States as the leading enforcer of international norms. Like it or not, we are the sheriff of much of the globe. If the United States were to lose the capacity or the will to defend its international interests, no other state would be capable of doing so, and we would be inviting military challenges to these interests.

Power Projection and U.S. Alliances

The capacity to project large-scale military power across large distances distinguishes the United States from every other nation today. As such, U.S. power projection capabilities are the sine qua non of viable alliances. Without these capabilities, our commitments to defend common interests in Europe, East Asia, the Greater Middle East, and elsewhere would be hollow. In such circumstances, we would quickly begin to lose influence over the decisions of the world's other important states. We would also see former allies moving to acquire more powerful means for their own defense, touching off destabilizing arms races in regions where important U.S. interests lie and reducing our ability to shape developments in those regions.

Our alliances are the cornerstone of U.S. national security strategy. Maintaining, adapting, and extending these alliances are the keys to shaping a world in which U.S. interests are secure and our values can flourish.

Optional and Mandatory Fights

Because the United States does not leave its most important interests unprotected, it is not possible to threaten those interests militarily without the application of substantial force. For example, a hostile state could not expect to defeat a U.S. treaty ally or seize an important objective, such as Saudi Arabia's oil fields, without undertaking large-scale aggression. Hence, for U.S. defense planners, defeating large-scale aggression is almost synonymous with defending important interests. Lesser U.S. interests can be challenged through smaller-scale attacks, as we have seen in places such as Grenada, Panama, Somalia, Bosnia, and Haiti.

The point here is that we can, in many cases, choose not to respond to smaller-scale challenges because these tend to involve less-than-important interests. However, we cannot choose not to defend important interests without grave consequences. The costs of failure in a major theater conflict are likely to be quite severe, both in terms of lives lost and in terms of the costs to our national interests, while the costs of taking a pass on smaller-scale challenges to lesser interests are likely to be tolerable.

Fungible Capabilities

Finally, it should be noted that the choice between fielding and preparing forces for large-scale theater operations, as opposed to fielding forces well suited to conducting smaller-scale operations, is not, in most cases, an "either-or" proposition. Forces and assets needed to deter and defeat major aggression often provide capabilities essential to commanders involved in humanitarian operations, noncombatant evacuations, intervention, peacekeeping, sanctions monitoring, punitive strikes, and other smaller-scale operations. Such capabilities as airlift, battlefield surveillance, mobile communications, maritime patrol, precision strike, and air superiority come readily to mind.

In short, prudence demands that the United States field forces capable of deterring and defeating aggression against its most important interests. And we must have sufficient aggregate capability to defeat, in concert with allies, threats to U.S. interests in more than one region at a time. For which threats should U.S. planners prepare?

Identifying Threats and Challenges

It is not possible to predict where or when the United States will fight its next war. Fortunately, it is also not necessary to do so. The key to defense planning is to identify which interests (and, by extension, which places) have to be defended from which threats.

Enduring Interests

Like other states, the United States maintains military forces to protect the nation from direct threats of attack. Unlike most other nations, the United States also fields and employs military forces to underwrite the security of other states. Put simply, the United States is an "exporter" of security and stability. Recognizing that the best way to protect and advance U.S. interests is to invest in stability in regions where our most important interests are engaged, the United States has built a network of security relationships with states in three regions:

➤ Europe and East Asia, because this is where most of the "movers and shapers" of the international community are. If we want to get something done internationally, whether it is controlling the spread of sensitive technologies, expanding international trade, or organizing an economic boycott against a rogue state, we start with our allies in these regions

➤ Southwest Asia and the Middle East, primarily, though not exclusively because of the critical and irreplaceable role played by petroleum in our economy

➤ Additionally, because of their sheer proximity, events in Canada, Mexico, and the states of the Caribbean and Central America can directly affect important U.S. interests.

Threats

In general, defense strategists and planners focus on threats that have one or more of the following attributes:

➤ The potential adversary (nation-state or otherwise) is pursuing (or may pursue) policies that conflict with U.S. preferences and objectives

➤ The potential adversary possesses (or may acquire) the military means to advance his policies

➤ The potential adversary's actions could threaten important U.S. interests

Threats that occupy the intersection of these three sets of conditions ("planning cases") constitute the most salient problems for defense strategy and force planning. Detailed operations plans are prepared for defending against such threats. Today, only North Korea and Iraq unambiguously constitute threats of this nature.

Threats occupying the intersection between two of these three sets ("hedging cases") generally demand our attention as well, constituting eventualities against which prudent strategists plan. Examples of cases against which force planners must hedge are Russia, China, Iran, and Libya.

This is not to say that our forces will never be called on to address threats that fall outside these zones of intersection. Presidents and geopolitics being what they are, it is very difficult to predict where and under what conditions U.S. forces might be engaged, especially when the United States confronts challenges that involve U.S. interests that are less than vital. In general, rather than trying to plan specifically for all such "lesser" contingencies, planners should develop generic scenarios against which to prepare and assess U.S. forces.[2]

This approach has the benefit of focusing the force planners' attention on the potential threats that they ought to worry most about:

➤ As noted earlier, nations that share our basic objectives and are unlikely to change their spots (for example, our NATO allies, Japan, the Republic of Korea, Australia, and so forth) need not be of concern, no matter how powerful their military capabilities.

➤ Nations that pursue policies antithetical to our own but that lack the capability to threaten important interests need not distract the force planner.[3] By acquiring weapons of mass destruction, however, such nations can vault themselves to the center of attention (for example, Libya).

➤ Nations that have sizable military forces and whose future geopolitical orientation is uncertain (for example, Russia, China) merit close attention, especially if these nations are located in regions where important U.S. interests lie.

This effort at identifying current and future problems worthy of attention could be further elaborated, but the basic point is made. When we plan forces for major conflicts, we need not worry about everything. Actors that lie within the interests-objectives-capabilities intersection are of primary concern. Actors that possess two of the attributes must also be considered in force planners' calculations. Actors that do not have at least two of the three attributes generally need not be of concern in the near term. However, strategy and force planning should address even these cases if a reasonable possibility exists that the actor might acquire two of the attributes in the future.

Enemy Capabilities and Strategy

If these are the adversaries and potential adversaries of interest, how might military challenges from them manifest themselves in the future? How one answers this question bears heavily on debates about force structure and modernization.

Obviously, prudence demands that we measure U.S. forces against the challenges that could be posed by representative adversaries that are reasonably competent and fairly well equipped. In positing future challenges, we should first recognize that regional adversaries generally do not need to defeat the United States and its armed forces to achieve their objectives. In the main, our adversaries in the post–cold war environment seek to undermine U.S. influence in their regions so that they may have a greater say in that region's affairs. This means that securing fairly limited military objectives—coercing neighboring states or seizing key territory or assets—might well serve to meet the adversary's policy objectives. And it means that clever adversaries will seek to avoid engaging U.S. forces in a major way if they can.

This fact, coupled with the realities that our adversaries will fight close to home and can generally be confident of having the initiative in the opening phase of a future war, suggests an approach that relies on surprise, speed of maneuver, and efforts to impede U.S. forces' access to the region and to suppress their tempo of operations.

Short Warning, High Speed

History shows that the wars U.S. forces fight are not the ones for which they prepare and deploy promptly. The Taiwan Straits, Korea (post-1953), and, perhaps, Central Europe throughout the cold war are examples of wars that did not happen, at least in part because of prompt or sustained U.S. deployments. Korea (1950) and Iraq's attack on Kuwait, however, suggest that a failure to anticipate or to react promptly to threats of aggression may invite attack. Prudence therefore dictates that the scenarios used to test U.S. defense preparedness include serious consideration of the possibility of surprise. Improved monitoring capabilities and a vigilant attitude can reduce the probability of U.S. forces having to defend from an unreinforced posture. But these cannot assure that warning indicators will always be acted on. Prompt action often relies not only on the speed of decision making in Washington but also on the cooperation of U.S. allies and friends. Building a consensus for action can take time. In short, a defense posture that relied for its viability on a lengthy period of reinforcement would be a poor deterrent and would subject U.S. forces and interests to substantial and unnecessary risks.

While all of this might seem obvious, it is worth noting that much of the work done in support of DOD's recent program review downplays these very factors. As was revealed in a study of the heavy bomber force conducted under DOD's supervision in 1995, the "base case" scenario for the Persian Gulf region assumes that U.S. forces will have nearly two weeks' reinforcement time before the commencement of hostilities.[4] During this period, the United States would be able to send more than a dozen fighter squadrons, two to three brigades of Army and Marine forces, and two to three carrier battle groups to the theater. Other U.S. forces continue to arrive during the course of the campaign. Not surprisingly, assessments of the outcome of such a conflict show U.S. and allied forces winning handily. But what rational adversary would wait to attack under such unfavorable circumstances? If potential adversaries learned anything from the Gulf War, they learned that they must strike before the United States deploys large-scale forces to their region and that they must do all they can to impede the progress of that deployment once it begins.

Countering U.S. Access and Optempo

A second way in which the canonical cases are insufficiently challenging is in their assumptions regarding the enemy's use of existing or emerging attack capabilities to deter or impede the deployment of U.S. forces to the region and to suppress their tempo of operations (Optempo) once deployed. A range of military capabilities that is well suited to this approach is available to potential enemies. Chief among these are air, missile, and special forces attacks on key airbases, command and control sites, logistics depots, and seaports. Likewise, regional adversaries have access to a growing array of weapons, including antiship missiles, submarines, and more advanced sea mines, that can be used to threaten naval combatants and merchant shipping. And it is widely recognized that all of our most plausible adversaries today, including North Korea, Iran, and Iraq, already have stocks of lethal chemical agents. It should also be assumed that despite our best efforts to the contrary, over the next ten years or so, biological agents and fission weapons will be in the hands of a larger number of countries than today.[5] Assessments of U.S. forces and modernization priorities must take account of these growing threats.

A generic scenario encompassing these considerations might depict a case in which a U.S. ally is attacked by a force of up to twenty-five divisions (half of them mechanized). The attack would occur with short warning and would be supported by modest numbers of advanced SAMs, fourth generation aircraft, and the types of capabilities mentioned above. A typical regional adversary (for example, Iran or Iraq) might bring to bear such forces in the middle or latter years of the next decade.[6] A more sizable nation, such as China, could certainly commit a larger force against its neighbors, though qualitatively, the threat would look much the same. This time frame— roughly ten years in the future—seems best suited as a basis for informing choices about today's defense program because it is set far enough in the future to account for lead times in fielding systems currently under development, yet it is near enough to the present to permit us to forecast factors, such as the U.S. regional posture and adversary objectives and capabilities, with some confidence.

In broad terms, it is assumed that the enemy's chief objective is to seize critical assets some distance from the prewar border. Hence, mechanized ground forces spearheading the enemy advance are instructed to move as rapidly as possible. We should also assume that the enemy is capable of a combined air and land operation, with reasonably modern surface-to-air defenses, interceptors, and attack aircraft.

Most important, force planners should assume that, for one reason or another, U.S. forces have not substantially reinforced the theater before the attack. In the vernacular, C-Day (the day that large-scale U.S. reinforcement begins) equals D-Day (the day that the enemy commences his attack). This could happen if U.S. indications and warning assets failed to detect or correctly assess enemy preparations for an attack, if U.S. decisionmakers delayed in reacting to warning, or if the leaders of countries that were threatened by the attack temporized in allowing U.S. forces access to their territory in the face of ambiguous indications of hostile intent by the neighboring country. This implies that the United States and its allies have, at most, modest-size forces available for initial defensive operations.

Obviously, this case represents a challenge for the defenders, even if weapons of mass destruction are not used in support of the attack. Nevertheless, it does not represent a "worst case." In August of 1990, the order to deploy U.S. combat forces to the Persian Gulf came four days after Iraqi forces marched into Kuwait.[7] If Saddam had chosen a more aggressive strategy, the first U.S. forces to arrive in theater could have found themselves fighting an enemy already well into Saudi Arabia.

Strategic and Operational Asymmetries

Finally, it is important that assessments of future U.S. capabilities reflect what might be called "strategic and operational asymmetries" between the United States and its potential adversaries. Projecting military power on short notice into the "backyard" of a major regional power is an inherently demanding enterprise. This is particularly true when that enemy is willing to accept vastly more casualties than the intervening outside power is. In this situation, there is a high premium on forces that can deploy rapidly, seize the initiative, and achieve their objectives with minimal risk of heavy casualties. Only by using plausibly stressing scenarios as the yardstick against which to measure the capabilities of future U.S. military forces can the importance of innovation and modernization be given fair weight.

An approach to force assessment that recognizes both the inherent asymmetries in the strategic and operational situations of the United States and its potential enemies renders moot many of the arguments that have been deployed in opposition to certain new systems currently under development by the Department of Defense. Some critics of ongoing modernization efforts seem to believe that if they can establish that a particular system under development by the United States is substantially more capable than those that will be possessed by our adversaries, they have made the case that the system is "not needed." However, an approach to force planning that encompasses strategic and operational asymmetries reveals that, in selected areas, U.S. forces may need capabilities far superior to those fielded by their opponents to prevail in future conflicts as quickly and as effectively as is called for by U.S. strategy.

Meeting Future Challenges: A New Approach to Theater Warfare?

The defense strategy outlined in the *Report of the Quadrennial Defense Review* (QDR) describes, in general terms, how the United States plans to harness its military power to an overall national security strategy designed to meet and shape future challenges.[8] DOD highlights the importance of deterring and defeating enemy aggression quickly, deterring and preventing the use of weapons of mass destruction, stationing and deploying U.S. forces abroad in peacetime, and other activities conducted by U.S. military forces. But it is not clear that defense resources are being allocated in ways that are fully consistent with this strategy. Rather, in important ways, the force structure, force posture, and investment priorities that emerged from the QDR seem to be grounded in a fairly traditional concept of future operations—a concept that is increasingly ill suited to emerging conditions.

Warfare by the Book: "Fire Enables Maneuver"

For centuries, land warfare has been dominated by the need to rely on close battle engagements to destroy the bulk of an enemy's forces. Longer-range firepower assets, such as artillery and aircraft, have been seen as useful chiefly as means of suppressing and disrupting enemy operations, but not in atritting enemy forces to a significant degree. Their effectiveness was hobbled in part by the difficulty of locating enemy forces quickly and reliably much beyond line-of-sight ranges. Such an approach places the burden of defense against an invasion primarily on large formations of heavy maneuver forces.

But this traditional approach will not work in situations similar to the scenario sketched out above. For one thing, in areas where potential conflicts might break out in the future, the United States does not routinely deploy large numbers of heavy ground forces forward. This is a function of both economics and politics. Manpower is expensive and stationing large numbers of forces abroad, especially ground forces, is manpower intensive. And in the Persian Gulf region, the United States must respect the views of host country governments that wish to minimize the impact of the U.S. military presence on their societies. Moreover, as weapons of mass destruction and the means to deliver them proliferate, the risks of placing large numbers of U.S. military personnel close to an attacking force will escalate inexorably.

A New Approach: "Information Enables Firepower"

Thanks to advances in sensors, communications, information processing, miniaturization, and other technology aggregates, U.S. military forces need not remain tied to this traditional approach. Today, our forces are acquiring new capabilities both to "see deep" (that is, into the opponent's operational second echelon and beyond) and to "kill deep." Future U.S. and allied commanders should be able to know with a high degree of confidence when and where large-scale enemy armored forces are moving. And with that knowledge, they should be able to direct highly effective firepower assets not only to slow and disrupt enemy columns but also to rapidly impose high levels of attrition on them.

One way to gain an appreciation of the significance of these innovations is to compare the capabilities of forces equipped with the most modern information and firepower systems to those of a previous era. In the 1970s, using route reconnaissance tactics and cued by reports from engaged ground forces, aircraft such as the F-4E relied chiefly on the human eye to locate and engage moving armor. This resulted in many sorties that failed to locate and engage enemy ground forces. Those sorties that did engage valid armored targets would, in a high-threat environment, deliver an unguided antiarmor cluster weapon, such as the Mk-20 Rockeye. Under these conditions and given the limitations of those weapons, several sorties would be required, on average, to achieve a high degree of confidence of killing a single armored vehicle. At night or in poor weather, sortie effectiveness—already quite low—declined markedly.

Contrast that operational concept with the capabilities of forces and assets being fielded today. Airborne surveillance platforms, such as the E-8 Joint Surveillance, Target Attack Radar System (Joint STARS) carrying moving target indicator (MTI) and other radar sensors, can detect moving vehicles at ranges of one hundred miles or more. Soon these assets will be supplemented by other platforms, such as unmanned aerial vehicles (UAVs) carrying multispectral imaging sensors. Together, such sensors will give commanders and control centers an accurate picture of the movements of large-scale mechanized formations in near-real time. Controllers can use this information to direct attack assets rapidly to the most important and lucrative targets. Weapons such as the wind-corrected munitions dispenser (WCMD) and the Army Tactical Missile System (ATACMS) can accurately deliver large numbers of smart, antiarmor submunitions, such as the Sensor Fuzed Weapon and the Brilliant Anti-Tank (BAT) weapon. Such weapons have demonstrated a level of lethality against moving armor that is an order of magnitude or more greater than earlier generation area munitions, such as Rockeye.

Thus, compared with our capabilities of a decade or more ago, many more of our long-range attack assets will find their targets, and those attacks will be vastly more effective. Moreover, because the new long-range sensors and specialized munitions are not degraded by conditions of poor visibility, enemy maneuver forces will have no sanctuary at night or in bad weather. The net result of these emerging capabilities should be a fundamental transformation in the way that U.S. forces fight wars against mechanized opponents. Under many conditions, enemy maneuver forces now can be engaged and neutralized before they have the chance to close with friendly ground forces. And with rapidly deployable firepower assets, such as fighter and bomber aircraft, playing a major role in destroying enemy armored forces, the United States should be able to protect its interests and its allies with relatively modest forces stationed and deployed abroad in peacetime.

Naturally, concepts relying on standoff surveillance and advanced firepower are best suited to situations in which enemy forces must move across fairly open or channelized terrain in large numbers to achieve their objectives. Other situations will arise, particularly in smaller-scale conflicts, where forces—perhaps infantry or irregular troops on foot and in urban or heavily forested terrain—would be far less vulnerable to this sort of approach[9]. Nevertheless, deterring and defeating attacks by large-scale armored formations remains an important objective—perhaps the most important objective—assigned to U.S. military forces. It appears that, with the proper levels of attention and investment, U.S. forces have the potential to render this form of warfare virtually obsolete for our opponents. Changes of this magnitude in capabilities imply the need for an equally fundamental revision of operational concepts, force mix, and investment strategy.

Conclusion:
Providing New Capabilities for Theater Warfare

In theater warfare, as in other levels of conflict, it will be essential that U.S. expeditionary forces be capable of rapidly dominating operations in the air, at sea, on the land, and in space. Only by fully exploiting advances in sensors, information management, and firepower will it be possible for U.S. forces to have high confidence in prevailing in the opening phase of future theater conflicts.

The key components of these capabilities include:

➤ joint forces deployed forward in peacetime that can monitor developments, train with allied and indigenous forces, and conduct initial defensive operations should deterrence fail;

➤ airlift, aerial refueling aircraft, and assets prepositioned in theaters of interest, for rapid deployment of reinforcements;

➤ forces that can protect rear-area assets, such as airfields, logistics hubs, command centers, and ports, from air, missile, and special operations forces attacks;

➤ forces that can quickly wrest from the enemy control of operations in the air, opening up enemy territory and forces to observation and attack from the air;

➤ airborne and space-based surveillance and control assets that can locate and characterize enemy maneuver forces and air defenses in near-real time and pass that information to attack platforms;

➤ forces that can damage and destroy attacking enemy maneuver forces and their lines of communication, using munitions that offer a high probability of kill for each round expended, regardless of weather; and

➤ modest-size, mobile ground forces that can be made available quickly and are capable of defending critical objectives against enemy maneuver forces that might survive or slip through highly lethal longer-range fires.

Forces and systems to provide these capabilities either exist today or are in advanced stages of development. If fielded in sufficient numbers, they would allow U.S. forces to halt armored invasions promptly, even under the stressing circumstances of a short-warning attack supported by concerted efforts to deny U.S. expeditionary forces access to the region of conflict. DOD today is underinvesting in key elements of this capability; most notably, advanced munitions, wide-area surveillance and control, and platform-weapon integration. Without a shift in resources toward these sorts of capabilities, U.S. power projection capabilities may erode over the coming decade, as potential adversaries field new, more powerful weapons and forces.

Notes

1. "Large scale aggression" is here defined as an attack by the forces of a state or combination of states against the forces of another state or states, with the objective of defeating those forces for the purpose of imposing conditions on the victims that could not be obtained by other means. Those conditions may include the ceding of territory or assets to the attacker, the termination of a security relationship with an ally, or a host of other policy changes. The form of aggression is assumed to be a combined arms operation involving land, sea, air, and missile forces.

2. For a clear statement of U.S. policy regarding the use of force and forces, see *Annual Report to the President and the Congress*, William J. Perry, secretary of defense, Government Printing Office (GPO), February 1995, pp. 14–17.

3. The exception here is the need to be able to evacuate American citizens from dangerous situations. The safety of Americans is always an important U.S. interest and their safety could be put at risk in virtually any country. Therefore, the DOD must be prepared to evacuate noncombatants anytime and any place.

4. See Paul G. Kaminski, "Heavy Bomber Force Study" (briefing charts), U.S. Department of Defense, Government Printing Office, 1995.

5. For an overview of the current and projected status of chemical, biological, and nuclear threats to U.S. interests, see *Strategic Assessment 1995*, National Defense University Institute for International Strategic Studies, GPO, 1995.

6. Les Aspin, *Report of the Bottom-Up Review*, U.S. Department of Defense, Government Printing Office, October 1993, pp. 13–15.

7. *Conduct of the Persian Gulf War*, U.S. Department of Defense, Government Printing Office, April 1992, p. 35.

8. See William S. Cohen, *Report of the Quadrennial Defense Review*, U.S. Department of Defense, Government Printing Office, May 1997, pp. 7–18.

9. For an in-depth assessment of the roles that modern air forces can play in defeating smaller-scale aggression, see Alan Vick, and others, *Preparing the U.S. Air Force for Military Operations Other Than War*, RAND, 1997.

CRISIS RESPONSE AND POWER PROJECTION IN NONPERMISSIVE ENVIRONMENTS AND ASYMMETRICAL CONFLICTS

Richard H. Shultz Jr.

A few years ago The Fletcher School's International Security Studies Program convened a conference with the Marine Corps to examine the role of Naval expeditionary forces and power projection in the post–cold war world. Was there a need for such a Naval capability and, if so, for what purpose or purposes? That was the theme. Within that context, what overarching strategic concepts should guide the development and employment of U.S. Naval forces?

This was not an easy question to answer at that time, given that the cold war had just ended and the international system was entering a period of great uncertainty and change. Estimating whether, and if so to what extent, conflict and instability would take place seemed problematic. The parameters of the conflict spectrum were hardly clear and the issue of emerging symmetrical and asymmetrical challenges was only beginning to be considered.

Recall that this was in the aftermath of Operation Desert Storm and in many parts of the U.S. defense establishment the Gulf War was seen as the paradigm for future U.S. military operations. Many at the 1992 conference did not agree with this prognostication, but they were clearly going against the tide. A year later, the Clinton administration's "Bottom-Up Review," with its emphasis on two major regional contingencies, confirmed the fact that Operation Desert Storm was the paradigm for mainstream defense thinkers. While the then new administration's first "National Military Strategy" document alluded to the need to address other nontraditional challenges, preparing for two conflicts that reflected the Gulf War dominated the document.

Here I will briefly look back at how the issue of strategic concepts for the post–cold war era was addressed at the 1992 meeting, as a starting point for examining the question of crisis response and power projection in nonpermissive and asymmetrical environments.

Strategic Concepts

What strategic concepts should guide the U.S. development of military strategy, forces, and their employment? In 1992 I argued that it was not going to be deterrence. Beginning in the early 1960s, deterrence moved to the forefront and remained the basis for U.S. strategic thinking and policy formation throughout the cold war. Deterrence works best when there are constants and certainty in the international system. Until 1991 the Soviet Union was a long-term and certain threat. In the early 1990s it appeared things were going to be different because the new international environment was not going to be marked by constants and certainty. Rather, the world of the last decade of the twentieth century would be fluid, uncertain, and characterized by diverse, diffuse, and incalculable conflicts that could threaten U.S. interests. New actors would be appearing, many of which would not be states but substate and transtate actors.

In hindsight, this proved accurate, and today many are predicting that we can expect more of the same in the new century. For example, the Defense Department's Joint Strategy Review concluded that the twenty-first-century security environment will be characterized by chaos, crisis, and conflict caused by political ideology, ethnic and religious animosity, proliferation of weapons of mass destruction, and competition for scarce resources. In 1992 there were some hints of this but not to the extent that it has actually burgeoned. There has been not just an increase but a proliferation of ethnic and religious conflicts, terrorism, insurgency, urban unrest, and international organized criminal activity.

In this setting, while deterrence would still have a place, it was asserted in 1992 that it would be a reduced one. Other strategic concepts would move to the forefront, including: (1) compellence, crisis response, and power projection, and (2) presence, peacekeeping, and peacetime engagement. Today this latter category is called "operations other than war." Why did I argue this in 1992 and does it still hold true today?

Compellence, Crisis Response, and Power Projection

The purpose of compellence is to employ military power to coerce an adversary into undertaking the following actions: (1) stop an activity or operation that he has initiated and is taking place, (2) reverse or undo an action that he has already accomplished, and (3) initiate an action that is otherwise unacceptable.

Compellence almost always involves the threat or use of force. It is offensive, action oriented, and particularly suited for crisis response situations that are not easily forecast in advance and deterred. The deterrence use of force is passive and seeks to prevent a known adversary from taking action. Compellence employs force actively and in a sequence of actions in situations that are not clear with foreknowledge. By definition, you are in a crisis response situation that involves attention to where, what kind, and how much military power needs to be projected to convince and compel an adversary to comply with your wishes.

Symbiotically connected to compellence and crisis response is power projection, the capacity to introduce military power over long distances into rapidly changing, unstable, and violent situations. In 1992 I argued that power projection requires an available military infrastructure that includes prepositioned forces and equipment, deployed naval support systems, deep reconnaissance capabilities, and advanced C3I networks. As I will elaborate below, while this remains a necessary prerequisite for power projection, it is not sufficient. The United States likewise will need a much better understanding of those actors against whom it may have to project power and of the situational context in which operations are executed. This is a major issue the U.S. defense establishment is only beginning to explore.

Still, the importance of compellence, crisis response, and power projection will hold into the foreseeable future. In an international security system characterized by difficult-to-forecast regional crises involving not only states but substate and transtate actors, the ability to project power to compel adversaries to halt an activity under way or undo a deed already accomplished will be essential. When a crisis erupts with little forewarning, a compellence—power projection capability—will be required by U.S. policymakers.

Operations Other Than War

In 1992 it was unclear the extent to which peacekeeping, peace enforcement, humanitarian assistance, and related nonconventional uses of military power were going to grow in importance. Over the last six years, they have received considerable attention in U.S. military doctrine. By the mid-1990s, operations other than war (OOTW) came to include noncombatant evacuation, humanitarian assistance and disaster relief, security assistance, support to counterdrug operations, combatting terrorism, peacekeeping, peace enforcement, and attacks and raids.

Joint doctrine divides OOTW into operations taking place in permissive and nonpermissive environments. The former includes the use of military resources in situations that may approach or involve sporadic political violence but fall below the threshold of armed strife. Missions range from routine training and presence actions to peacekeeping, humanitarian assistance, and democratization operations.

OOTW taking place in nonpermissive environments can involve adversarial situations that result in violent armed conflict short of conventional conflict. It encompasses countering international organized crime, combatting terrorism, peace enforcement, insurgency and counterinsurgency support operations, and attacks and raids.

Unclear in 1992 was the extent to which operations other than war would grow in importance on the U.S. national security agenda and proliferate as a result of the growing number of internal wars, state disintegration, and ungovernability taking place in several of the world's regions. Substate and transstate actors are increasingly the cause of this post–cold war instability.

The linkages between crisis response and power projection and operations other than war were likewise not obvious in 1992. A lack of understanding existed of what the actors against the United States might confront in nonpermissive OOTW and the situational context in which these substate and transtate actors conduct military or paramilitary operations.

What has become increasingly apparent is that the situational context of future crises in which the United States will find itself projecting power to protect its interests will not be Gulf War-type conditions. Future conflicts are much more likely to be Chechnya or Bosnia-type situations.

The Future of Conflict: The Rise of Substate and Transstate Actors

Many international relations specialists have come to believe that substate and transstate actors will be among the major sources of violence, conflict, and war in the post–cold war world. While states will remain important actors and, as in the past, will use force to defend and promote interests, substate and transstate actors will increasingly be able to initiate violence in unprecedented ways. Technological advancements and the availability of modern weaponry will contribute to the rise of these new (and not so new) sources of instability.

These new actors will challenge the viability and survivability of existing states. The outcome of these developments may be that states in many parts of the world will be unable to function and disintegrate into ungovernability. This appeared to be accelerating in the late 1990s.

What motivates substate and transstate actors and what kinds of movements and groups will be involved? In terms of the former, the ideologies of ethnonationalism and religion, in their extreme radical forms, are playing an important role. The challenges of radical ethnonational factions, religious militants, secessionists, ethnic-based international criminal organizations, terrorists, and insurgents are all at play today. Among the threats they pose to international and regional instability are the following:

➤ The challenges of terrorism continue. The end of the cold war did not bring an end to terrorism. Groups and movements motivated by transcendent religious ideals and ethnonationalist passions are more than willing to employ these tactics to achieve desired ends. For example, instability is currently being generated by radical Islamic factions employing terrorism and other tactics of subversion in several Middle Eastern states, most notably Algeria, Egypt, and Israel. Ethnonational groups like the PKK and Tamil Tigers also employ these tactics.

➤ Secessionist movements are employing armed force and executing strategies of protracted conflict and insurgency to gain independence from states that seek to prevent their secession. Kashmir, Chechnya, and Sri Lanka are but three examples. Secession is an important contributor to nation-state disintegration and regional instability.

➤ Radical religious movements are likewise challenging government authority in various parts of the world through violence. The rise of transnational Islamic radicalism in the Middle East and Southwest Asia, and the cooperation between various radical Islamic factions and states, illustrates this potential. Radical Islamist political groups are able to compete for political power through the use of violence, as well as other political and social measures. Radical religious movements and cults in India, Israel, and Japan have proven capable of similar violent actions.

➤ Organized criminal groups also contribute to the declining ability of various existing governments to govern. State disintegration provides an environment in which criminal organizations, many of which are ethnic based, can flourish. They are able to threaten the stability of states, have a major impact on local economies, and corrupt officials and financial institutions. The Andes region of South America is a poignant example. The linkages that exist between organized crime, ethnic and religious movements, and terrorist and insurgent groups multiply the seriousness of this challenge. The successor states of the former Soviet Union and Eastern Europe are likewise threatened by such criminal syndicates.

The aggregate impact of these substate and transstate challenges will be political fission in which a state splits apart and its government disintegrates. Recent examples include Rwanda, Bosnia, Liberia, Lebanon, and Somalia. There are other states that, if they collapse, could destabilize important world regions. These include Pakistan, India, Egypt, Algeria, Iraq, Indonesia, Nigeria, and even Turkey and Mexico.

Contributing to these challenges will be the fact that radical substate and transstate actors have access to modern conventional arms, information technologies, and weapons of mass destruction. These weapons are available through states and on the black market.

While there is growing attention to instability generated by substate and transstate actors, there is little agreement over the extent to which this instability will affect U.S. interests in those regions of the world where it is taking place. I believe that these developments cannot be ignored. U.S. intervention in northern Iraq, Somalia, Haiti, and Bosnia are all illustrative of this fact. Substate and transstate actors will engage U.S. interests abroad and, as we have already experienced, will carry out operations inside U.S. borders.

The development by the Pentagon of doctrine for OOTW, including peacekeeping and peace enforcement, supports the contention that the United States will be unable to ignore substate and transstate instability. However, defining such conflict as OOTW may not portray the true nature of these conflicts in the most accurate light. In many ways, this is analogous to the old debate over the concept of low-intensity conflict (LIC). A look back at several of the conflicts classified as LIC reveals that, "on the ground" they were anything but low in intensity, if measured by killing, maiming, and destruction. Likewise, several situations categorized as OOTW have everything to do with the violence and carnage associated with warfare. While new doctrine is crucial, it is also important that doctrine accurately identify the context in which U.S. soldiers are deployed.

Instability caused by substate and transstate actors has important ramifications for U.S. military strategies for the future. The current debate over the need to restructure the armed forces cannot ignore these new trends or characterize them as secondary contingencies. As we explore the impact of the revolution in military affairs and information warfare on future U.S. military strategies, it is important that new approaches reflect the threats the United States is likely to face. What the United States wants to avoid is finding itself in 2010 in the position of being most prepared for the least-likely contingencies and least prepared for the most-likely challenges.

A few specialists have attempted to describe these "most-likely" conflicts as they are likely to appear in the years ahead. The images they present are not ones that can be found in the theorizing about the revolution in military affairs (RMA), information warfare (IW), or academic analysis of future conflict trends. These analysts, who can be described as iconoclasts, describe situations that are odious, beastly, and bewildering. What they tell us is that the future "faces of battle" in the years ahead will be very different from what the United States experienced in Desert Storm.

I count myself among the iconoclasts and believe we need to assail the cherished beliefs of the RMA and IW theorists, who subscribe to an abstract, highly managed, technologically dominated, and almost bloodless image of future conflict and war. They presume that future enemies, if they choose to fight our way, will be unable to do so effectively against us or, if they select other methods of fighting, we will be able to rout them through our way of fighting.

The Future Faces of Battle: Insights from International Journalists and Strategic Iconoclasts

Lebanon, Afghanistan, Chechnya, Bosnia, Somalia, Colombia, Israel, the Kurdish conflict, Rwanda and Burundi, and the civil wars in Sudan, Sri Lanka, and Angola all are taking place today and all need to be examined and understood in new ways, employing concepts and frameworks not commonly found in the mainstream national security literature. If these are the kinds of conflicts that will occur in increasing numbers in the years ahead, it is imperative that we not analyze them through Western lenses.

Conflicts and internecine wars taking place today differ in important ways from the Western understanding of the causes, conduct, and termination of war. We need to get in touch with these differences because they have consequences that are measured in blood and treasure. If we get it wrong, it matters.

We must come to understand "the otherness of others." In the West we like to think everything we have experienced, including how we fight war, has universal application. For example, our political values and institutions are seen as the undeniable basis for all others in this "new world order." Is this not how we think of democratization? We continue to believe this, even as the age-old principles of the desire for despotic power and the emotional appeal of virulent ethnonationalism oppose the spread of the political and cultural foundations on which Western civilizations rests.

So it is with war and conflict. If it must take place, the West likes to believe it will occur in the ways that we have come to understand and experience it. Looking at Lebanon, Afghanistan, Chechnya, Bosnia, Somalia, Colombia, and so on through these lenses will not tell us all we need to know, especially if we are contemplating intervention.

International Journalists

A handful of journalists who are "on the ground" covering today's conflicts provide searing accounts of war in its most brutal and often most indiscriminate form. One of the first to do so was Robert Kaplan. His expose, "The Coming Anarchy," shattered the hope that the post–cold war era would be orderly and peaceful. Rather, Kaplan proposed that as states disintegrate in West Africa and elsewhere, they will be characterized by "disease, overpopulation, unprovoked crime, scarcity of resources, refugee migration, the increasing erosion of nation-state and international borders, and the empowerment of private armies, security firms, and international drug cartels," that will have no interest in using force within the context of the Geneva Conventions of 1864 and 1906, the Lieber Code of 1863, and the Hague Conventions of 1899 and 1907.[1]

In Kaplan's description, we see many of the substate and transstate actors, identified above, that constitute a burgeoning source of violence, conflict, and war in the post–cold war world. He takes us out of the realm of the theoretical and into the extremely unpleasant and shocking real world of state breakdown and the violence it generates.

In many parts of the underdeveloped world are found the withering away of government structures and controls; the rise of ethnic, religious, tribal, and regional power centers; and the unchecked spread of violence and warfare. Africa is the prism through which Kaplan believes we should come to see what internal war will be like for the twenty-first century.

In his analysis of future internal wars, he explores several factors that will shape the contours and dimensions of these situations. He begins with the destructive effects of environmental scarcity and degradation. Next, he details how internal conflicts in the third world are being fought along racial, ethnic, tribal, and religious lines.

Kaplan's initial work focused on West Africa. Many argued that while the situations he described are tragic, these states are of little consequence to U.S. interests. In subsequent articles, Kaplan focuses on states that, if they begin to disintegrate, will create instability that the United States will not be able to ignore. Egypt is a case in point. In "Eaten from Within," he details how the Egyptian state, a pillar of U.S. foreign policy, is slowly disintegrating. If it collapses, it could destabilize the entire region of the Middle East and Southwest Asia.[2]

Journalistic accounts of Bosnia likewise present disquieting evidence of the new faces of battle. *Love Thy Neighbor: A Story of War* by Peter Maass is a stinging example. Maass reported from the Balkans during the most nightmarish period of that conflict. What he found was that neighbors who had lived side by side for years were capable of undertaking the most savage acts against one another. He presents a side of human nature that would make Thomas Hobbes flinch—and Hobbes was no optimist.[3]

Maass's description of the nature of the conflict in Bosnia is laced with the following language: atrocities, concentration camps, ethnic cleansing, genocide, rape, mutilation, sadism, torture, war crimes, and crimes against humanity. To be sure, these can be found in all wars, but in Bosnia they have become that war's raison d'etre. There are no rules or regulation of armed conflict and there are no noncombatants. His account of each of these activities is gruesome and horrifying.

Journalistic accounts of the civil war in Algeria are equally grisly and frightful in the day-to-day details of the conflict. As in Bosnia, there appear to be no rules and no noncombatants.

Strategic Iconoclasts

While journalists like Kaplan and Maass provide an "on the ground" view of the new dimensions of warfare in specific cases, a small number of strategic thinkers have sought to place post–cold war conflicts in a broader context. Probably the first to do so was Martin van Creveld in his 1991 book, *The Transformation of War*.[4] He was ahead of the curve in asserting that the state-centric international system was about to undergo a fundamental change in terms of the sources of instability. While he goes too far in suggesting that states "are decreasingly able to fight each other" and are withering away, he has proven prescient in terms of predicting the growing phenomenon of state disintegration and ungovernability.

According to van Creveld, as this century is coming to an end, the state's ability to monopolize violence is faltering. He envisions the emergence of new "warmaking organizations of a different type." These will include "groups whom we today call terrorists, guerrillas, bandits, and robbers. . . . Their organizations are likely to be constructed on charismatic lines rather than institutional ones, and to be motivated less by professionalism than by fanatical, ideological-based, loyalties."[5] They will fight in ways that do not fit our laws of war framework. He goes on to propose that the ways in which these groups fight will be more analogous to the warrior societies and classes of the Middle Ages.

What about technology? He hardly sees it as the panacea of the RMA and IW theorists. For van Creveld, there are elements of war that are not easily constrained by technology, especially in the unconventional realm of internal conflicts. These include violence, suffering, pain, death, and irrationality. The kinds of unconventional conflicts that he sees on the rise in the next century are likely to place greater emphasis on these dimensions of war. Such conflicts will be "protracted, bloody, and horrible." If the Western states are to cope, key changes in doctrine and force structure will be required, according to van Creveld.

There are two authors in this study who likewise provided early strategic insight into the future faces of battle. Both have been pilloried for their heretical arguments. Ralph Peters focused on adversaries U.S. soldiers may have to face. For Peters, they are not just emerging or in our future but are already present in several places. He asserts that "thanks to a unique confluence of breaking empires, overcultivated Western consciences, and a worldwide cultural crisis, the warrior is back, as brutal as ever and distinctly better-armed."[6] His description of substate and transstate actors involved in several ongoing internal wars contains much that is accurate and worrisome.

In failing states, the rank and file of substate and transstate groups and movements will emerge from four social pools. These include: (1) the underclass, which has no stake in society, little education, no legal earning power, and no future, (2) young males who enter warfare in their early teens and learn to do nothing else for a decade or more, (3) men who fight for strong and radical beliefs, whether religious or ethnic, and (4) disposed or otherwise cashiered soldiers.[7] From these social groupings come the militias and gangs that can be found fighting in Lebanon, Rwanda, Afghanistan, Chechnya, Bosnia, the West Bank and Gaza, and Somalia.

As states disintegrate in the years ahead, they will appear elsewhere. In "The Culture of Future Conflict," Peters accurately observes that future violent conflicts "will be shaped by the inabilities of governments to function as effective systems of resource distribution and control, and by the failure of entire cultures to compete in the post–modern age."[8]

The reasons for the disintegration of a growing number of states are complicated and structural. They involve many states created after World War I and World War II that have unresolved problems of assimilation, access to economic opportunity, ethnic or religious preferential legal structures, and unequal status. In several such situations, the existing state structures cannot cope with these challenges. There is no common identity or national homogeneity. The prospects for differences over religious or ethnic origin leading to major political confrontation and armed conflict are increasing because these problems are ensconced in the political, economic, and social structures of such states.

As states disintegrate they will generate the kinds of substate and transstate actors described above. Peters asks what these developments mean for the U.S. military? He believes that U.S. forces will more likely fight warriors rather than soldiers like itself in the years ahead. While RMA and IW technologies may be helpful, alone they will not equip the Army "for the conflicts we cannot avoid." He observes that "although there are nearly infinite variations, this kind of threat generally requires a two-track approach—an active campaign to win over the populace coupled with irresistible violence directed against the warlord(s) and warriors." To address the former, the

Army has been developing the doctrine of OOTW and the forces to support it. For the latter, the Army will require "skilled infantry and special operations forces."[9]

Finally, Peters cautions that we must come to grips with the ugly, brutal, and often intractable nature of these internal wars and those who fight them. "We will fight men who do not look, think, or act like us. . . . We will fight in cities, and this brutal, casualty-prone and dirty kind of combat will negate many of our technological advantages while it strains our physical and moral resolve."[10]

Charles Dunlap seeks to give us a close-up look at the kind of warriors the U.S. military will find itself fighting in the future. He speculates on how war might be fought asymmetrically against a technologically superior United States in the early twenty-first century by developing a scenario in which a mythical radical religious regime invades a weaker state in which the United States has vital national interests at stake.[11]

Washington undertakes a high-tech military solution, using a downsized force that has undergone major changes consistent with the RMA to expel the occupiers. The opposite transpires, and it is the United States that is compelled to withdraw. The religious regime refuses to fight on U.S. terms. Instead, it devises an indirect strategy that is extremely brutal and odious in the tactics employed. Indeed, through Western eyes it would be considered absolutely uncivilized.

The enemy's strategy entails "a vicious form of confrontation that extends across the spectrum of warfare. It differs from more traditional total war by, among other things, the propensity of the aggressor to focus on shattering the will of an opponent by employing brutality openly and unapologetically against combatants and noncombatants alike."[12] The United States quickly learns that recognized standards, laws of armed conflict, and Western values are not part of the enemy's strategy.

The invented American adversary practices what the historian John Keegan describes as primitive warfare. Such warfare is part of a culture "where the young are brought up to fight . . . and think killing in warfare glorious."[13] In Dunlap's scenario, the warrior society practices uncompromising zealotry and ferocity against a United States that is not prepared for this kind of fighting. There is no "winning without fighting" in this future conflict, as promised by the RMA and IW proponents. Rather, the U.S. adversary conducts military and paramilitary operations in ways that confuse, shock, and paralyze America, eventually shattering its will to fight. How is this possible?

First of all, while refusing to fight along the lines prescribed by the United States, the warrior society takes advantage of information-age technologies in several ways. For example, it uses cheap communications to devise redundant networks to exercise effective C3 over its military and paramilitary forces and to avoid the communications paralysis promised by the IW. It also manipulates the global media to spread its message that in this conflict the most insidious tactics will be used without reservation. The instant reporting of U.S. deaths and the savage treatment of its POWs produce powerful images. There is a Mogadishu every day. The global media also serves as the warrior regime's intelligence service, providing vital information on the U.S. domestic setting.

The warrior regime seeks to identify asymmetries in the conflict that it can exploit. It does so by extending the battlefield to the United States. For example, it destabilizes the Mexican economy through "cyberassaults" on its banking system and financial institutions. It also circulates billions of counterfeit pesos and provides support to insurgent groups in Mexico. The result is that Mexico is thrown into chaos, with millions fleeing across the U.S. border.

Domestic targets likewise come under terrorist assaults. As Dunlap explains, "unrestrained ethically or legally, my notional adversary chose to strike America's growing population of the elderly. Bombs were placed in parks and elder care facilities."[14] Environmental warfare is also employed by sinking oil tankers off the U.S. coast.

In the actual theater of operations, the United States finds itself long on information units but short on combatants needed to fight an enemy that disperses its forces. On the ground, digital warriors do not do well against primitive warriors. Dispersing its forces not only makes it harder to locate enemy troops for the United States but results in our using up precision weapons inventories.

Finally, the radical regime sacrifices its own people through what many believe is an unlikely scenario. What they do is induce the United States to use precision weapons against a biological warfare laboratory. As the U.S. weapons hit the target, the enemy leadership detonate their own nuclear weapon, sacrificing thousands. This brings world public opinion crashing down on the United States, which is blamed for the detonation. It also allows the warrior state to commit savage abuses against female U.S. prisoners of war. The domestic repercussions in the United States result in a call for withdrawal now.

Dunlap's study has come under considerable criticism. It is said to be unrealistic. No one behaves as his notional U.S. adversary.

Conceptualizing Future "Faces of Battle"

Since the end of the cold war, internal wars have grown in number and intensity. As a result, increasing attention has been paid to the causes of these conflicts, with particular attention given to ethnicity, ethnonationalism, and religion. The international dimensions have also received attention.

However, only a few specialists have begun to attempt to describe these internal wars in ways that reflect how they are actually being fought and what their impact is on the political, economic, and social setting in which they take place. Internal war today differs considerably from what John Keegan terms the Western approach to warfare.[15]

More systematic attention should be paid to understanding the dimensions and nature of internal war by the U.S. defense community. What has become increasingly clear today is that we do not know enough about the situational contexts of the most likely kinds of conflicts in which the United States may find itself projecting power.

One approach would be to develop an analytic framework that identifies and illuminates the various elements of these conflicts in a systematic manner. Such a framework would focus on the ways in which such internal wars are actually fought, the strategies and tactics employed, combatant training and behavior, and the impact of internal war on the locations in which they take place. Such an understanding of the post–cold war "face(s) of battle" in internal wars is essential.

This analytic framework should include attention to a host of variables, many of which are not part of the mainstream national security literature. In fact, it will require attention to concepts and frameworks found in other disciplines. The following variables, which are framed in terms of questions, are among the most apparent:

➤ 1. What are the organizational structures of warrior armies, militias, gangs, and criminal organizations involved in internal wars today? We are not likely to find this information in the annual *Military Balance* published by the International Institute for Strategic Studies. Not knowing can be costly, as the Russian army found out in Chechnya. How these nontraditional paramilitary organizations structure themselves for operations is important.

➤ 2. What kinds of training do the fighters who make up these warrior armies, militias, gangs, and criminal organizations receive? In what ways are they taught to fight? What kinds of actions are they prepared to undertake? Are there any constraints or limitations on actions inculcated during the training process, based on legal and moral concepts that inform the training of soldiers in the West?

➤ 3. Who becomes a warrior or fighter in these conflicts? How are they recruited and at what age are they inducted? How long is a tour of duty? Is there even such a concept as a tour of duty present?

➤ 4. What is the scope and nature of the type of operations that are carried out in today's internal wars and what objectives do they seek to achieve? To what extent does the concept or concepts of operations differ from what exists in Western military experience and doctrine?

➤ 5. What are the targets selected to attack? Who is considered a legitimate target and what kinds of actions can be taken against a target? Are there any distinctions made between combatants and noncombatants in today's internal wars?

➤ 6. What type of killing and destruction is taking place? How extensive is it? To what extent does it constitute war crimes and wanton destruction?

➤ 7. What is the impact of internal war on noncombatants in terms of the creation of refugees, displaced persons inside the territory where the conflict is taking place, and migration across borders?

➤ 8. To what extent do those who plan and execute these conflicts adhere to the laws of armed conflict? Do these regulations have any application in these situations? Are there other codes of conduct being employed to govern combat and the use of force? What are they?

➤ 9. To what extent has the personalization and localization of conflict generated the fomentation of blood feuds, vendettas, and hatred? How deeply are these entrenched and how do they affect perceptions? Do they create cultures of violence, and if so, what are the implications for more war fighting?

➤ 10. How are these wars financed by third parties? Who are these third parties? To what extent are international criminal organizations involved? What is the role of other outside actors, both state and nonstate, in the conduct of internal combat?

While these variables are not meant to be exclusive, each would have a prominent place in the framework envisioned. Each would require conceptual elaboration and the development of propositions that could be tested across cases. The development of each of these categories will necessitate an interdisciplinary approach that is likely to lead far from mainstream security studies.

A case in point is item three. Who becomes a warrior in these conflicts? How are they recruited and at what age are they inducted? How long is a tour of duty? Is there even such a concept as a tour of duty present? There is some very interesting work that has been conducted on this subject by non-governmental organizations. The analysis can be found in the publication *Children:The Invisible Soldiers*.[16] Why is this important? It is important because in many of the internal wars mentioned earlier, warrior armies, militias, gangs, and criminal organizations are increasingly recruiting or abducting out of the ranks of young teenagers. Their growing involvement has important social ramifications for the development of cultures of violence and prolongation of conflict.

Another example is the extent to which the personalization and localization of today's internal wars generate the fomentation of blood feuds, vendettas, and hatred. To what extent do we understand this in Bosnia? Here I am not talking about age-old vendettas and hatreds but about ones provoked in the 1990s.

Once developed, the framework could be used to guide case study analysis of several post–cold war internal conflicts. Such analysis has a valuable contribution to make to the understanding of policymakers and military planners as they contemplate intervening in these internal wars through U.S. power projection.

Notes

1. Robert Kaplan, "The Coming Anarchy," *Atlantic Monthly* (February 1994), pp. 44–76.

2. Robert Kaplan, "Eaten from Within," *Atlantic Monthly* (November 1994), pp. 26–58.

3. Peter Maass, *Love Thy Neighbor: A Story of War* (New York: Vintage, 1996).

4. Martin van Creveld, *The Transformation of War* (New York: Free Press, 1991).

5. Ibid, chap. 7.

6. Ralph Peters, "The New Warrior Class," *Parameters* (Summer 1994), p. 16.

7. Ibid, pp.17–19.

8. Ralph Peters, "The Culture of Future Conflict," *Parameters* (Winter 1995-96), p. 18.

9. Peters, "The New Warrior Class," p. 24.

10. Ibid.

11. Charles Dunlap, "How We Lost the High-Tech War of 2007," *The Weekly Standard* (January 29, 1996), pp. 22–27.

12. Ibid, p. 24.

13. Ibid, p. 22.

14. Ibid, p. 27.

15. John Keegan, *A History of Warfare* (New York: Vintage, p. 1993).

16. Rachel Brett and Margaret McCallin, *Children: The Invisible Soldiers* (Sweden: Radda Barnen, 1996).

THE HOURGLASS WARS

Ralph Peters

Despite all of the good money and muddled thinking dedicated to the revolution in military affairs and information warfare, the United States military remains a twentieth-century force in its organization, strategy, and, above all, materiel. We have made startling progress in the manipulation of information within the services to create battlefield efficiency and dynamism. But this progress is blunted by parochial leadership, the sclerosis of tradition, fear of change and loss, and industrial-age fleets of ships or aircraft supporting unwieldy ground formations designed not to facilitate victory but to minimize the commander's liability. Were it only more relevant to the world as it is and as it will be, we might content ourselves with this best-of-all conventional force.

The materiel is the key issue today, because in our deformed system procurement dictates everything else of import. Defense industries are our masters and, so long as they employ us when we retire, we in the military stuff our honor in our wallets and keep our mouths shut. As a result, our major weapons systems are so expensive and psychologically disarming that we shape our "needs" and forces to fit the gear, instead of the other way around. We are entrapped in our purchasing habits, and they have become a whopping mismatch for the conflicts we face. We struggle, through exercises such as the Quadrennial Defense Review, to adapt our requirements to our procurement plans. This is the precise opposite of a sound military policy, and we only get away with it because we are so wealthy and powerful.

We continue to buy breathtaking, inappropriate "new" systems that are only dressed-up versions of yesterday's solutions to the day-before-yesterday's problems. We do this out of habit and greed. Our national process for buying weaponry is corrupt and corrupting. Defense industry is the only field of American business endeavor wherein the key producers do not have to worry about the real needs of the consumer and are not held accountable for products that fail to work as advertised. We will continue to get fragile, budget-buster airplanes, such as the B1, B2, F22, and Joint Strike Fighter, that cannot fly regularly, strike efficiently, or survive independently. We will continue to buy ships that the fighting Navy does not want and cannot use. And we will cut real combat power to do it.

We do not want a revolution, nor do we want revolutionary systems. We just want sexier versions of the same old stuff. We insist on buying Porsches when we need pickup trucks. Our military is a magnificent national ornament of bombers, fighters, and obese fleets too valuable to risk in combat, too inefficient to use in conflict, and too unreliable to trust in crisis.

Meanwhile, we send soldiers and marines in patched-together task forces with jerry-rigged equipment to the broken places of the earth to do good that is ineffective, to create order that is unsustainable, and to defend clients we cannot respect, trust, or improve. Our useable forces—primarily those same soldiers and marines along with transport aircraft and vessels—are starved. They are undermanned, underfunded, improperly equipped, and overextended. We have achieved an old military dream: one force for parades, another for battle. But even for us such luxury is unaffordable. And it is the battle force that has been paying the bill.

The profile of our future enemies has begun to emerge from the fog of peace (contrary to Clausewitz, war is a great clarifier). With increasingly rare, anachronistic exceptions, these enemies will not be so foolish as to attempt to compete with us in the heavy-metal combat of ships, aircraft, and tanks. They will not bankrupt themselves in a conventional arms race or expose themselves to defeat in "honest" battle. They will arm themselves with the most basic killing tools and with sophisticated information technologies: sidearms and cell phones, machetes and modems, incisive low-density technologies and genocidal masses of humanity, child warriors and weapons of mass destruction. They will wage psychological and information warfare campaigns on levels we do not credit as military areas of responsibility. They will fight not for the transient human romance with statehood, but for belief systems, blood ties, clans and tribes, nationalisms exclusively defined, personal gain, revenge for incredibly imagined wrongs, and for the ineradicable joys of subjugating, destroying, and killing.

A graphic depiction of these enemies would look like an hourglass—the bottom broad with that most expendable resource of bullies, excess population. Simple armaments, from personal weapons to antiaircraft missiles and bombs, will be widely available to them. At the top of the hourglass, our most capable enemies will concentrate their resources on off-the-shelf technologies for communications, information manipulation, and cyberattack; on lawyers and propagandists; on media coercion; on eliciting sympathy from third parties who can impede us in international fora; and on weapons of mass destruction. Their Pattons will be programmers, their Jacksons men of iron will, obsessive vision, and enthusiastic cruelty. From drug lords to warlords, and from charismatic nationalists to religious furies, the common trait of these enemies is that they will not present suitable targets for the military we have constructed.

Our forces are designed to strike where this new breed of enemy does not exist. For all of our intelligence and targeting capabilities, we will be shooting at thin air. We are aimed at the middle of the hourglass, at a mirror image of our own force. Despite recent technology purchases, our heavy combat systems remain so dominant in our thinking and practice that our information systems automatically become slaves to yesterday's combat tools instead of being used to expand the horizon of combat. Also, we are bound by extremely conservative, state-limited notions of the legitimate parameters of military activities. We are focused on boundaries—between states, between departments of government, between units. Yet, the state with its component institutions—no matter the degree of federalism—remains a hierarchical unit that reached its apogee in the late nineteenth and first half of the twentieth century. Today, some enemies we face are unrestricted by bureaucracy, charters, or laws.

Because of our dominant conventional power in all spheres—and our growing cultural-economic power—we feel no pressing need to change. Yet, the world is changing, and our own country is changing. There is evidence of our government's inability to adapt to this accelerating pace of change on many fronts. Congress has transitioned—without realizing it—from a proactive legislative body that shaped the country to a reactive body that struggles to catch up with the dynamism of our culture, economy, society, and technology. Our organs of justice are incapable of maintaining basic civility in our cities. The Immigration and Naturalization Service is increasingly part of our national security and has become a defender of our shores. We cannot even measure our economy accurately. Our private sector and culture are the most advanced, creative, resilient, and successful on earth. America dominates the world—our government muddles through, looking backward with longing.

Our new enemies, by contrast, are creatures of change—although they are by no means uniform in the changes they desire. Some seek regressive change, a return to an imaginary golden age. Others want to impose an unprecedented local dominion over their neighbors. Some just want the gold, while others cherish messianic dreams of a collective destiny. But they all will do whatever it takes to reach their goals, without counting the cost in human misery. Timothy McVeigh, not Albert Schweitzer, is the international model of the committed man.

We will fight saints and opportunists and everyone in between. Greed tends to be cleverer than Belief, but Belief is more enduring. We will encounter remarkable combinations: enemies intoxicated by medieval religious practices who nonetheless employ brilliant software programmers, mass murderers who understand the manipulation of our humanitarian impulses, and international gangsters whose most effective defenses are our own laws. But our laws and humanitarian affectations otherwise mean nothing to men who will be delighted to employ weapons of mass destruction so hideous they are ultimately suicidal. The elation of man at the suffering of others—especially, but not only, that of his enemies—is just one of mankind's dirty little secrets. (It is difficult to find a moral difference between yesteryear's gleeful spectators at public tortures or burnings and the audience spikes when CNN covers genocide, mass rape, or terrorist attacks—we find horrors inflicted on others titillating, life-affirming, entertaining, and satisfying on a level for which the English language, at least, does not have a term.)

We are at the end of the Western conceit of rational man. The Enlightenment—coincident with the largest-scale wars in European history—is finished as a philosophical or sociological model. Future historians will see it as a foolish and futile attempt to match the social sciences to the Newtonian revolution, an endeavor equivalent to expecting men to behave with the predictability of beams of light. Well, we are the darkest of creatures, by far the most destructive, and we revel in it. The most powerful weapon our future enemies will bring to bear against us will not be submarines, or strike aircraft, or tactical missiles, or software viruses—or even nuclear weapons. Their most powerful weapon will be hatred.

Man loves, men hate. While individual men and women can sustain feelings of love over a lifetime toward a parent or through decades toward a spouse, no significant group in human history has sustained an emotion that could honestly be characterized as love. Groups hate. And they hate well. Despite the lurking evidence in today's society, the unique quality of the American experience and its galvanizing myths has disarmed our understanding of the enduring, invigorating power of group hatred. In many societies, it is the fundamental human bond outside of the family.

While psychology—an infant discipline that is little more than astrology for the educated classes—has not begun to explore the layered paradoxes of mass behavior, first-hand observation makes several things clear: While individuals can readily sustain love for years or even a lifetime, it is rare for an individual to sustain hatred, which tends to wither quickly into mere dislike. We might even blurt out that we want to kill the boss, but we only rarely get around to it, occasionally even developing a perverse retrospective affection for him or her as we suffer under a successor.

Masses hate. In turn, hate bonds the masses. Love is an introspective emotion, while hate is easily extroverted. Americans—cultural descendants of religious zealots who survived only because of their ability to hate rigorously—reject this out of hand, conditioned by a heartless liberalism of culture that ignores human reality until its devastations begin to touch our elites. We refuse to believe that the "civilized" peoples of the Balkans could slaughter each other over an event that occurred over six hundred years ago. But they do. Hatred does not need a reason, only an excuse. Until Americans begin to grasp the depth, extent, and seductive appeal of the hatreds revived in our grave new world, we are unlikely to fashion an appropriate or fully effective military policy.

We have chosen not to examine mass behavior. Our dying century was one of mass *mis*behavior, of illogical descents into madness: brilliant Germany celebrating the most hideous cult of death since the Aztecs, Russia exterminating its natural leaders and culture, Japan embarking on a national killing spree, divided India's confessions painting themselves with blood upon independence, African tribes slaughtering each other until the death toll reached millions—these are just highlights. But such events have been so horrible, so inexplicable in terms of notions we cherish, that we have done our best to ignore them, studying the facts in neutered atonement, but avoiding the least serious study of the underlying causes. The truth is that we do not want to know the truth about ourselves.

And the truth is that human beings are different in mass. Our primitive level of science cannot yet differentiate the psychological from the biological changes when humans group together, but profound changes do occur. That is why military organizations work. We take an eighteen-year-old, condition him or her to our organizational values, norms, and goals; and accelerate group bonding through stress and ritual differentiation from human beings who are not members of the club. As a result, we can get that eighteen-year-old to do things under the intoxication of group identity that he or she would never do if left to his or her own devices. Psychologically, at least, masses are much greater than the sum of their parts.

Anyone who has ever been part of a mob, or who has observed one first hand, has experienced sensations beyond the power of language to articulate. We change in groups and the stronger the group focus, the richer the change, taking us to Srebrenica and Rwanda. There is a programmed longing for the group's approval—for belonging—that trumps biological self-interest as well as those values taken for granted over a lifetime. Fools, heroes, and monsters are all creatures of the mass.

Group behavior is self-accelerating until sated. That is why we see noble self-sacrifice, and that is why we see a half-dozen average college boys get drunk and commit a rape. There is a rapture in dynamic participation in group activities, from team sports, to warfare, to the slaughter of the innocents. While group behavior is too intertwined with other basic impulses—still little understood—to explore further here, it appears that mankind is a violent herd animal hardly more domesticated than the wolf. Our understanding of our bodies, brains, and souls remains so primitive that future specialists will laugh at our ignorance the way we mock Renaissance plague doctors. And mass behavior is only part of the bad news.

Men like to kill. Not all men like it, and not all of those who do kill like it to the same degree. Some are surprisingly indifferent to it. Others dislike it and suffer from their participation in the act. But the latter are few; tearful regrets and self-pity do not equal repentance. We need to get past the lecturing of those who have never experienced violence to face the world as it is. Violence is psychologically rewarding for the victor, and it is addictive. It is cathartic and exhilarating, and lying about it will not change any of this. Violence and killing are as addictive as heroin and as intoxicating as crack cocaine. That is why spouse abusers do not commit abuse just once; it is why child warriors rarely can be redeemed; it is why gangs flourish and prisons fill; and it is why agreements signed in Bosnia bring pauses but not peace. For many men, there is no more empowering act than taking a human life. For some, it is the only empowering experience they will ever have. Just as junkies often do not have more attractive options than heroin in their lives, so do the killers among us lack competitive satisfactions. The Balkan bullies were losers or also-rans in peacetime. Civil war is the best thing that ever happened to them.

Many men—especially those who have lived privileged lives under conditions of peace—have had the killing impulse subdued. It is dormant, if not deadened. Likely the great majority of human beings today are not natural-born killers. Only future science will determine the proportions of popular tendencies, but it is enough to rupture continents if only a small part of mankind remains psychologically "uncivilized." Conflicts, such as those in the wreckage of Yugoslavia or in Central Africa or in the Caucasus, are not triggered by well-organized mass movements, but by smaller groups of men unsatisfied with the recognition life has given them. Most men have something to lose; the most dangerous do not. Before catalytic events, the masses gossip and meander. Then the hard core of misfits begins the killing, and the spirit of violence proves contagious, activating the lethargic mass. The murder in an alley at night turns into the next morning's pogrom.

In the cathartic mass-violence phase, the misfit often becomes the messiah. And messiahs are best sustained through killing, through the creation of a threatening opposition that can be imagined as a force of evil, through fear. Nothing sustains collective violence like the individual's fear of retribution. After the mass intoxication, reality sets in. So does self-knowledge. In the former Yugoslavia, the biggest obstacle to an exhaustion we might pass off as peace is the individual's fear of what he or she has done, and the group's shame at its actions—a shame impossible to admit, which is why the shouting continues. As of this writing, Karadzic and Mladic survive, defended by their people, because, to admit their wrongs would be to admit "our" wrongs.

We Americans are amazed again and again that others could continue to believe for so long in Hitler, or Stalin, or Pol Pot, or the media's thug of the week. We have been blessed by a lack of leaders who devour our individual identities. But those enemies with whom we must deal today and tomorrow cannot bear their inherited identities and will sacrifice themselves to alter them.

Even in the pogroms and slaughters, the majority rarely participates in direct physical violence. The crucial violence is usually perpetrated by a smallish number of actors, with lesser violence enacted by a larger circle, with still a larger group enjoying the spectacle of the violence and, perhaps, looting. Even in the atmosphere of the mob, different personalities crave different satisfactions. Mobs—and mass movements—can be uniform in their effects without being uniform in their behavior; although they desensitize members to behavioral standards and fears, the degrees of courage and energy still vary from individual to individual—and from mob to mob, from cause to cause, from upheaval to upheaval.

Usually, when the eruption is about deeply held values and supernatural convictions, the violence is worse and participation fuller. Fights between religious parties or groups of different racial or blood identities tend to excite the broadest participation—especially if the different parties have long coexisted in the same space, since nothing excites jealousy, hatred, and fear as does the mystery of the different neighbor (even if the differences appear inconsequential to outsiders). We expect foreigners to be foreign; we demand that the folks next door conform to our beliefs, values, language, and appearance—and damn them for the slightest transgressions. Interestingly, one of the most enduring and pervasive themes in the ignition of human conflict is the myth of the abducted child taken for ritual purposes by members of an evil minority come among us, from horrid medieval fantasies of Jews kidnapping Christian infants for blood worship to contemporary propaganda about third world children kidnapped so that the rich can use their body parts for transplants or arcane cures. (The story that AIDS is a Western tool to ravage the third world is a reverse play on this—and it has been given remarkable credence abroad; a related confabulation is a Malaysian leader's recent insistence that financier George Soros "diseased" his region's economic success; yet another is the Russian and Romanian conviction that Westerners willing to adopt disabled orphans are out to weaken the local gene pool.) We may dehumanize those whom we do not know, but those we do know are more likely to dehumanize us.

There are near-infinite variations in the details of mass behavior, and the phenomena must be explored scientifically, dispassionately, and honestly. For initial purposes, however, the commonalities are key: men like to kill; humans change in mass; masses hate instinctively; a small number of instigators can lead the mass to commit atrocities its individual members would shun in isolation; violence is addictive and cathartic; the fear of retribution long outlives the joy of action. Perhaps worst of all, the most effective ways to deal with mass behavior are either to let it run its course or to kill so many of the participants the effect is debilitating and intimidating for a generation. Both options are unacceptable to the Western conscience (at least as embodied by our elites). We will continue to focus on human rights, while our enemies enjoy an excess of the human commodity.

The next century will be one of excess population in the least absorptive regions; of destabilizing informational availability decoupled from the capacity to understand it; of continued sociobiological revolution; and of enraging wealth for a minority of the Earth's peoples, with real or perceived deprivation elsewhere.

Information is already the most destabilizing factor in our world, and the situation will worsen. Exacerbating the confusions of information overload, we are engaged simultaneously in altering patterns of human behavior—the relationship between men and women, and the content of work—that have existed largely unchanged since human beings began to self-organize. We live in a period of such powerful change and dislocation—physical and psychological—that the collapse of the Roman Empire looks glacial by comparison. The grail of individuals and masses alike will be the quest for an excuse for their failures. They will find it in a return to crude, intoxicating systems of belief and valuation—wronged gods and stolen patrimonies. The result will be intermittent euphorias of hatred, stunning violence, and ultimate failure that then begins the cycle again. Much of humanity is returning to the days of witches, anti-Christ, and self-willed apocalypse. Only today the forces of evil are associated with female emancipation, computers, and satellite television. And, to a great degree, these neotraditionalists are accurate in their fears. While we concern ourselves with markets and quality of life, much of humanity will imagine itself engaged in a struggle between good and evil. Even if the entire world learns English, we will never understand one another.

The broad pattern of discontent, disruption, and violence is predictable. Specific events often are not. Violent mass movements develop after the pattern of epidemics, not classic wars. The visible build-up period may be only a matter of weeks or months, or perhaps a few years. Governments tend to believe it is in their self-interest to hide the symptoms until it is too late. The infection breaks out—usually in a densely populated urban area. (Villages are capable of great cruelty, but it takes a city to get genocide moving efficiently.) It spreads rapidly, if not ruthlessly contained, and the pattern of its spread is not fully predictable with present tools. The "epidemic" feeds on itself, with intercommunal violence taking ever more victims on both sides (or on multiple sides), constantly upping the ante. You go from a backstreet confrontation, to a pogrom, to an ethnic cleansing campaign and civil war, to attempted extermination and regional destabilization—roughly the pattern in the former Yugoslavia, in the multiple murder fests in the Caucasus and Transcaucasus, in the Indian neighborhood. The alternative pattern is state- or leadership-sponsored genocide, as in much of Africa, in the Armenian holocaust, in Germany's culturally suicidal campaign against the Jews, in regional efforts against the Kurds, in Chinese efforts against minorities, in Indonesia.

An objective examination of these phenomena might find them far more predictable than present analytical tools allow. We eventually figured out where plague and cholera originated. Far from examples of spontaneous combustion, these disturbances tend to occur in societies that have slipped from or have been thrown out of equilibrium. Intercommunal violence appears to be the programmed response of unbalanced societies seeking to "right themselves." The formula may prove as simple as high school physics.

When, as during the cold war, cultural ecosystems are kept artificially in disequilibrium through the exertion of external pressure, they are apt to react explosively in a self-correcting action when that pressure is finally removed. (Freedom can very quickly become the freedom to kill.) The notion is so crude and fundamental it is probably true. If so, inserting large foreign entities—such as the 10th Mountain Division—into the system, seeking a new balance, will only delay resolution. Should this model be correct, the success of our interventions would be statistically predictable: the greater the degree of resolution achieved by the target society before our arrival, the likelier we are to facilitate recovery. Intervention in a society in the fits of disequilibrium would be wasted effort, except to the extent it made us feel good about ourselves or we were willing to remain as occupiers.

There are a great many related issues deserving study, from the devaluation of human morality that occurs with urbanization to the anthropology of normative behaviors and their regulatory role in restricting individual and mass violence. The issue of appropriate—and necessary—weaponry is vast in its possibilities, import, and moral dilemmas, from crowd control weapons to new weapons capable of altering human behavior. But the fundamental requirement is for an open confrontation with ourselves that demands truth seeking as to who we really are and why we behave as we do. We must begin by overcoming our vanity about the level of our self-knowledge. If it is to deal with humanity's violent diseases and not merely their topical manifestations, our military must study mass behavior.

Finally, our future struggles will resemble "hourglass wars" in yet another important respect. Time will forever run out on us. We face a century of terrific violence ignited by enduring problems, and we—especially the Army and Marines—will be asked to fix many of those problems in a matter of months (or even weeks). It will often prove an impossible mission, even if we arrive at a deeper understanding of root causes. But greater understanding will nonetheless be worthwhile. It will help us keep our service members alive—while the great rotting bombers sleep in their hangars and the fleets dream of an enemy. Honesty is the best policy.

INTERNATIONAL CRIMINAL ORGANIZATIONS: A GROWING SECURITY THREAT

John F. Kerry

Over a span of about eight or nine years I served as chairman of the International Operations Narcotics and Terrorism Subcommittee on the Foreign Relations Committee. Through the work of that committee, we uncovered an extraordinary network, which was not only involved in narcotics trafficking, but was also involved in many other activities, including wheeling and dealing in proliferation, in the movement of human beings, in money laundering, and in a host of different criminal activities. These activities had enormous implications.

We stumbled onto General Manuel Noriega and his network. We stumbled onto the BCCI, the Bank of Credit Commerce International. My committee was first in exposing that bank and its activities, which resulted ultimately in the bank's shutdown. In the course of this, I came to understand linkages involving an increasingly pervasive, interconnected set of criminal activities that worked together and that was beginning to steal whole countries, thereby threatening the fabric of the international network in new ways.

Through this effort I have come to agree with General Charles C. Krulak that we need to be thinking in a new paradigm about where the military is going and the kind of conflicts in which it will find itself involved. I concur with that up to a certain point. I do not believe that we are entitled ever to let down our guard or believe that we do not need simultaneously to maintain the capacities that sustained our strength over the course of the last fifty years. There is too much that is unsettled. There is too much yet to be determined. We have to think in traditional, conventional terms to a certain degree; but we have to make a wiser set of choices about the nonconventional and about this new paradigm.

In my judgment, we should not think of the last century as a century of individual wars. This has really been the century of war, in its own way. World War I was sort of the outgrowth of much of what had preceded it in terms of warfare. You can go back and read these remarkable accounts today of people being thrown at each other in the trenches and the extraordinary expenditure of person power. World War II, then, was the absolute unfinished business of World War I. It led up to the cold war, which was the clear outgrowth of Stalin and Communism and the division at Yalta, as well as the unfinished business of World War II.

We have had almost this entire century consumed by the same conflict, in essence, until the Berlin Wall fell and we found ourselves at this new moment. I would respectfully suggest to you that the lessons of Somalia, Haiti, Bosnia, Korea, Vietnam, back to World War II, would say to us that the likelihood—not the certainty—but the likelihood of us fighting a similar kind of war again is probably pretty low. It does not mean we will not. But, if the lessons stick, and if the experience we gained from those experiences really has lodged itself in our strategic thinking, the likelihood is that we are not going to see a great nation-state war again in the foreseeable future.

Because, in fact, the strategy of those years worked. Deterrence works. Weapons of mass destruction, the concept of mutual-assured destruction, worked beyond anybody's expectations. In point of fact, the reason we never invaded Hanoi was not because we could not, but because of the fear of great power intervention—either the combination of China and Russia, or China alone.

We are in a different world. What is this world? I would respectfully suggest to you that there are probably five principal areas of confrontation. First of all, there is obviously proliferation. The proliferation will be nuclear, chemical conceivably, and biological. Recently, we have been in the middle of a confrontation with Saddam Hussein and Iraq. There is no question in my mind that I would rather face him today than in the future. There is no question in my mind that this is serious. In many ways, more serious, or as serious, as Desert Storm. Because if he gets away with this, I absolutely guarantee you he will press the future development of weapons of mass destruction. He is a man who has invaded five countries, has used chemical weapons against other troops, and has murdered his brother-in-law. So, we have a very tough set of choices ahead of us. But, in my judgment, these are choices we can manage. Obviously, it is complicated, because we have to manage the international community. Clearly, the French and the Russians have a different attitude about how fast you get where and what they are willing to do at the outset. But I invite all of you to go read the resolution of the United Nations. It is not a namby-pamby resolution. It is clear that all of these nations have signed on to the absolute, unconditional, immediate, nonreservational recommencement of the United Nations Special Commission (UNSCOM) process. Now that is one area of conflict with which we are going to have to deal.

The second area is that of nationalism and fundamentalism, as they will evidence themselves increasingly in either terrorism or localized conflicts. The third is a set of environment-induced crises that will come as countries continue to deforest, to pollute their rivers, and to diminish the capacity of their fisheries to be sustainable. All you have to do is travel in the Far East today to understand the consequences of the lack of choices about leaded gasoline or air pollution standards, or so forth, and to recognize that, ultimately, those could be inducements to instability and, certainly, to great dislocations of population.

The fourth is what I call the human condition issues. Issues of population, refugees, food, famine, and the kinds of things we have seen in Africa, where there is just a total implosion as a consequence of the human condition. We are either called on, or not called on as the case may be—Rwanda versus Somalia—to respond, and the clear question is, how you do it?

The fifth is international crime. International crime will exploit every single one of the previously discussed four crises. International crime will profit from the exploitation of every single one of those four by illicitly dumping toxic waste; by being the inducer of arms proliferation; by stealing weapons and selling them to renegades, terrorist, or otherwise; by exploiting the human condition with prostitution rings, with extortion, with money laundering; and by a whole set of other actions.

So, the truth is that all of these things are really at the mercy of some of these new syndicates that have emerged and ultimately threaten the stability of nation-states. These therefore have now risen to a new level of national security issues, which obviously involves all of our armed forces, but particularly the Marines and the Navy, for reasons I will discuss later in this chapter. When James Woolsey was the Director of the CIA, he testified before my committee on this issue. He explained: "There's a major difference between the challenge posed by international crime and that posed by nations who have been our adversaries. As a rule, nations do not exist in a constant state of conflict. Even during the long struggle of the cold war, when cooperation was not feasible, communication was possible. From quiet diplomacy to public démarches, from hot lines to summitry, the means could be found to try to settle disputes. Often the negotiation table was just a phone call away. With organized crime, there is no such table. The tools of diplomacy have no meaning to groups whose business revolves around drug trafficking, extortion, and murder. And when international organized crime can threaten the stability of regions and the very viability of nations, the issues are far from being exclusively in the realm of law enforcement; they also become a matter of national security."

Let me give you another example of the predicament we face. William Olsen, the former deputy assistant secretary of state for narcotics and a fellow at the National Strategy Center in Washington, testified to my subcommittee: "You know, we're dealing with an antique legal system. Our common law system, our method of prosecuting criminals, is an antique of the eighteenth century. It is perfectly suited for the stealing of a cow on the village common. The jurisdiction is clear; you can identify what has been stolen; you can identify the villain; you can identify the victim; and you can send someone to jail. Get yourself into an international case that involves a drug cartel, an arms smuggling ring, a bank fraud, and you've got hundreds of thousands, if not millions, of documents in dozens of languages, with many, many witnesses, many of whom are from different cultures, different backgrounds; and, now you take this mess into court and you try to prosecute. And the jury is hopelessly, totally lost and confused. So, our legal system is not really suited for complicated international crime."

Let me tell you what Boris Uveroff, the chief investigator of major crime for the Russian attorney general said: "It's wonderful that the Iron Curtain is gone. But, it was a shield for the West. Now we've opened the gates and this is very dangerous for the world. America is getting Russian criminals; Europe is getting Russian criminals. They'll steal everything. They occupy Europe. Nobody will have the resources to stop them. You people in the West don't know our mafia yet. You will. You will."

Now, those are dispassionate and nonpolitical and fairly fundamental warnings to us about what we face. I will tell you as a former prosecutor that this is not insignificant, what has just been described. Because the purposefulness of today's crime winds up with a hit man from Moscow killing somebody in Queens in New York, and getting the fake papers to come here by supplying Sicillian mafia with Soviet Army surplus ground-to-air missiles, which are then smuggled into the Balkans to supply the Bosnian Serbs for their military forces.

The question is: Who do you prosecute? How? Where? How do you begin to get at this? This is a new war, literally. It is a different kind of war from anything we have fought before. We talk about a war on poverty, a war on crime, a war on poverty among the elderly, and so forth. Unfortunately, in political life in America, we have declared war far more than we have been willing to actually fight it. But with organized crime, we face a different set of choices. Because people believe it can triumph in the following ways: You can have partial control taken of a country, such as Colombia. Or you can have a nascent democracy set back or even brought down. The story has yet to be determined with respect to Russia. Or you can literally corrupt every one in a society and, then eventually, take over the state, as we are beginning to see in a number of countries.

In Russia, we now are being told by Russian authorities that there has been a hijacking of their economy in many ways. You have got racketeering, murder, fraud, auto theft, assault, drug distribution, trafficking in weapons, radioactive material, prostitution, illegal aliens smuggling, extortion, embezzlement, infiltration, and purchase of banks. Government officials in Russia say that 90 percent of the businesses there have some kind of mafia tie and that 40 percent of their economy is totally controlled by criminal activity.

Between 70 and 80 percent of the businesses pay 10 to 20 percent of their profits for protection. There is a long tradition, in Russia, of a certain level of criminal activity; but, obviously, with the Communists in charge and with the Iron Curtain, that was diminished and held down. But, in 1995, twenty-four bankers were assassinated; a Russian official has estimated that two hundred to three hundred billion dollars, which should have been used for investment in this nascent democracy, was shuttled out of the country. Instead, these funds were shuttled off to investment in other parts of the world by these criminal elements, including the former KGB.

I will give you three examples of how this threatens us in terms of national security. In 1995 twenty-seven crates of Russian weapons—high-grade nuclear materiel—were intercepted in Lithuania, en route to a buyer in Switzerland. The presumption by intelligence organizations is that the buyer was North Korea, for its weapons program. That affects our national security. Similarly, we uncovered in a shed in Amman, Jordan, missile components that had been removed as we had gone through the dismantlement of Russian weapons systems. These components, which had been taken out of their missiles, were destined for Iraq. Three Russians were arrested in Munich, carrying a lead-lined suitcase containing materiel needed to build a nuclear weapon. This materiel was being offered on the market for the price of some three hundred and fifty million dollars. Now, that takes us to Japan. The reason I jump to Japan is that in that nation for the first time we have seen terrorist use of a weapon of mass destruction in a terrorist act. Subsequently, the investigatory process uncovered documents that showed that the terrorists had priced nuclear weapons and nuclear materiel. So, we have clear documented evidence of a terrorist organization attempting to secure those weapons of mass desctruction that are of principal concern—loose nukes. By the way, in Japan you have some three thousand criminal groups, perhaps eighty-five thousand strong, involved in significant international criminal endeavors.

In China, similarly, you have major enterprises that are engaged in almost every kind of criminal activity ranging from the transfer of human organs to a hundred thousand illegal aliens, who at $30,000 a head, are transported to Russia and then to the United States. The United States is the ultimate destination. This travel across the high seas increasingly has become a concern of ours in terms of interdiction and naval activity. This is a continuing threat to our immigration system, as are the types of people that come in unknown to us. For example, the Chinese gangs and Chinese criminal activity in our country, the FBI tells us, are increasingly identifiable and active today.

With respect to China, we are told that there is a five hundred billion dollar-a-year business in both drugs and other kinds of criminal activity, ranging from loan sharking and extortion through Britain; heroin trafficking through Pakistan and Rotterdam; gambling, robbery, and contract murder through Germany; money laundering through Prague, some of the Eastern European Bloc countries, and the Caribbean; weapons to Romania; and a whole lot of alien smuggling that takes place through Moscow.

In Thailand, not so long ago, a great scandal broke revealing that the cabinet had abused its privilege of enrichment. Cabinet members had too many Mercedes and too many ill-gotten houses. This level of corruption threatens the capacity of our businesses to do business on a level playing field. It ultimately breeds a level of corruption that is so pervasive that the capacity to build treaties you can rely on, to have agreements that become tenable, to have a government with which you know you are really dealing is literally challenged.

Look at Mexico. It is on the verge of moving down the road of a Colombia. And, it is right on our border; some of our DEA agents have died there, which has vastly complicated our law enforcement capacity and could have a profound impact on NAFTA, and on our capacity to continue to build a relationship and to have the kind of stability in the hemisphere that we seek.

Let me mention Colombia again because Colombia is a country that is very distressed. In Colombia, one of the things you are dealing with is the capacity of criminal elements to achieve a level of weaponry and sophistication that puts us to great test. Encryption is an example of that. They have the highest level of encryption capacity. That becomes an increasing threat to us, to both law enforcement and intelligence gathering.

Equally important, we have got to understand the kinds of money with which they are dealing. For example, one former Mexican crime boss was found to have the following network: In Panama, he had $22 million in the bank; in Colombia, he had $42 million in the bank; in the United States, he had $2 million; in Luxembourg, he had $39.4 million; in England and Germany, he had $4.25 million; in Switzerland, he had $10.3 million; in Austria, he had $5.9 million; in Hong Kong, he had $6 million; and, he had $150 million in cash buried in the ground in his backyard, because he did not have time to put it anywhere else.

And then there is the violence. Again, take Colombia. Four presidential candidates were assassinated. Almost the entire supreme court, thirteen judges in the chambers of the supreme court, were assassinated by gunmen who simply walked in and blew them away because of the issue of extradition. Sixty journalists, seventy judges, and more than a thousand policemen have been assassinated by the criminal element that succeeded in changing the constitution of their country, to prohibit the one thing that the criminals most feared, which was extradition and transfer to the United States so they might serve real time.

The final issue is money laundering. A five hundred billion dollar-a-year business—the third largest business on this planet and an extraordinary capacity to undermine traditional business and, ultimately, the social fabric that holds us together as a democracy. Now suddenly in America, we are beginning to see more police corrupted, more judges perhaps paid off, and that the money is beginning to have an influence with border guards and with other people in ways that we have not known until recently. If we fell on harder economic times, if unemployment again rose, it is hard to predict what the implications of that could be on the capacity of money to corrupt. The assets held in the Cayman Islands doubled in the 1990s. This is a tiny island, but it has 533 banks that are licensed, 29,298 companies that are registered, and $420 billion in assets, which is $15 million per person on the island.

The burgeoning of international criminal organizations threatens what we fought for over the course of the last century: for a civilized structure, for rule of law, for democracy to be able to grow and flourish. Criminal organizations of the kind I am describing are the opposite of democracy. They are authoritarian, they are ruthless, they clearly are nondemocratic. They will resort to anything to achieve their ends, and they do not believe in anything except money.

That brings us to the question of what the role of the U.S. military is in thwarting these activities.

Well, that is what is happening today. You have the Coast Guard pursuing a known drug dealer. They go into the Caribbean islands and they have to stop at the three-mile limit and get permission in order to pursue. By the time they do pursue, the drug dealers are gone. I have seen videos, taken by the DEA and others, of twin-engine airplanes that we have tracked all the way up from South America, coming out of Colombia or Uruguay, flying up over the Bahamas. The video has shown these planes kicking out bales of marijuana, or packages, at 100 feet above the water. Completely unmarked and at night. You see the bales going. You see them over the water and you see them take off.

Now, in my judgment, they ought to be shot out of the sky. I tried to get that passed in the United States Senate. We had a huge debate about it, but I lost by several votes. But if we are going to get serious about this, we have to raise this on the international scale. At the next meeting this needs to be front and center on the agenda. Because here are the things we desperately need in order to be able to fight back.

We have got to have international partners. We do not have them now. We have to commit the resources. Today we have not done that. We need to modernize our approach. We need to think differently about the overall paradigm, we have got to think differently about the paradigm of international law enforcement and cooperation. I am not suggesting that we ever give up American sovereignty to anybody else. I am not talking about international cops. What I am talking about are joint investigation and commonality of standards.

The issue of transparency is critical. Under the banking treaty, you are supposed to know your customer. But the truth is that many banks are obviously far more meticulous about whom they lend money to than they are about from whom they get it from. We could have far more cooperation from the private sector in guaranteeing that we are really holding people accountable to this notion of knowing your customer.

Most critical of all, you have to go after the money and you cannot allow the criminals to have the havens that they have today that are institutionalized in the global order. The Cayman Islands, Hong Kong, and these places, we have to leverage. Using the leverage of our marketplace, using the leverage of our chip system for clearance of checks and money in New York. Where most people want to legitimize their money ultimately is by coming into the stock market, or the securities, and so forth. That is where we have to pressure people to rise to this standard of behavior. The powerful economic leaders of the world, who are the democracies by and large, have the ability economically to demand the kind of transparency about which I am talking. You must shut down the offshore capacity to hide. Nothing would do more to raise our standards of accountability than if we were to do that.

There is much more that the military could do. Clearly, the Navy's capacity for the over-the-horizon radar is critical to that tracking. But, equally important, the platform you provide, and will continue to provide, to the Coast Guard for law enforcement purposes has been essential to whatever minimalist, and I emphasize minimalist, interdiction capacity to which we have been willing to commit.

In my judgment, there is significantly more that we can do. We have got to make up our minds as to whether we are really serious. The number of ships, the level of smuggling on the high seas, reminds me obviously of the difficulties we faced in trying to interdict in Vietnam and elsewhere. It is clearly not foolproof. It is difficult. But, there is a lot more we could do to raise the cost of doing business and to make it difficult for people to be able to hide. So, interdiction is clearly one component of it.

Forced projection and termination is another. The termination that I talk about is shooting down an aircraft or with special operations covertly undermining some of these criminal enterprises engaged in other countries. We have done that quietly in certain ways. I think that we ought to be prepared to embrace that to a greater degree. Unless we are prepared to do that, we are not going to be able to turn the corner in some of these countries where there is such a criminal stronghold. There is no countervailing force, whatsoever, to create enough fear in the opposition, in the enemy, and enough confidence in the people you are trying to bring along down the road to democracy.

Those are the things that need to be considered as we try to deal with this issue. I have no illusions; I have been in law enforcement long enough to know that we have never stopped loan sharking, we have never stopped prostitution, we have never stopped other things that are criminal on our books today. But, there is a distinction. Those things have, at least in this country, essentially been rendered a nuisance. They do not tear at the fabric of our society. These criminal enterprises, however, do. They do tear at the fabric of our society. In my judgment, these criminal organizations have declared war on our nation, on civilized structures. They are prepared to engage in any kind of activity to perpetuate the capacity to continue to make money illicitly, and we need to rethink the paradigm that treats law enforcement as a mere criminal activity.

The level of the threat is real and, given the experience of some of these other nations, significant enough that we have seen whole nations stolen by them. We should never be sanguine enough to believe that we are eternally immune to that.

ASYMMETRICAL WARFARE AND THE WESTERN MIND-SET

Charles J. Dunlap Jr.

The concept of asymmetrical warfare is a popular and much discussed issue in U.S. defense literature these days. *Joint Vision 2010 (JV 2010),*[1] the *Report of the Quadrennial Defense Review* (QDR),[2] and the *National Military Strategy* (NMS)[3] are just a few of the documents that express concern about it. Understandably, addressing the phenomena is a central theme of the administration and of the secretary of defense.

All of that said, what exactly is meant by asymmetrical warfare? In broad terms it simply means warfare that seeks to avoid an opponent's strengths. It is an approach that tries to focus whatever may be one side's comparative advantages against its enemy's relative weaknesses.[4] In a way, seeking asymmetries is fundamental to all warfighting. But in the modern context, asymmetrical warfare emphasizes what are popularly perceived as unconventional or nontraditional methodologies.

For most potential adversaries, attacking the United States asymmetrically is the only warfighting strategy they might reasonably consider for the foreseeable future. The Gulf War was an object lesson to military planners around the globe of the futility of attempting to confront the United States symmetrically, that is, with like forces and orthodox tactics.

This chapter will briefly examine how cultural disposition and mind-set affect the West's concept of asymmetrical warfare. It will contend that the West's current focus may leave it vulnerable to asymmetrical challenges that arise from opponents whose cultural perspective differs significantly from that of the West.

Technology-oriented Asymmetries

In the West generally, and in America specifically, asymmetrical warfare is frequently conceived in technological terms. *JV 2010* states, for example, that "Our most vexing future adversary may be one who can *use technology* to make rapid improvements in its military capabilities that provide asymmetrical counters to U.S. military strengths."[5] Not surprisingly, therefore, weapons of mass destruction and information warfare are often proffered as illustrations of the asymmetrical warfare genre.[6]

The technological orientation of the Western mind-set is to be expected. In his book, *On the Origins of War*, Donald Kagan writes that the scientific revolution ongoing since the sixteenth century has had a profound effect on the West. As a result, he maintains, "It is a special characteristic of the modern Western world, as opposed to other civilizations and the premodern Western world, to believe that human beings can change and control the physical and social environment and even human nature."[7] As a result, faith in the efficacy of technology and scientific methodology invaded thinking about warfare. The fact that technology proved important to the military dominance of the West for over a century only reinforces the idea that it will continue to drive military success in the future.[8]

Furthermore, focusing on technology reflects the quintessential American approach to waging war. Historians Allan R. Millett and Peter Maslowski declare that since the mid-nineteenth century (but particularly in the twentieth century) the United States has relied on "increasingly sophisticated technology to overcome logistical limitations . . . and to match enemy numbers with firepower."[9] This emphasis comports with America's sense of itself. General George S. Patton Jr.'s comments typify the classic American view: "The Americans, as a race, are the foremost mechanics of the world. . . . It therefore behooves us to devise methods of war, which exploit our inherent superiority. We must fight the war by machines on the ground, and in the air, to the maximum of our ability."[10]

This concentration on technology continues today. *JV 2010*, the "operationally based template"[11] as to how America will fight future wars, centers on the question of how to "leverage technological opportunities to achieve new levels of effectiveness in joint warfighting."[12] Clearly, the American "mind-set" (if not that of the West generally) tends to see all difficulties— even the complex challenge of war—as technical problems subject to engineered solutions.[13]

Culturally-oriented Asymmetries

War does, of course, present technical problems but is not itself one. It is instead a contest of human wills that transcends the logic of the physical sciences. Importantly, it is also more than simply a violent form of a Westernized notion of politics. Indeed, the Clausewitzean mantra of the U.S. defense establishment, that is, that war is an extension of politics by other means, has been much deconstructed by the work of John Keegan and others who address war's cultural basis.[14]

Complementing Keegan's thesis is that of Samuel Huntington. He argues that future conflicts will likely be clashes between civilizations with fundamentally different psychological orientations and value sets. Huntington maintains that certain ideas define what it is to be Western and therefore add to what might be called the "Western mind-set." These include such concepts as "individualism, liberalism, constitutionalism, human rights, equality, liberty, the rule of law, democracy, free markets, [and] the separation of church and state."[15]

What is important about Huntington's work is that he reminds us that the rest of the world does not necessarily share these values. Thus we should not expect that they will think the same way as the West about many subjects, including warfare. In June 1997, Lieutenant General Li Jijuan of the Chinese People's Liberation Army, observed that "each civilization has its own notion of war which cannot help but be influenced by its cultural background."[16]

Nevertheless, an appreciation for the fact that other civilizations may look at war from a fundamentally different perspective is not only disregarded by many in the West (and Americans especially) but is wholly counterintuitive to them. Americans persistently seem to assume that other peoples think basically the same as they do. Along these lines, Edward L. Rowney, a retired flag officer and former U.S. arms control negotiator, commented recently that: "Our biggest mistakes stem from the assumption that others are like us, when in fact, they are more unlike than like us. We insist on ascribing to others our cultural traits, not recognizing that we have different objectives due to our unique historic backgrounds and sets of values. In short, 'We fail to place ourselves in the other person's moccasins'."[17]

When this obtuseness toward the mind-set of our adversaries is allowed to affect strategic thinking, asymmetries result. H. R. McMaster argues in his book *Dereliction of Duty*, for example, that the graduated application of airpower during the Vietnam War—intended to signal our resolve to support South Vietnam yet to do so in a way that the United States believed demonstrated restraint—wholly misperceived North Vietnamese thought processes. McMaster contends: "Graduated pressure was fundamentally flawed. . . . The strategy ignored the uncertainty of what was *the unpredictable psychology of an activity that involves killing, death, and destruction*. To the North Vietnamese, military action, involving as it did attacks on their forces and bombing their territory, was not simply a means of communication. Human sacrifice in war evokes strong emotions creating a dynamic that defies systems analysis quantification."[18]

The technological orientation of the Western mind-set along with the assumed universality of Western values distorts the analysis of asymmetrical warfare. Consider the potential dangers of technology-based asymmetries. The West readily examines them because solving that kind of problem plays to the West's own notion of its comparative advantage, that is, in the areas of weapons innovation and production. Such perceived "technological" asymmetries are almost welcomed by the West's military-industrial complex.

The much-ballyhooed revolution in military affairs (RMA) exemplifies this trend. The RMA seeks to produce radically more effective militaries through the widespread application of emerging technologies, especially advanced computer and communications systems.[19] While it provides enormous opportunities for sales of new equipment to Western forces fearful of technological obsolescence, much of the new weaponry too often seems optimized for high-tech, peer-competitor war. In other words, it is aimed principally at a form of warfare that is symmetrical (in relation to the West) in its essence. In truth, few potential adversaries will wage symmetrical, high-tech war against the United States, because doing so presents enormous training, logistical, and resource requirements, and these are "demands that few societies can meet."[20]

The characterization of weapons of mass destruction (WMD) as asymmetrical threats is a further manifestation of the West's analytical distortion. In truth, the premise that WMD constitute asymmetrical threats vis-à-vis the West—at least insofar as interstate war is concerned—deserves challenge.[21] Given the West's still-sizable nuclear arsenals and its *relatively* robust capability to deal with other-than-nuclear WMD warfare, are WMD really asymmetrical to the West? So long as the West maintains its current capabilities, it seems rather unlikely that an adversary could *decisively* employ WMD against it. In a very real sense, using WMD against the United States and other Western nations would represent an ill-considered attempt to match the West *symmetrically*.

The use of WMD in the context of terrorism committed by nonstate actors is, of course, a profound and different challenge. As serious a problem as terrorism is—especially when WMD are involved—it is not likely to actually defeat the West. It does not yet appear that nonstate actors could mount a sufficiently comprehensive attack to physically vanquish a nation like the United States. Martin Van Creveld has pointed out that terrorism has never succeeded in the West because the nature of modernity is that it provides redundancies that give advanced societies resiliency against the sort of sporadic attacks that terrorists carry out, even though individual incidents might be quite costly.[22]

The "Real" Asymmetrical Challenge

Quite clearly, terrorism principally aims to affect its targets more *psychologically* than physically. To that extent, it does suggest the real asymmetrical challenge for the West. Major General Robert H. Scales Jr., the commandant of the Army War College, argues that in future conflicts an enemy may perceive his comparative advantage against the United States and the West not in technological terms, but in the "collective psyche and will of his people."[23] In turn, this generates an obvious question, that is, how will an enemy attack the West's psyche and will? The answer makes Americans and others in the West uncomfortable because it raises the specter that basic Western values, the very things Huntington sees as defining the West, are in fact the asymmetries that future adversaries will most likely seek to exploit.

The potential asymmetrical vulnerabilities about which the West should be concerned are not so much technological, as the Western mind-set believes (and even prefers), but rather are those that turn the fundamentals of the West's culture and political system against themselves. For example, among the things that adversaries have learned in the latter half of the twentieth century is to exploit the West's democratic system. Consider the remarks of a former North Vietnamese commander: "The conscience of America was part of its war-making capability, and we were turning that power in our favor. America lost because of its democracy; through dissent and protest it lost the ability to mobilize a will to win."[24] Thus, by stirring up dissension in the United States, the North Vietnamese were able to advance their strategic goal of removing American power from Southeast Asia.

More recently, by dragging the body of a U.S. soldier through the streets of Mogadishu, the Somalis were able to destroy the public support on which the United States and other Western democracies depend to sustain military operations. We should expect such strategies to proliferate as new communications technologies vastly enhance the news-gathering and dissemination capabilities of international media organizations.[25]

Enemies may perceive vulnerable asymmetries in what the West views as its virtues. While the mind-set in the United States and the West sees the "moral strengths" and the "ethical standards" of its troops as keys to military power,[26] adversaries willing to abandon Westernized legal and ethical regimes may well consider them as things to exploit and manipulate.[27] Increasingly, opponents will seek to present Western militaries with moral and ethical conundrums. For example, the Serbs were able to discourage high-tech NATO air attacks by the simple expedient of chaining hostage UN soldiers to potential targets. The idea of purposely killing friendly troops in order to destroy an enemy target will be very difficult for Western forces to rationalize.

Where once the "Western way of war" meant that adversaries risked wars often characterized by decisive battles where the annihilation of enemy forces was sought,[28] today we see the emergence of a Western mind-set markedly more sensitive to casualties on *both* sides.[29] Enemies may consider this humanitarian concern as yet another asymmetry on which they can capitalize in ways the Western mind-set considers unthinkable: they may purposely put their own people in jeopardy if doing do complicates or adversely affects the West's use of its military power.

Indeed, Somali warlords used women and children as human shields against coalition forces during the intervention of the early 1990s. This led analyst James F. Dunnigan to caution that "if the opponents are bloody-minded enough, they will always exploit the humanitarian attitudes of their adversaries."[30] Along similar lines, the Libyans have threatened to encircle a facility alleged to be involved with the production of weapons of mass destruction with "millions of Muslims" in order to deter attacks by the West.[31] Most recently, when Western military action seemed imminent, Saddam Hussein surrounded his palaces and other buildings with noncombatant civilians (some of whom may have genuinely volunteered) to discourage attacks by Western forces sensitive to the effect on their publics of civilian deaths, regardless of the circumstances.[32]

Even those opponents—including possible peer competitors—who seek to achieve technological asymmetries over the West may likewise find it profitable to use our values against us. The West's free market, open competition economic system encourages innovation and quickly produces technological advances. But the nature of that system in a democracy makes turning new ideas into deployed weapons a cumbersome and lengthy process, something extremely worrisome in an age of rapid technological change.

An adversary less constrained by the political realities of a capitalistic democracy may be able to gain an asymmetrical advantage by deploying the latest systems more rapidly than can the bureaucratically restrained Western militaries. Author David Shukman explains: "While the Western military struggle for a decade on average to acquire new weapons, a country with commercially available computer equipment and *less rigorous democratic and accounting* processes could field new systems within a few years. It is the stuff of military nightmares."[33]

Parenthetically, it is unlikely that the openness of democratic societies will allow the achievement of an asymmetrical advantage via technological surprise against future adversaries, despite the West's best efforts. Ephraim Kam asserts in *Surprise Attack* that "since it takes a long time to produce and deploy new weapons in sufficient quantities capable of changing the military balance between nations, information on their characteristics usually becomes available in the interim."[34] While many opponents will lack the resources to develop technologically superior countermeasures, they may nevertheless be able to develop low-tech offsets as has been done with some regularity in the past.

In fact, an overemphasis on technology can cause the West to overlook the many low-tech ways in which adversaries might asymmetrically respond to gadgetry-obsessed—and gadgetry-vulnerable—Western opponents.[35] What is so remarkable about this is that so few seem to remember the lessons of relatively recent history. Two senior U.S. military commanders warn against the siren song of technology in *Parameters*. They point out that: "[Technological] supremacy could not prevent Holland's defeat in Indonesia, France's defeats in Indonesia and Algeria, America's defeat in Vietnam, the Soviet Union's defeat in Afghanistan, or Russia's more recent defeat in Chechnya. All these episodes confirm that technological superiority does not automatically guarantee victory on the battlefield, still less the negotiating table."[36]

Future adversaries may wage asymmetrical warfare by combining available low-tech equipment with a culturally oriented strategy. For example, marines should expect to face opponents who deploy relatively unsophisticated mines, much as Iraqis did during the Gulf War, in the hopes of replicating Iraq's success in deterring an amphibious assault following damage by mines to the USS *Tripoli* and the USS *Princeton*.[37] Similarly, opponents will likely acquire small, diesel-powered submarines to present the same threat.[38] What is important here is that such schemes might not be able to stop a determined assault, but an adversary may aim to simply exploit the growing aversion to casualties in the West's culture by causing some losses.

Surface ships may face an even more insidious threat: an enemy could use a civilian airliner covertly loaded with explosives to launch an attack on a high-value target such as an aircraft carrier. The plane might be flown by a suicide pilot (or automatically guided) and carry a hostage or even volunteer group of civilian passengers. Recalling the recriminations that followed the accidental shootdown of an Iranian airliner by the cruiser *Vincennes,*[39] the adversary may hope to create just enough hesitation on the part of the crew to allow the aircraft to successfully penetrate the defenses. Again, simply causing casualties—in this scenario both U.S. military personnel and enemy civilians—would be the aim.

It is rather paradoxical that these kinds of enemy actions against forward-deployed American forces might engender a completely different reaction than acts of terrorism against the U.S. homeland would. Although the aim of both might be to simply maximize casualties, the former could succeed in undermining public support for an overseas operation, while the latter may well evoke a demand for extreme measures against the perpetrators. Such is the mercurial nature of contemporary U.S. public opinion.

In any event, the kind of asymmetrical warfare future adversaries may wage is not that which seeks to actually defeat U.S. or Western military forces, but that which assaults the psyche and will of the populations whose political support is required by Western democracies to sustain military operations.

Summary and Conclusions

Hopefully, this chapter will not be interpreted as an antitechnology, Luddite manifesto. To the contrary, no one–least of all the author—disputes the dictum that "technology and warfare have never been far apart."[40] Moreover, it is unquestionably true that decisionmakers need to be extremely concerned about procuring the finest technology for U.S. forces. Analysts Ronald Haycock and Keith Neilson warn that to a great extent military applications of technology have "permitted the division of mankind into ruler and ruled."[41] And it is also true that technology is, in fact, the West's comparative advantage.

One of the great dangers, however, is that decisionmakers may delude themselves into thinking that the challenge of asymmetrical warfare is *exclusively* technological. It is especially a concern as more and more of the civilian leadership lacks first-hand military experience. This has led some military officers to worry, as the *Wall Street Journal* reported in 1995, that such leaders might believe that "gadgets can somehow substitute for the blood and sweat of ground combat."[42]

The West must recognize that consideration of war as a technological or engineering problem has its limits. The engineer's culture is an "aggressively rational one," where technical problems are solved with a logical application of scientific principles."[43] War, however, is something different. Lieutenant

General Paul K. Van Riper explains: "Technology permeates every aspect of war, but the science of war cannot account for the dynamic interaction of the physical and moral elements that come into play, by design or by chance, in combat. War will remain predominately an art, infused with human will, creativity, and judgment."[44]

What is necessary for the United States and the West is to expand their assessment of asymmetrical warfare. Asymmetrical warfare needs to be examined from the culturally distinct perspective of potential enemies. As unpleasant as it may be, the West must consider that enemies may try to turn against us the very values that the West is seeking to protect. In particular, the United States and the West must not allow their technologically oriented mind-set to blind them to the fact that modern war remains, as already noted, a struggle of psyches and wills.

The West must be prepared to meet the moral as well as technical challenge of future war. Enemies may concede that physically defeating militarily the forces of the United States and the West is beyond their capability, but they nevertheless may attempt to achieve their war aims by overcoming the will of the United States and the West and testing them in new and innovative ways. That is the essence of the challenge of asymmetrical warfare in the twenty-first century. If we indulge ourselves with visions that success in future wars can be reduced to finding high-tech "silver bullets," all that the West holds dear is in peril.

Notes

1. Chairman of the Joint Chiefs of Staff, *Joint Vision 2010* (1996).

2. William S. Cohen, *Report of the Quadrennial Defense Review*, May 1997.

3. Chairman of the Joint Chiefs of Staff, *National Military Strategy of the United States of America* (September 1997).

4. Other authorities define asymmetrical warfare somewhat differently. For example, in its unclassified report on the exercise STRATEGIC FORCE '96, the Air Force discussed the issue as follows: "The symmetrical battles have classically pitted steel against steel in slow wars of attrition. Asymmetrical warfare departs from this thinking. Asymmetrical warfare avoids traditional force-on-force battles. Asymmetrical warfare favors pitting your strength against an enemy's strength or weakness in a nontraditional and sometimes unconventional manner.," Department of the Air Force, *Strategic Force* (1997), p. 8.

5. See *JV 2010 supra* note 1, pp. 10–11.

6. See, for example, Ibid, p. 11 (information technologies); *QDR supra* note 2, at 4 (NBC [nuclear, biological, and chemical] threats, information warfare); and the *National Military Strategy supra* note 3, p. 9 (WMD and information warfare).

7. Donald Kagan, *On the Origins of War and the Preservation of Peace* (1995), p. 3.

8. See Michael Howard, *War in European History* (1976), pp. 116–35.

9. Allan R. Millett and Peter Maslowski, *For the Common Defense* (2d ed., 1994), p. xii.

10. As quoted by Colin S. Gray, "U.S. Strategic Culture: Implications for Defense Technology" in *Defense Technology* (Asa A. Clark IV and John F. Lilley, eds., 1989), p. 31, citing George S. Patton Jr., *War as I Knew It* (1947; Bantam reprint 1980), p. 345.

11. General John M. Shalikashvili, p. ii.

12. Ibid, p. 1.

13. See Robert N. Ellithorpe, *Warfare in Transition? American Military Culture Prepares for the Information Age*, a presentation for the Biennial International Conference of the Inter-University Seminar on Armed Forces and Society, Baltimore, Maryland, October 24–26, 1997, p. 18 ("American military culture historically emphasized scientific approaches to warfare to the point of holding an almost mystical belief in the power of technology to solve the challenges of war.)" (Unpublished paper on file with author.)

14. See John Keegan, *A History of Warfare* (1993). Harry Summers maintains that Keegan makes a false distinction between "politics" and "culture." See Colonel Harry G. Summers Jr., USA (Ret.), *The New World Order* (1995), pp. 40–42.

15. Huntington's original thesis (first published in 1993), together with thoughtful critiques have been published. See Council on Foreign Relations, *The Clash of Civilizations? The Debate* (1996). Huntington has expanded his thesis to a book-length treatise entitled *The Clash of Civilizations and the Remaking of World Order* (1996).

16. Lt. General Li Jijaun, *Traditional Military Thinking and the Defensive Strategy of China*, LeTort Paper No. 1, U.S. Army War College, Strategic Studies Institute (Earl Tilford, ed., August 29, 1997), p. 1.

17. Edward L. Rowney, "Tough Times, Tougher Talk," *American Legion Magazine*, May 1997, pp. 24, 25–26.

18. H. R. McMaster, *Dereliction of Duty* (1997), p. 327 (emphasis added).

19. For a discussions of "the revolution in military affairs" in the information age see generally, "Select Enemy. Delete.," *Economist*, March 8, 1997, p. 21; Eliot A. Cohen, "A Revolution in Warfare," *Foreign Affairs*, March/April 1996, p. 37; Andrew F. Krepinevich, "Cavalry to Computers: The Pattern of Military Revolutions," *The National Interest*, Fall 1994, p. 30; and James R. Fitzsimonds and Jan M. Van Tol, "Revolutions in Military Affairs," *Joint Force Quarterly*, Spring, 1994, p. 24.

20. Geoffrey Parker, "The Future of Western Warfare," in *Cambridge Illustrated History of Warfare*, Geoffrey Parker, ed., (1995), p. 369.

21. Military historian Martin Van Creveld makes the interesting observation that, ironically, "in *every* region where [nuclear weapons] have been introduced, large-scale, interstate war has as good as disappeared." Martin Van Creveld, "Technology and War II," in *The Oxford Illustrated History of Modern War* (Charles Townsend, ed., 1997), p. 304 (emphasis in original).

22. Van Creveld, *Technology and War*, pp. 307–08.

23. As quoted by James Kittfield, in "The Air Force Wants to Spread Its Wings," *National Journal*, November 8, 1997, at 2264.

24. As quoted in "How North Vietnam Won the War," *Wall Street Journal*, August 3, 1995, p. A8.

25. Douglas Waller, a *Time Magazine* correspondent observes: "The same technology that is revolutionizing the way the Pentagon fights wars is also changing the way the media cover them. The media can now provide viewers, listeners, and even readers almost instant access to a battlefield. With lighter video cameras, smaller portable computers, cellular phones, their own aircraft, and worldwide electronic linkups, the media can report on any battlefield no matter how remote and no matter how many restrictions the Defense Department tries to place on coverage." Douglas Waller, "Public Affairs, the Media, and War in the Information Age," in Robert L. Pfaltzgraff Jr. and Richard H. Shultz Jr., *War in the Information Age: New Challenges for U.S. Security* (Washington/London: Brassey's, 1997), pp. 321–31

26. *JV 2010, supra* note 1, pp. 28 and 34.

27. In a fascinating piece in *Parameters*, Ralph Peters, then a U.S. Army major, described what he called the rise of "The New Warrior Class," a multitude which he contends "already numbers in the millions." Peters says that in the future America will face warriors "who have acquired a taste for killing, who do not behave rationally according to our definition of rationality, who are capable of atrocities that challenge the descriptive powers of language, and who will sacrifice their own kind in order to survive." Ralph Peters, "The New Warrior Class," *Parameters*, Summer 1994, p. 24.

28. See generally, Victor Davis Hanson, *The Western Way of War* (1989), Doyne Dawson, *The Origins of Western Warfare* (1996), and Russell E. Weigley, *The American Way of War* (1973).

29. Walter J. Boyne notes "two unique demands that have since Vietnam come to be made by the American public. . . . The first of these demands is that we must fight our wars with a minimum of casualties to our forces. America wants no more Vietnams where our troops are forced to fight and die in unconscionable numbers. The second of these demands is unusual in history, for it is that we must also win our wars with a minimum number of casualties inflicted on the enemy." Walter J. Boyne, *Beyond the Wild Blue: A History of the U.S. Air Force 1947–1997* (1997), p. 7.

30. James F. Dunnigan, *Digital Soldiers: The Evolution of High-Tech Weaponry and Tomorrow's Brave New Battlefield* (1996), p. 219.

31. See "Libyans to Form Shield at Suspected Arms Plant," *Baltimore Sun*, May 17, 1996, p. 14.

32. See Barbara Slavin, "Iraq Leaves U.S. Few Options," *USA Today*, November 14, 1997, p. 13A.

33. See David Shukman, *Tomorrow's War: The Threat of High-Technology Weapons* (1996), p. 8. See also Michael Loescher, "New Approaches to DOD Information-Systems Acquisition" in *Cyberwar: Security, Strategy and Conflict in the Information Age*, Alan D. Campen and others, (1996), p. 127 ("In a world in which state-of-the-art is off-the-shelf, industry, and potentially our foes, can obtain better information systems [IS] technology cheaper and faster than DOD because our current acquisition system buys computers in the same way we buy bullets."); and Jeffery R. Barnett, *Future War* (1996), p. 17 (stressing the need to compress the procurement time for information technologies).

34. Ephraim Kam, *Surprise Attacks* (1988), p. 19.

35. See, for example, Charles J. Dunlap Jr., "How We Lost the High-Tech War of 2007," *Weekly Standard*, January 29, 1996, p. 22.

36. Lt. Gen. Paul K. Van Riper, USMC, and Maj. Gen. Robert H. Scales Jr., USA, "Preparing for War in the 21st Century," *Parameters*, Autumn 1997, p. 4, 5.

37. Although the absence of an amphibious assault during the Gulf War was later characterized as a deception operation, General Schwarzkopf's memoirs make it clear that concerns about mines were key. See General Norman H. Schwarzkopf, *It Doesn't Take a Hero* (1992), p. 446; See also Rick Atkinson, *Crusade* (1993), pp. 239–40.

38. For a discussion of how a few submarines can complicate a military operation, see, generally Admiral Sandy Woodward, *One Hundred Days* (1992) (Falklands War).

39. On July 3, 1987 the cruiser USS *Vincennes* shot down Iranian Air flight 655 over the Persian Gulf when it mistook the civilian aircraft for a military threat. A total of 224 adults and 65 children were killed. See Sandra Mackey, *The Iranians* (1996), p. 331.

40. Ronald Haycock and Keith Neilson, *Men, Machines, and War* (1988), p. xi.

41. Ibid, p. xii.

42. Thomas E. Ricks, "Gingrich's Futuristic Visions for Re-Shaping the Armed Forces Worry Military Professionals," *Wall Street Journal*, February 8, 1995, p. 16.

43. Robert Poole, *Beyond Engineering* (1997), p. 209.

44. Lt. Gen. Paul K. Van Riper, "Information Superiority," *Marine Corps Gazette*, June 1997, pp. 54, 62.

THE ROLE OF THE NAVAL SERVICES IN OPERATIONS OTHER THAN WAR: PEACETIME ENGAGEMENT AND CHAOS MANAGEMENT

Alberto Coll

An essential component of American policy and strategy over the next two decades will be "operations other than war," designed to achieve specific political objectives around the world. The naval services will be indispensable in the two major dimensions of operations other than war: peacetime engagement and chaos management. The crisis over Iraq's refusal to comply with the United Nations's inspection regime illustrates the naval services' unparalleled versatility as a strategic instrument for both peacetime engagement and chaos management.

But first, a word about the place of operations other than war in American policy and strategy is in order. The chief challenge of the United States for the foreseeable future will be far broader than simply containing a few troublesome or potentially aggressive regional powers. It will be nothing short of shaping a rapidly changing international system in order to guide it in directions congruent with long-term American political, economic, and military interests and values. The task of American grand strategy will be the day-to-day exertion of influence and power in multitudinous places and situations in which American interests are at stake in varying degrees, so as to secure outcomes beneficial to the United States and its allies. At times this will require the projection of military power across a broad spectrum of potential uses, all the way from operations short of war to war itself.

Part of what is involved in this broad task is what in earlier centuries might have been described as "imperial maintenance." At the dawn of the twenty-first century, the United States stands at the head of an empire, a global network of closely interconnected interests, values, international relationships, and institutions ultimately backed by the United States's vast military power and its willingness to use that power in its defense. It is not a classic empire held together by coercion. Rather, to use Thomas Jefferson's phrase, it is an "empire of liberty" in two senses. First, its chief principle is the preservation of liberty and its enlargement to any societies that may desire to adopt it as their guiding principle of public life. Second, the empire is more properly described as a league of societies that have freely chosen to be associated with it and that are free to leave it anytime they wish. The American empire is radically different from traditional empires. It is more akin to a league of free states whose members expect the United States to play the role of leader or "senior partner" as long as the American agenda provides sufficient benefits to the league's wider membership. In spite of these critical differences, however, many of the tasks associated with "imperial maintenance" are relevant to the future health and vigor of the *Pax Americana*.

These tasks include: the containment or co-opting of potential adversaries, the strengthening of existing alliances and relationships, and the creation of new ones whenever it is cost-effective; the enlargement of influence and power over important regions; the defusing of disruptive crises before they can damage the existing order; and the overall enhancement of credibility and security. All of these require the continuous application of the full panoply of instruments of statecraft. Among the latter, political-military operations short of war are likely to play a major role.

Naval Services and Peacetime Engagement

Peacetime engagement refers to those activities carried out before a crisis exists, or at least before it has crossed the threshold into armed violence. As former U.S. Senator Sam Nunn has put it repeatedly, one of the chief purposes of peacetime engagement is to carry out preventive or preemptive action to address smoldering crises before they erupt fully. Another purpose of peacetime engagement is simply to foster a political climate beneficial to American interests so that crises do not arise at all. The core of peacetime engagement is the development of political and military relationships and the strengthening of existing alliances. There are many dimensions of peacetime engagement in which the naval services have a vital role to play.

The first dimension is forward presence. A Marine contingent or a naval task force is a powerful symbol of American will and leadership. Whether permanently stationed, or sent to an area periodically, naval forces convey American power and commitment in a manner that is often both more sustainable economically and less intrusive politically than ground or air forces would be. "Showing the flag" in key areas of the world signals American involvement and interest in such areas. The same is true of port visits to countries with which the United States wants to maintain or enhance political relations and cooperation. The projection of forward presence by the naval services reassures allies and friends, deters and discourages adversaries, and provides a substantive basis for exploring new avenues for cooperation among interested powers.

Another dimension of peacetime engagement is the whole range of activities encompassed under the rubric of "military-to-military contacts." These include training exercises with the naval services of allies and friends, exchanges of naval personnel across different organizations, the intense connections that take place year after year at the Naval War College and Naval Postgraduate School between American naval and Marine officers and those of foreign countries, and the participation of American naval personnel in the military educational institutions of other countries. All of these add up to an extensive world-wide network of strategically significant connections of great value to American security. American military strategy rests on the assumption that the United States will need the help of its allies and coalition partners in handling future security threats in various regions. The military-to-military contacts carried out under peacetime engagement will facilitate such future coalition cooperation. Combined training exercises will make it easier for the military forces of different countries to work together during actual crises. And the personal relationships, understanding, and trust developed through exchanges and shared educational experiences will enhance military cooperation at the operational and strategic levels.

Naval Services and Chaos Management

Operations other than war also include the management of crises or chaotic situations in which the risk of war is real and American military forces must be ready to respond to armed violence. Unlike peacetime engagement, chaos management in its various forms—humanitarian intervention, peacekeeping, and peace enforcement—carries high risks of the use of military force. At a minimum, the American military have to go into such situations prepared to use force, and they must make it clear to all potential adversaries that they will indeed use lethal and effective force if attacked. The sad fate of the U.S. Marines in Beirut in 1983 shows the disastrous consequences that befall the U.S. military when it assumes a peacekeeping role without preparing to defend itself against acts of war by parties hostile to the peacekeeping mission. The American experience in Somalia, Haiti, and Bosnia shows to varying degrees that chaos management operations are most effective when the American military is ready to defend itself against those local factions that stand to lose the most from a peaceful settlement of the crisis.

Chaos management operations have two dimensions: warfighting and political-military operations. Although warfighting itself is not associated directly with operations other than war, it is an indispensable backdrop to it. Unless U.S. military forces assigned to peacekeeping or humanitarian intervention operations in hostile circumstances are prepared to wage war, they will lack the credibility to carry out operations other than war. This was amply validated by the American experience in Somalia, and it has been confirmed to this day by the Bosnian intervention. Much of the effectiveness of the U.S. forces in Bosnia has come from the belief by the warring factions that the American forces are heavily armed for combat and are prepared to use deadly force if challenged or threatened.

Since 1991 critics of the effort to assign peacetime engagement and chaos management missions to the U.S. military have argued that such missions detract from the primary warfighting mission by diverting focus and resources away from it. By fostering the illusion that they carry little risk and low costs, they can therefore serve as substitutes for warfighting. Such criticism contains a valuable grain of truth, but it also can lead to a distorted picture of the problem. It is true that operations other than war are expensive, and that, if resorted to excessively without any criteria of selectivity to limit their application, they can damage overall military readiness and cause political exhaustion on the part of the American public toward all kinds of international involvement. This is why operations other than war must not be seen as cheap, or as easy solutions to complex long-standing problems. It is also true that there are many situations in which operations other than war can never be a substitute for warfighting.

The warfighting mission of the U.S. military, including, of course, the naval services, must remain the primary mission and the recipient of the largest share of bureaucratic attention and resources. In contrast to the more frequent low-intensity conflicts or crises other than war, conventional war breaks out rarely. But when it does break out, it usually involves vital or highly significant American interests, and the United States must be prepared to win decisively. The odds of a regional power using conventional war against major U.S. interests may be low at any given point, but when such war does occur, the United States cannot afford to ignore it or to run the risk of fighting under anything but the highest probability of success. Hence conventional warfighting, and preparations for it, must remain the top priority.

All of the above, however, should not serve as an excuse for blurring the equally obvious point that operations other than war still deserve significant attention and resources because they involve activities that underpin American interests and values around the world on an everyday basis. As long as policymakers use operations other than war selectively and are willing to secure adequate funding for them from Congress, the U.S. military can do both warfighting and operations other than war with the same degree of excellence. Moreover, both types of activities are to some extent mutually supportive. When carried out skillfully, peacetime engagement and chaos management operations can obviate the need for later, and costlier, direct American military involvement. And when forces carrying out operations other than war demonstrate readiness to engage in warfighting, their credibility and ability to deter potential enemies are enhanced, thereby improving their prospects for success.

The core of chaos management in any of its variants—humanitarian intervention, peacekeeping or peace enforcement—is a political-military operation in which the operational use of military force is tightly controlled in a highly disciplined manner by the underlying political logic, and nonmilitary instruments play a vital complementary role in relation to the military. To play an effective role in such political-military operations, the naval services will have to encourage greater development by their personnel of certain political-military skills to which the American military traditionally have not paid as much attention as is required today. Among the naval services, the

Marine Corps is far more comfortable with many of those skills and has recognized their importance to a greater degree than the Navy has, a fact corroborated by the venerable place held to this day in Marine Corps officer education and training by the 1940 *Small Wars Manual.*

First, the naval services will need to invest more in language training and regional specialization, so that more of their members will be comfortable with the delicate and often highly sensitive political-military tasks required in chaos management operations. Language skills and regional specialization need to receive greater encouragement and career recognition instead of being treated as superfluous idiosyncrasies useful mainly for naval attachés in their last posting before retirement. While foreign-language skills are not necessary for every member of the naval services, they need to be more widely available than they are today.

Second, military personnel need to be more knowledgeable about the political logic and implications of military operations. Knowledge of, and a high level of comfort with, the interagency policy process, the functioning of multinational coalitions, the world of nongovernmental transnational organizations, and the relationship of military operations to grand strategy and policy are all essential to success. Such broad knowledge is best developed not only through experience but also through education at senior military educational institutions. Every Marine and Navy officer attending the Naval War College, for example, spends one year in residence studying Clausewitz and other strategic theorists on war and the primacy of politics in military operations, the functioning of the Washington bureaucracy and the processes of national security decision making, and the problems of combined and joint military operations. The naval services should ensure that all of their most promising officers, who sooner or later are likely to play a leadership role in future operations other than war, go through such a residential program of studies. Whether in Somalia, Haiti, or Bosnia, the success of American military power cannot be measured in strictly military terms alone; clumsiness and missteps in the political dimension on the part of militarily brilliant but politically inept officers can be exceedingly costly in human terms, diplomatically, and politically, often tarnishing or completely negating the benefits of operational military success.

There are other skills, not necessarily political in nature, that are valuable in operations other than war and that can have significant political repercussions for good or for ill. For example, American military forces in such operations often have to perform complex governmental, administrative, public health, engineering, and police functions for which warfighters are not necessarily well equipped. Vast reservoirs of such knowledge exist in the reserve component and even more so in the private sector. The naval services need to reexamine their reserve component policies with an eye to determining how to use reservists with valuable nonwarfighting skills that are essential to the smooth functioning of such operations more effectively in operations other than war. Experience has shown that skilled civil affairs or military police personnel and prompt attention to issues of basic sanitation, food distribution, and public welfare can make the difference between political success and failure.

The former commandant of the Marine Corps, General Charles C. Krulak, has also put forward the idea of developing closer ties between the naval services and the private sector, so that in operations other than war the military can draw on private-sector support and skills in addressing some of the practical, technical nonmilitary problems that military personnel lack the capability to handle. Given current advances in information technology and communications, it would be feasible to develop databases and networks that would enable the military to draw quickly and precisely on private sector sources of expertise to deal with problems that may arise unexpectedly in a peacetime engagement or chaos management operation. This kind of active working relationship between the U.S. military and the highly resourceful U.S. private sector could be the powerful catalyst for fresh approaches and solutions in handling the wide array of complexities typical of most operations other than war.

Need for Greater Integration among the Naval Services

In an era of shrinking defense budgets and forces, the Navy and the Marine Corps need each other more than ever before, and this is especially true in the realm of operations other than war. The U.S. Navy no longer believes *a la Mahan* that its main function is to fight and defeat other blue-water navies. By adopting as its strategic blueprint *From the Sea,* the Navy has recognized in true Corbettian fashion that one of its chief tasks will be to support the insertion of Marine Corps and Army forces into the theater of war. With regard to operations other than war, tremendous opportunities exist for mutual support and cooperation that will enhance the effectiveness of the naval services in this critical area. Too often in the past, and unfortunately even to this day, both services have looked at each other as rivals in a zero-sum competition for resources, instead of as partners in a number of significant ways.

The Marine Corps and the Navy bring complementary assets and strengths to operations other than war. The Corps, on the one hand, has a centuries-old tradition of political-military operations in far-flung corners of the globe. Many of the tasks involved in peacetime engagement and chaos management are familiar elements of this tradition; unlike its sister services, the Corps has never seen warfighting as its sole mission. The Navy, on the other hand, has unparalleled capabilities for global reach, including large numbers of ships and personnel that allow it to perform operations other than war without denigrating its warfighting skills. Throughout its long history, the Navy also has made room within its larger culture for a small group of officers with diplomatic and political skills who are comfortable with many of the cultural and political complexities entailed in political-military operations. One of the top priorities in the next three years for the senior leadership of the naval services should be to explore, with as much creativity and imagination as possible, new ways in which these complementary strengths can be brought together to enhance effectiveness in operations other than war. In an age of complex global responsibilities for the United States, the time has come for the two naval services to move more aggressively in the direction of becoming a truly integrated team.

PART II

DIMENSIONS OF THE TWENTY-FIRST CENTURY SECURITY ENVIRONMENT

INTRODUCTION

The second part of this volume has two primary objectives: First, it provides a conceptual overview of present and future regional conflict environments. Here, Dr. Susan L. Woodward identifies and discusses the kinds of instability that will take place and the actors that are likely to be involved. Second, it assesses the security challenges facing three key regions. Lieutenant General Martin Steele, Mr. Fred Smith, and Brigadier General Richard J. Quirk examine Asia and the Pacific Rim, Southwest Asia and the Persian Gulf, and Latin America and the Caribbean, respectively. Each also considers the future to address the question of whether stability or instability will predominate in the years ahead.

Dr. Susan L. Woodward, in her essay "Failed States: Warlordism and Tribal Warfare," analyzes emerging challenges to the current international security environment, focusing on the problem of failed states, a phenomenon that represents a growing source of regional instability and conflict. She observes that there is little consensus about what to do about it. This creates the following policy conundrum. On the one hand, the post–cold war world is experiencing burgeoning state disintegration, the rise of warlordism, and increased access to arms by a growing number of nonstate actors. On the other hand, there is a lack of interest by major powers in these new problems and a view that they are internal matters based on old rivalries and ethnic hatreds. This has resulted in little agreement over whether or not to intervene at all, let alone to act early through collective action.

Woodward touches on a number of cases—Somalia, Bosnia, Croatia, Rwanda, Haiti, Liberia, Afghanistan, Zaire/Congo—in her discussion of the characteristics of the threat and the operational problems resulting from insufficient collective interest, reluctance to intervene, and an inability to deal with counterparts on the ground, the most problematic of which are "warlords," who try to fill a vacuum of authority by controlling territory through arms and population allegiances based on fear and insecurity. The resort to older forms of solidarity (that is, ethnic and religious identities) reflects the breakdown of legal norms and institutions and is the result of the collapse of formal structures of government.

Woodward identifies the following two dimensions of this challenge that have to be addressed for the United States and the international community to respond adequately to these fragmented states. First, the threat posed by failed states is increasing, but our perceived interest in the problem is declining. Second, there is a growing gap between the willingness of governments to devote the amount of resources required to respond effectively to these problems.

The chapter concludes by arguing that there is a mismatch between the nature of these new regional challenges and current training, equipment, and doctrine of the U.S. armed forces. Furthermore, political constraints also inhibit what can be done when we do intervene, as the homefront demands zero casualties, a quick solution, and withdrawal.

The next three chapters discuss future security challenges from a regional perspective. The authors argue that each of the regions contains important U.S. interests, which require a military presence to encourage stability and promote democracy. Each area also faces the following security challenges: weapons of mass destruction proliferation and arms races; state disintegration, the rise of substate and transstate actors, and ethnic and religious violence; and drug trafficking, other international criminal activities, terrorism, and insurgency.

In Asia and the Pacific Rim, Lieutenant General Martin Steele, who served as director for strategic planning and policy at Pacific Command and currently is the president and CEO of Intrepid Sea-Air-Space Museum, identifies economics, population, and security as central to this region's stability. They are the keys to determining whether order or chaos will reign, who the primary regional actors and competitors will be, and whether the United States maintains its strong interests. He views these elements as interconnected—in particular, the increasing economic influence of the region, which requires a foundation of security.

Accomplishing these objectives will not be easy, because the region is also experiencing all of the sources of instability noted above. In South Asia, India's and Pakistan's nuclear tests open a Pandora's box of security issues. Elsewhere we find the buildup of arms and state-to-state confrontations. Asia and the Pacific Rim have also seen the emergence of nonstate actors, ethnic conflict, warlords, international organized crime, and state fragmentation.

Steele concludes that in light of the importance of the U.S. presence in creating stability for Asia and the Pacific Rim, the United States must remain engaged both economically and militarily. Given the vast differences in the region, he advocates the continuation of a strong forward naval component.

Fred Smith, principal deputy assistant secretary of defense for international security affairs and visiting professor at the United States Naval Academy during the period August 1999–July 2000, examines regional security in Southwest Asia and the Persian Gulf by first reviewing the evolution of U.S. policy over the last three decades. He then considers the vital interest (oil) and key challenges to U.S. policy, particularly with regard to force protection measures and the use of sea-based forces.

Smith proposes that three factors will remain constant in the twenty-first century: U.S. interests will remain vital in the Persian Gulf and Southwest Asia. This will continue to be the most challenging region involving our vital interests, and our ability to operate in it will become more difficult. With respect to the latter, he argues that this will result from evolving threats; local domestic factors, including economic, demographic, political, and religious elements; and shrinking U.S. defense budgets, force structure, and public support for a strong presence in the region. In light of U.S. vital interests, Smith concludes by strongly supporting the role of naval and Marine forces in the region as a clear priority now and in the future.

Finally, Brigadier General Richard J. Quirk, former chief of Southern Command's Intelligence Directorate and current deputy commanding general of the U.S. Army Intelligence Center, examines the challenges facing Latin America and the Caribbean in the twenty-first century. He notes that this region is vast, covering a wide range of nations with different languages, histories, and cultural heritages. Homogeneity is not characteristic of the region and presents some formidable challenges.

In the last decade, Latin America and the Caribbean have undergone some important changes, most notably the spread of democracy and decline of dictatorship. Quirk asserts that the United States played an important role in this evolution and continues to do so through the strategy of cooperative peace engagement. This includes the promotion and support of democracy; the protection of U.S. interests; and the modernization, innovation, and development of interoperability among the forces in the region.

While the region has undergone important and positive changes, security challenges still exist. Quirk identifies a range of transnational threats, including drug trafficking, illicit arms sales, terrorism, international organized crime, illegal migration, and environmental attack. Adding to these forces of instability in the future will be social and economic inequalities, strong nationalist sentiments, and reduced U.S. presence.

Within this regional security context, and in preparation for an uncertain future, Quirk proposes that naval forces will be important for flexible presence, readiness to support emergency requirements, military cooperation, and balancing the potential of an arms race with appropriate force modernization. Naval presence will contribute to each of these endeavors and must be structured to engage actively and be prepared to adapt to the unique circumstances in the region.

FAILED STATES: WARLORDISM AND "TRIBAL" WARFARE

Susan L. Woodward

The problem of failed or failing states in our current international system is like the uninvited guest at a party. The overwhelming impulse is to ignore it, to treat it as insignificant to the real show, and to hope it will go away. The horrifying image on global television in October 1993 of the corpses of American soldiers being dragged through the streets of Mogadishu led to a prompt retreat by American forces from such a situation in Somalia.[1] It also strengthened convictions within the American military that they should stay out of Bosnia and bolstered the argument of resisting intervention in a sure "quagmire."[2] For all the current chest pounding about the consequences of not sending bombers over Vukovar or Dubrovnik in Croatia in 1991 or not intervening in Bosnia in 1992 or in Rwanda in spring 1994, those who made the decisions still believe they were correct. Similarly, fights over the defense budget pay little attention to funding and preparation for such operations, still labeled with a derogatory connotation, "unconventional warfare," "operations other than war," and "political-military operations," despite major changes in doctrine.

Few would challenge the thesis that the phenomenon of failed states has become a serious source of global instability and conflict, or even that it represents an increasing proportion of current threats to international order. But few could also defend that thesis for long. It has become a kind of conventional wisdom without much consensus on why or what to do about the problem. The very fact that we have such a concept—a failed state—and use it with ease shows how far into the new international era we have come since the fall of the Berlin Wall. The lack of agreement on policy, within both civilian and military leaderships, shows how far we have yet to go.

The reason for these contradictions is that the phenomenon of failed states challenges the key operating assumptions of the current international order. That order is organized around the Westphalian state system, in which the basic elements are sovereign actors and rules of behavior among these actors are governed by the norm of sovereignty, or nonintervention in the internal affairs of states. Failed states represent a collapse of states and sovereign capacity. That international order is also characterized, however, by increasing globalization, which is said to erode sovereignty, making states ever less important. Yet the consequences of failed states reveal clearly how crucial states remain. Globalization requires states that function—governments capable of giving sovereign guarantees, exercising sovereign power and responsibility, controlling sovereign borders.[3]

In addition, the end of the cold war was said to make the contest over the domestic order of countries less relevant to the exercise of global power, whether by the United States, as sole remaining superpower, or by other major powers of the global economy. Geostrategic criteria of international significance and national interest have reasserted themselves. A large number of states whose internal order and very existence were shaped by cold war rivalry and superpower competition have lost strategic significance and superpower patronage since 1989–91. But the subsequent disinterest and withdrawal of resources to governments from Liberia and Somalia to Afghanistan and Yugoslavia have been the primary cause—at the least, the triggering catalyst—of their collapse. There is a powerful association between internal disintegration, fragmentation, massive civil violence, and the rise of warlordism, on the one hand, and states' lack of strategic significance to major powers and the uncontrolled proliferation of conventional arms since the end of the cold war, on the other. Yet to reinforce this new order of strategic interest, a new ideology—reminiscent of colonial discourse—has emerged that talks of a resurgence of tribalism and unresolved historical (even prehistorical) conflicts and hatreds, as if to remove any sense of external obligation in these conflicts. Failed states are said to be the result of ethnic conflict as opposed to the "old" ideological conflict, thus of internal genesis having nothing to do with international change and all to do with cultural particularities about which outsiders can do little.[4]

This series of paradoxes arises from the way we currently organize the international system and the foreign policy and defense establishments that operate within it. Although reorientation to challenges of the future is a global task, the challenge is greatest for the United States, as the sole remaining superpower in an international system still organized around the power of a hegemon to manage the primacy of national interest. No future challenge demonstrates this problem more clearly than that of failed states and the polarized debate over whether to intervene militarily in such conflicts. A threat to global order in general, and particularly through global communications and the slippery moral fabric that underlies any order, failed states raise a generalized problem without the specific national interest (with the partial exception of an influx of refugees) necessary to motivate action. The issue poses the classic problem of collective action.

Thus calls for American intervention, in its role as global guardian, are more frequent than should be necessary. American refusals to act undermine its global authority far more than the specific instances would seem to warrant. But the knowledge available to make a change is ignored. Explanations for failed states are by now quite developed, but policymakers appear to consider it largely irrelevant. The threat to international stability, and the likelihood that the problem will continue or worsen in the future, if most of the current explanations are correct, would seem to create a booming concern for taking preventive action. In fact, the substantial early warning and local knowledge now available do not lead to early action.

Identifying the Problem Correctly

The problem of failed states is not the failed states themselves but our lack of preparation for them. To paraphrase the old Pogo saying, "the enemy is us." This lack of preparation can be seen in three disproportions. The first is a disproportion between the threat posed by failed states and our perceived interest in the problem. As a result, secondly, there is a disproportion between the resources we commit and are willing to spend on these threats and the response that is needed. Third, there is a sharp disparity between the characteristics of the threat, the conflict, the context, and the combatants, on the one hand, and what we are prepared—and are preparing—to deal with, on the other.

Disproportion Number One: Threat versus Perceived Interest

Many dispute that the problem of failed states is increasing. They show levels of civil violence and internal conflict as quite steady for many decades. Others dispute only that failed states represent an increasing proportion of conflicts that seem to require international response, pointing out that the conflicts of Northern Ireland, Cyprus, or the Middle East may continue but they present no greater external threat than they ever have. But this confuses civil conflict with failed states, although an argument could be made that failure of governance is likely to provoke civil conflict. The focus on the conflict, or failed state, itself, moreover, prevents us from understanding *why* failed states are a problem. The problem lies in the change in the international environment. The ability of states to govern *matters* much more to global order, but we think it matters less. The threat may be rising but our interest is definitely declining.

The end of the nuclear stalemate and superpower competition has lifted the restraining mechanisms that kept general equilibrium during the cold war, but without anything to take its place. At the same time, increasing globalization, interdependence, and transnationalism make international order and stability, and even our national well-being and way of life, increasingly dependent on the capacity of governments to function and rulers to exercise sovereignty effectively and responsibly. Whether the focus is on the needs of nonstate actors such as businesses and banks or the affairs of state and interests of citizens, it is states that give sovereign guarantees, provide conditions for trade and foreign investment, control borders, prevent proliferation, keep populations sufficiently satisfied to remain at home, and provide enough protection of human rights and welfare not to need international relief or evoke cries in domestic arenas for action.

Yet the end of bipolar competition has also reduced dramatically the motivation to use aid and trade politically to obtain allies and keep them in power. One consequence has been that superpower or major power patrons have withdrawn the foreign financial and military support that governments had come to depend on for domestic power and governing capacity. Dependent more on foreign resources than on a domestic tax base, and on the skills aimed at obtaining foreign resources more than on those necessary to winning allegiance at home, controlling factional fights, generating tax revenues, and enforcing their collection, such regimes collapse rapidly when the resources go. Verbal support has replaced the funds, arms, and legitimacy that had been used to neutralize or co-opt other contenders for power, buy domestic support, and distribute the minimal welfare necessary to social equity and to the peaceful resolution of differences over inequality. One need only mention in this regard the former Yugoslavia,[5] Afghanistan,[6] Somalia,[7] Liberia,[8] and Zaire/Congo to make the point.

There has been a radical shift in international resource allocation, from buying friends in an ideological and strategic contest to conditioning domestic reform in exchange for loans in a globalizing economy. But this reform process is guided by an economic ideology of neoliberalism that is intentionally reducing the authority and resources of states through policies of liberalization, privatization, budgetary cuts and devolution, and overall fiscal conservatism. The consequences, however, have also been increasing regional inequalities and grievances, social polarization and abandonment, and creating a power vacuum that opens the door to demands for regional autonomy or secession, to alternative elites who aspire to total power through ethnic and nationalist appeals, and to the vicious cycle of public protests, police repression by weak governments, communal violence, and local insurgencies. In some cases, the predatory character of rule protected by cold war patrons comes home to roost. In others, the delicate balance of social comity and welfare is disturbed, and the speed and thoroughness demanded of reform allows no time to work out new political accommodations. To the countries cited above might be added Rwanda, Algeria, western Africa, and possibly many countries in Asia in the wake of the current financial crises and international response.

Thus, while some of the causes of state failure may only be transitional, withdrawal symptoms of a change in patterns of international resource allocation, others are related to the new order of things and thus predict more occasion for concern. Because the global decline in aid and the changed terms for external resources have also been accompanied by an inclination to view failure as a solely domestic problem, not one to which outsiders contribute, and by a disinclination to act early with the aim of prevention, the neglect is reinforced, and their frequency to rise can be predicted.

Disproportion Number Two: Resource Commitments versus Need

What matters about failed states is not their failure but its consequences: mass violence and atrocities transmitted instantaneously and worldwide on television screens; reports by nongovernmental organizations of famine, star-talk to, finding a government, offices, and staff. The longer local politicians delayed in meeting prescribed deadlines, the more outsiders managing the implementation began to take on the authority they originally refused—to dictate, and even to impose legislation as emergency measures to get the process moving.

Whether in Bosnia or Somalia, operations assumed the existence of hierarchy and some organized command and control, but in its place found tenuously controlled armed men acting with local interests, for personal vengeance or gain, only partially under the control or authority of people who claimed to be leaders, and often shifting their alliances for tactical reasons. Those who claim authority may not be able to exercise it, or may not want to demonstrate to their ostensible followers that they lack the power they claim by attempting to implement what they have signed up to. Most problematic for the intervenors is that such "warlords," persons whose power depends on the gun, may be seeking to work with outsiders to get the legitimacy necessary to securing that fragile power—to gain external recognition of their claim to authority as the precondition for domestic authority and as leverage with supporters and against rivals.

This condition is not tribalism, which is based in the classic analysis of authority types by Max Weber on military organization and success in battle. Truly "tribal" warlords would be easier to deal with than the wide variety of informal, fragile, competitive, and personal relations of authority that do abound. They either earn leadership through the test of battle or they inherit it along with elaborate norms of honor and social obligation, not as the conduit to international resources or the recipient of nationalist loyalty against international condemnation. The difference can be seen where remnants of the disintegrated army still retain their professional identity and codes of behavior, or where a professional army can be reconstituted.

Instead of the hierarchy and earned personal loyalty to leaders characteristic of tribes, the vacuum of legal authority is filled by those who claim to control some patch of territory and cache of arms and who then seek to capture popular allegiances on the basis either of the fear and insecurity generated by the absence of reliable authorities or the informal bonds of obligation and solidarity that already exist in society but are more like kinship groupings. In Somalia, a northern insurgency and breakaway led to breakdown along regional lines and the revival of loyalty and reciprocal obligations of the system of segmentary lineages. In Bosnia and Herzegovina, Yugoslavia first broke apart with the breakaway of Slovenia and Croatia and then from further competition for regional power on the basis of national self-determination that forced people to choose loyalties and dependence according to individual ethnonational identities. Regional conflict on the Zairian border with Rwanda allowed a leader to take advantage of ethnic differences and conflict in a regional insurgency and eventually to challenge the collapsing Zairian autocracy. In Afghanistan, the vacuum of state collapse was filled by territorially identified clans with linguistic or religious association. These loose bonds between leader and follower are based more on reciprocity, however, and thus require those who claim power to provide services (directly controlling and channeling such resources as they can obtain from outsiders, or through permission to loot—a mutual understanding that does not promote the clean command demanded by outsiders and is more likely to evolve more toward criminal gangs, protection rackets, and local defiance). This reciprocity tends to prolong the personalized and unaccountable nature of such power, deepening the anarchy, because any formal or legal regulation of such control over resources would give rivals access to those resources.

The resort to solidarity groupings and older forms of solidarity—what outsiders call ethnic conflict—also reflects the prior breakdown—or increasing marginalization—of legal norms and of an industrial or service-oriented class structure. These societies are not premodern as the theme of historical hatreds would have it, but the very result of rapid urbanization, growing urban unemployment, and a collapse of the middle class under austerity policies aimed at macroeconomic stability in countries with high foreign debt or trade deficits, leading people to cope through an informal and household sector outside the formal economy. Family-based and locally based networks of support and loyalty, evoked often through the emotion of manipulated cultural symbols or the religious identities and proselytizing of churches providing charity and succor, become substitutes for formal welfare and employment. But these identities can become the source of exclusion and conflict when the distribution of resources is at stake, and if that conflict or claims on loyalty turn violent, the distinction between soldiers and civilians, between battlefield and home front, on which international convention and morality are based, does not exist. Intervening forces face indirect warfare, waged against the population, and attrition tactics, not the soldier-on-soldier battles they know how to assess.

In responding to such conflicts, moreover, it is easy to see such ethnic, religious, linguistic, or clan differences as the essence of the conflict when they are in fact only a result (and for quite some time a reversible result) of the collapse of formal structures of governance and economic activity. When groups seek outside assistance, as some eventually do, on the basis of those same loyalties—ethnonational identity, religion, cultural values, membership in the same "civilization"—the tensions and competition can be made much worse by *outsiders'* views that the violence is caused by ethnic hatred, for they begin to treat those differences and presumed hatreds as essences rather than contingencies that are a matter of alterable conditions. This is especially the case if outsiders need to organize in terms of enemies and victims and thus take sides, for they help to harden the lines of conflict within the society rather than strengthening the instances of and capacity for cooperation.

The loss of a state's hegemonic power and authority to legislate, tax, enforce, and define the right to bear arms also creates a situation of relative balance in resources, especially arms, and in access to finances for war (such as regional control over trade routes and customs posts as can be seen in Bosnia, mineral resources as we see in Angola today, or lucrative financial offers from international businesses seeking local monopolies over natural resources that have no scruples about dealing with warlords and that do not condition their monies on certain behavior and reforms as do the United States and international organizations). Contrary to the stabilizing results attributed to balance-of-power arrangements in interstate relations, the most likely result of this relative balance of resources (particularly military ones) resulting from domestic anarchy is unending wars of attrition.[9] The equilibrium result—a negative equilibrium in economists' terms—is, according to Laitin, "stable anarchy" in which "all resources would be spent in fighting rather than production." They may lead to battlefield stalemates, but they do not have an internally generated completion.

The other result of this relative balance is to create layer upon layer of security dilemmas. The spiraling dynamic of mutual fears then continues to feed such wars once they begin.[10] The disintegration of Yugoslavia or the Bosnian war cannot be understood, for example, without recognizing that, once the federal state had no more authority and each group was pressuring for its own national rights and claiming to be at risk of exploitation and even survival from other nations who had once been members of the same state, then it was critical that each group was a numerical minority and could perceive themselves at risk and as acting only in defensive terms. Interventions that attempt to remain impartial, delivering food and shelter to all civilians but not intervening politically to stop the spiraling dynamic, thus are most likely to perpetuate these perceptions and the stalemate, while those that do intervene politically but take one side without going to war in support of that side also perpetuate the conflict by demonstrating to the others that their perceptions were correct and that they cannot disarm (psychologically as well as physically).

Finally, the search for sovereign actors in interventions prevents us from seeing the regional complexes that surround these conflicts. Three cases illustrate this point: Rwanda, Burundi, and Zaire/Congo; Afghanistan, Pakistan, and central Asia; and the complex of former Yugoslavia, where Slovenia led directly to Croatia, then on to Bosnia, and with developments in Yugoslavia, Kosovo, and Macedonia. The domestic conflicts can be fed and exacerbated by neighbors where there are transborder minorities they feel compelled to support (as in the military and political involvement of Croatia and Serbia in Bosnia-Herzegovina), or where they obstruct the restoration of central state capacity because they perceive it as a threat to their own sovereignty (as in Pakistan toward Afghanistan). The consequences of internal war, refugees, and cross-border flows of arms and armies resulting from state failure can also destabilize an entire region (as in the effect of Rwanda on Burundi, Zaire/Congo, and much of central Africa, or the potential effect of the arms that flowed from the chaos in Albania during 1997 to transborder Albanians in Macedonia and in Kosovo, Serbia). And efforts to restore peace and stability to one state can be hindered by neighboring instability (as demonstrated by the extension of conflict in 1999 to Kosovo and the continuing potential to undo much of the work to create a Bosnian state and political stability by the NATO-led mission attempting to implement the Dayton peace accords). Intervention in internal conflicts cannot ignore the fact that such failing states are likely to be surrounded by insecure or even failing states themselves in which the power shifts in one state reverberate rapidly in the others and the construction of one stable political order requires a regional strategy.

There are obvious mismatches between these characteristics and the current training, equipment, and doctrine of the armed forces. Military interventions in such circumstances are not conventional operations, but they are far more than police actions. The enemy is chaos, meaning a lack of the kind of order we know, and it is violence—guerrilla warfare, urban violence, small arms, snipers, terrorists—but in the hands of people who may have access to technologically sophisticated, deadly weapons of biological and chemical warfare, modern air power, shoulder-launched mortars, and antiaircraft artillery. Their mission is usually to protect civilians and aid workers, negotiate cease-fires, and give support to civilian relief organizations in the lead, not to do battle or run the show themselves. Often the most endowed and best organized of the organizations in such an effort, they must nonetheless play the supporting role and accept the inefficiencies, delays, and lack of coordination emanating from the civilian side.

The following mandate is provided to soldiers and officers sent into such conflicts: be impartial with locals, use minimal force, and give priority to force protection and at the same time to political relations that will maintain or improve support at home. One may enter with robust rules of engagement and equipment, but one quickly learns that it is psychological robustness that matters because the weapons are not suited to the situation, making the deterrence logic shaky, and because the home front demands zero casualties. These rules of intervention, however, risk accusations of inaction (made famous by the exchange at a cabinet meeting early in the first Clinton administration when the U.S. representative to the United Nations, later secretary of state, Madeleine Albright, asked Chairman of the Joint Chiefs of Staff, a Bush appointee, General Colin Powell: "What's the point of having this superb military that you're always talking about if we can't use it?"[11]), or worse, of immorality for being impartial. In the effort to end hostilities or to prevent them from resuming by talking to any and all factional leaders, they risk being accused of strengthening villains. Their mission is to do only what the military can do, but the primary tasks on the ground are political. Even the criteria for success are highly political and are defined by others. The most likely outcome is a stalemate where cease-fires last but there is no restoration of the political capacity and singular authority necessary to independently sustainable peace. This means having to stay far longer than intended.

In those cases where the military is sent to help implement a negotiated agreement to end the violence, its mandate is even more likely to be a vague, political compromise. The tendency for wars of attrition encourages foreign intervention to stop the killing long before leaders are ready to concede and reach a genuine agreement. The political reunification of warring factions and local leaders is not a given, and to move in that direction the military often has to do the local work of building the mutual confidence, trust, and command structures that are absent. While tactical agreements may make the separation of forces, cantonment of heavy weapons, and initial demobilization a relatively simple matter of mandate authority and the imbalance of forces favoring the intervenors, the longer-term problem of restoring government is a matter of internal security. One of the first offices to collapse in failed states is the police.

Much of the after-action literature on such operations so far emphasizes the crucial role of intelligence and of political savvy. Yet the very nature of such interventions is a crisis response to a locale considered unimportant. No preparation for local knowledge is likely, not because these conflicts cannot be predicted—they can be—but because of the low priority attached to such interventions and locales. The skills needed are either available as a matter of luck, or they are in the reserves. Some even argue that the fascination with military revolutions and technologically driven change tends to bias against the skills and weapons needed to succeed in these conditions.

In contrast to the autonomy of conventional military engagements, at least at the operational level, these operations require close and clear political direction. Yet, while these operations are immensely public and politicized, political direction is most often indecisive, erratic, and contradictory. Sending the military for humanitarian or containment motives, political leaders are unprepared for the political issues at stake or the expenditure of resources that are necessary. To complicate matters more, the lessons learned from recent operations tie success directly to the flexibility that only delegated leadership on the ground can achieve. A contest between field and capitals appears to be an inevitable ingredient added to the problems of coordination between military and civilian organizations that still serve as a substitute for combined political and military strategy. And the absence of clear political direction at the level of objectives and mission is reinforced by the obligation, for reasons of legitimacy in the post–cold war environment, to intervene multilaterally. Multinational operations create their own issues of unity of command, interoperability, political direction, and authority—a result in part of the anarchy that also characterizes international relations.

Conclusion

To conclude, these disproportions are particularly acute for the United States and its naval forces. Our reluctance to get involved in a preventive mode, including the use of force if necessary, is often a contributing factor to these disasters. The longer we wait, the more conditions deteriorate to the point where military force is needed. We are now emphasizing the need to develop a capacity for rapid deployment, but the political conditions necessary to early deployment are not being laid. And the security problem in a state that has failed tends to require a long ground presence. We are also emphasizing a greater role for regional powers and organizations in these conflicts, as against the United Nations, but the United States—and especially its naval reach—is the only global power and member of most regional organizations. We want to retreat from global policing, yet most such operations require the logistics, communications, and intelligence that only the United States can provide.

There is no doubt that the problem of failing and failed states will be a major threat to international security and American leadership in the coming decades. There also seems no doubt at the moment that the response will remain ad hoc and late in the game, plagued by political indecisiveness and confusion or contest at home and by conflict with allies over the interests at stake. In the public's outrage at the consequences, they demand a military response, but without much information or debate about its proper role or the place of military assets in this problem.

For the armed forces, this situation appears to leave only two choices: to adapt doctrine, train for these contingencies directly, and be prepared to move early, or to push harder for prevention. As it is now, the problems presented by failed states can only be stopped by reversing the failure: to seat a sovereign and rebuild state capacity. The United States military will increasingly be used to assist in the state-building that politicians resist, to provide military governors and occupations, and to think harder about strategy for such operations, including the careful integration of military and civilian capacities into one effort—an integration that thus far the United States military has resisted. As Barnett Rubin concludes from the case of Afghanistan, "The main lesson is that resolution of conflicts in states that have been failed by the international community requires a sustained cooperative effort by that community."[12]

Notes

1. A clear analysis can be found in Terrence Lyons and Ahmed I. Samatar, *Somalia: State Collapse, Multilateral Intervention, and Strategies for Political Reconstruction* (Washington, D.C.: Brookings Institution, 1995), pp. 57–60 and *passim*.

2. Although only a rephrasing of the Weinberger (some would say Nixon) Doctrine, this resistance of the military leadership in 1991–92 became associated with the sitting chairman of the Joint Chiefs of Staff, Colin Powell, and was relabeled, the Powell Doctrine.

3. See Francis M. Deng, Sadikiel Kimaro, Terrence Lyons, Donald Rothchild, and I. William Zartman, *Sovereignty as Responsibility: Conflict Management in Africa* (Washington, D.C.: Brookings Institution Press, 1996) on this argument

that the grant of sovereignty must include responsibility, including to international standards and conventions.

4. The best known are Robert D. Kaplan, "The Coming Anarchy," *Atlantic Monthly*, 1994, and *Balkan Ghosts: A Journey through History* (New York: St. Martin's Press, 1993), and Samuel Huntington, *The Clash of Civilizations and the Remaking of World Order* (New York: Simon and Schuster, 1996). But see Chaim Kaufman, "Possible and Impossible Solutions to Ethnic Civil Wars," *International Security*, vol. 20, no. 4 (Spring 1996), pp. 136–175, for an even more influential example of this new fad, in which he divides internal conflicts into two categories: cold war conflicts are ideological and post–cold war conflicts are ethnic.

5. The argument for Yugoslavia can be found in Susan L. Woodward, *Balkan Tragedy: Chaos and Dissolution after the Cold War* (Washington, D.C.: Brookings Institution, 1995).

6. See Barnett R. Rubin, *The Fragmentation of Afghanistan: State Formation and Collapse in the International System* (New Haven: Yale University Press, 1995) and *The Search for Peace in Afghanistan: From Buffer State to Failed State* (New Haven: Yale University Press, 1995).

7. See Terrence Lyons and Ahmed I. Samatar, *Somalia: State Collapse, Multilateral Intervention, and Strategies for Political Reconstruction* (Washington, D.C.: Brookings Institution, 1995), and Mohamed Sahnoun, *Somalia: The Missed Opportunities* (Washington, D.C.: U.S. Institute of Peace, 1994).

8. The work of Adekeye Adebajo emphasizes this factor for Liberia.

9. David Laitin applies this model from biology and industrial organization to the case of Somalia, in "Somalia—Civil War and International Intervention," forthcoming from Columbia University Press in a volume edited by Jack Snyder and Robert Jervis on the security dilemma and ending civil wars.

10. See one example in Barry Posen, "The Security Dilemma and Ethnic Conflict," *Survival* vol. 35, no. 1 (Spring 1993), pp. 27–47.

11. Cited by Colin Powell in his autobiography, written with Joseph E. Persico, *My American Journey* (New York: Random House, 1995), p. 576. He then adds, "I thought I would have an aneurysm. American GIs were not toy soldiers to be moved around on some sort of global game board."

12. Rubin, *Search for Peace*, p. 145.

ASIA AND THE PACIFIC RIM

Martin Steele

In this chapter, my task is to examine the Pacific region of the future. My outlook is colored by two distinct points of view: as a former Marine from headquarters Marine Corps and also as the former J-5 from the U.S. Pacific Command. My focus will consider the following six questions:

➤ What are the strategic and cultural challenges in this region?

➤ To what extent will the region be characterized by stability, conflict, or chaos?

➤ Who will be the principal actors—that is the state, substate, and transstate actors?

➤ What are the U.S. interests, both vital and important, in the region?

➤ What is the likely U.S. role?

➤ How will naval forces contribute to U.S. strategic and operational roles within the region?

Cultural and Strategic Challenges in the Region

In the Pacific region, with 105 million square miles, forty-four countries, and eight of the ten largest militaries, the Pacific Command is faced with huge challenges. Chief among these is the tyranny of distance. Furthermore, there are three factors that are of particular importance: economics, population, and security.

Growing, urbanized, predominantly male populations will put pressure on the economic boom to continue to provide jobs and create an increasingly chaotic security situation. As new nation-states mature, they will search for their individual identities, both culturally and on the world stage. China and India, demographically the two largest countries in the world—with India forecast to surpass China early in the twenty-first century—present a foreboding problem with regard to available resources and the ability to provide food for their respective populations. How they act and react within the region and on the global scene will be a concern for the next twenty-five to fifty years.

After I had spent twenty months in the Pacific Command, including five trips to China, one of the most significant events I witnessed was watching a country's populace migrate from the hinterlands to the urban centers on the coast. Within twelve months, a Chinese city with a population of six million grew to a city of eighteen million. It is almost inconceivable to imagine how these masses struggle to survive in a labor market without any infrastructure, without any shelter, without any electricity, and without any water, but this is the reality in China today.

In China at six o'clock on a Sunday morning in any of its major cities, in excess of one million people are already up and striving to get a piece of the market economy. Where else in the world can you see a million people in a metropolitan area up and about? The fact is that this condition exists in every major city in China. The idea of throngs of people going to the marketplace has not been understood by the United States, nor have the implications of a billion, three hundred million people trying to survive been fully grasped. The survival of its population is a major factor in how China deals with the rest of the world and affects how we must deal with China in the future.

Strategically, this region is most likely to produce a peer competitor to the United States. It contains a number of growing powers and is home to many ancient animosities, ongoing conflicts, authoritarian governments, growing regional arms races, and multicountry territorial disputes, such as the dispute over the Spratly Islands. While nominally a point of contention based on historic territorial claims, this conflict is really a controversy based on the vast amounts of oil thought to exist in the region. Currently, we recognize none of the claims of any of the disputing countries. Conflicts of this type, which involve a finite supply of a particular resource, are likely to increase and may expand over time to include other resources.

Another factor that is particularly important in this region is technology. Whether it is cyberwar or information war, this is a technologically rich region. India, Japan, China, South Korea, and many others have thriving or emerging technology industries. They are often the source of significant breakthrough technologies, which pose security issues that affect our lives and the way we fight.

All of this is strategically connected to a condition that is unique to Asia, in that there are no major security alliances—such as NATO—in the region. ASEAN has proven a little bit better than anticipated with its growth over the last three to five years. Still, the fact remains that our relationships in the region are fundamentally bilateral. This presents specific challenges for the United States and our policymakers because what is fundamentally good for one country may not necessarily be good for the country—or countries—on its immediate borders. This creates a tremendous challenge in dealing with the region.

In sum, trends in economics, population, and security affect our thinking and planning for the Asia and Pacific Rim region. These three trends are the main source of cultural and strategic challenges and are key to resolving whether order or chaos will reign. These three factors will also determine the primacy of regional actors—state, substate, or transstate—in the region and on the world stage. The future U.S. role in this vital area will be measured against each of these trends.

Economics

The economic importance of the Asia and Pacific Rim region, and the reason it can be justifiably labeled an area of U.S. interest, has been vividly demonstrated by current events. As mentioned above, these nations' economies and stock markets are now globally linked, if not in fact, at least—and perhaps most important—psychologically. A vivid example of this is the recent Asian financial crisis. News reports in the morning now include the results of overnight trading in Asian markets as a routine part of their economic report. This was not common before the recent crisis, and this news often serves to set the tone for the day's trading on Wall Street. The link, though, is more than psychological—it also involves the very real effect of changing currency rates and their impact on trade. U.S. trade with this region is increasingly important to our economy.

The amount and importance of U.S.-Asian trade, and the resulting economic link, continue to expand. While some experts point to a cooling of the superheated Asian economies, one trend does not seem to be in decline. The demand for resources, both raw and material, and energy continues to climb. Competition for these resources will fuel regional competition in all of its forms. Growing economies and growing competition can also create divisions between "haves" and "have nots." These can be sources of both interstate and intrastate conflict. Moreover, economic rifts can be exploited by transstate actors, as witnessed by the steady growth of "drug empires" across national borders. All of these "competitions" pose a threat to the stability and growth of U.S. investments in the region.

Population

There may be no clear way to determine which came first, but the growth of Asian and Pacific Rim economies is coupled with growth in population. This growth is every bit as explosive as the recent economic boom. In addition, there are two subtrends to this population growth. It is increasingly male, especially young male, and people are migrating to urban areas, creating megacities.

The pressure inherent in crowded urban settings, as I described in China, but prevalent throughout the region, especially when they are tilted toward a predominantly male environment, create a fertile environment for unrest. Mix in the myriad religions of the region, "different" moral standards, conflicting cultures—some still tribal or clan oriented—and the mounting mass of humanity in the region may become a source of constant conflict.

Security

The security environment of this region is very complex and the trend indicates that it will get even more so. Sorting out all of the players can be difficult. The idea of a nation-state, in the modern-European-Western sense, is new. Many countries have ancient animosities, which create conflict even today. The economic boom may trigger a regional arms race and lead to more potent regional militaries. Totalitarian regimes, ongoing conflicts—both external and internal—and multistate territorial disputes, like the Spratly Islands—also cloud the security picture.

All of these problem areas are fueled by the trends in economic and population growth. Additionally, the region contains at least two nuclear powers and several growing powers. If an adversary or peer competitor develops, the technology and urbanization of the battle space presents an asymmetric threat. Weapons of mass destruction proliferation also complicates strategic planning. Overcrowding, access to money and weapons, and competition for resources between the "haves" and "have nots" serve as tinder in a dry region.

To What Extent Will the Region Be Characterized by Stability, Conflict, or Chaos?

Based on the above trends, I believe the region will become increasingly chaotic as we move into the twenty-first century. This will be especially true if there is a void in U.S. presence, because the United States is such an important stabilizing factor.

The small conflicts of today are very likely to grow, especially as the population of urban males develops into a warrior class, with a thin veneer of technology, particularly the technology associated with high-technology weaponry. The asymmetry of the environment in which they live will make asymmetric action almost a given. Another area of "growth" with incredible potential for chaos is the population of refugee warriors, and, as economies grow, the ability of these warriors to procure increasingly sophisticated arms.

Who Will be the Principal Actors— State, Substate, and Transstate?

As Professor Richard H. Shultz Jr. points out in his contribution to this volume, the ideas of ethnonationalism and religion, especially in the radical, extreme form, are playing an increasing and important role, both in the Pacific region and throughout the globe. Many of the nations in the region are "young," or relatively new. These "young" nations may not have the culture or national identity to survive the coming chaos. Many of the nations in the region, both "young" and established, have internal religious, cultural, tribal or clan differences. This will result in challenges from radical factions, religious militants, secessionists, ethnic-based international crime organizations, terrorists, and insurgents.

The changes and growth among the three factors—that is, the economic trend, the population trend, and security trend—will determine the primacy of actors in the region. As competition for resources, including labor, increases, transstate actors will grow in importance. For example, pirates operating in choke points and the littorals—the Strait of Malacca with its significance to the flow of oil from the Persian Gulf, or drug cartels operating across international borders, such as the Golden Triangle—will have an impact on the United States.

Other pressures, whether from transnational corporations or illegal drugs, will strain both the order of the region in the future and the basic stability that now exists there, despite the challenges in places like Myanmar, Sri Lanka, and East Timor.

What Are U.S. Interests, Vital and Important, in the Region?

First, it is obvious that global stability and security, and therefore stability in the Pacific, is fundamental to U.S. interests and to our role and responsibilities there. Second, the worldwide stock market reverberations were triggered by fluctuations in the Hong Kong exchange, which were motivated by the financial downturn in Thailand. The Hong Kong and Taiwanese markets also dipped at the start of the Taiwan Straits missile crisis, but rebounded when our aircraft carriers arrived on station. These examples highlight the current level of economic interconnectedness with security issues and the challenges they pose for the future.

This global economic linkage will only grow with time. It is exemplified by the projection that tanker traffic to Asia, for fossil fuel and other trade goods, is expected to triple within the next twenty years. Japan still imports 90 percent of its oil from the Middle East, causing significant challenges if there is instability in the region. China's imports of oil are growing at 5 percent a year, as it is no longer able to supply its domestic needs internally. Again, with its existing population and projections of substantial growth, oil imports will only continue to increase.

The long-term prosperity of the United States, particularly in light of this global-connected economy, rests on stability, and particularly on stability within Asia and the Pacific Rim. Additionally, we have many long-standing allies in the region. We need to ensure that these allies remain solid, as they move into the potentially chaotic world of the twenty-first century. These allies have stood firm with us in times of trouble, and we will continue to honor our commitments to them.

There are, however, already indications that some countries in the Pacific do not believe we will continue to provide security in the region, for whatever reasons. They question our resolve, and because of the successful economies in the region, they are not sure we are going to stay.

The Marine Corps commissioned Dr. Dov Zakheim and a team of his specialists to examine this phenomena in the region. They visited eleven countries, soliciting leaders—from the political, business, and economic communities—on their views about the need and desire for continuous U.S. presence in the region. The results, on the one hand, are what you would expect. On the other hand, they are quite phenomenal and alarming with regard to their implications for our responsibilities in this area of the world and our need to remain connected to the Asia-Pacific region.

For example, in Malaysia, the report included a quote from the assistant minister of defense, who stated that the United States is an unreliable partner because of the lack of predictability of U.S. public support for continuation of a role in the Pacific. Prime Minister Mahathir in Malaysia made a statement in July in a public speech that, "We appreciate the offer to defend us, but how can we be sure the promised help will be forthcoming, when we see so many countries being abandoned to their fates as soon as they are in trouble?" In Indonesia, the take-away for Dr. Zakheim and for the Marine Corps and naval forces was a quote from the former Indonesian ambassador to another Asian country, in which he said, "The Chinese people can wait. Indonesians question how long will the U.S. bear the burden." These types of attitudes and the challenges we face with them can only lead, in the long term, to destabilization. It is hoped they will not lead to open conflict, but there still remains a responsibility for us to maintain a presence in the region to prevent conflict from escalating.

Another concern is the access to arms that is afforded by the wealth generated by growing economies. Many countries in the region are arming themselves at a shocking rate. The problem is exacerbated by the glut of arms on the world market as many cold war adversaries draw down and as arms makers look for emerging markets to maintain profit margins. Unless the arms trade is controlled, this can only lead to destabilization and conflict.

What Is the Likely U.S. Role?

Our best method of ensuring peace is to insure peace. That is, much like an insurance policy, we must pay a little every month to avoid a major catastrophe. The form of this payment is engagement. Abandoning the Asia and Pacific Rim area as a risky firetrap can only lead to a greater expenditure of both U.S. monetary and human capital if and when the region ignites. We must reassure our allies that we are with them for the long term. We must demonstrate our resolve and commitment to the region consistently. We must sell American-backed security as the coin of the realm. This may lessen the perceived need in many countries to arm themselves. We must illustrate, at every occasion, that the economic health of the Pacific region, and every country in it—as well as the global economy—rests on a safe, secure environment in which to do business where conflict serves no one.

So we must remain engaged, economically and militarily. This engagement must go beyond jointness—for that matter, it must go beyond interagency—and include contributions from all forms of our national power. This is true not only in Asia and the Pacific Rim, but around the globe. This means that we have to bring academia, the business community, technology, and nongovernmental organizations (NGOs) as elements of our national power, into the security plan. These "new" partners should serve not just as links to a military security force, but in the conflict prevention phase. By thinking in a forward manner in regards to stability and economic viability and coordinating all forms of national power, we can better prevent conflicts and resolve them more quickly if they do erupt. Fundamental to this is continued, forward presence. This presence must be sustainable, flexible, responsive, and most important, credible. In so vast an area, the presence force cannot be tied down geographically. This points to a strong forward naval component—the Navy-Marine Corps team. They are already in the region and they are a proven performer, regionally and worldwide.

How Will Naval Forces Contribute to U.S. Strategic and Operational Roles?

As Dr. Zakheim found out, throughout Asia, the end of the cold war did not change the view of regional leaders toward the continued presence of U.S. military. The United States is viewed by countries throughout the Asia and Pacific region as the stabilizing factor in what they all consider to be a very uncertain area. Sea power will also be the key to economic stability.

This goes beyond visits and port calls, or over-the-horizon forces. The major impact is philosophical and what mental images it creates for the leaders and populace of the region: the stability that a presence force brings with it *by its mere presence.* As an increasing number of countries begin to lose patience with having a permanent U.S. presence on their soil, naval forces will become even more important.

Will we be able to keep about a hundred thousand troops in Asia for the foreseeable future? That is the projection and the desire. But the facts and the reality are that we have to be less obtrusive with the peoples of the region so that we can remain to ensure their security. Factors such as the reunification of Korea will most certainly affect the size of the land component of any force we keep in Asia.

The trend of NIMBY, or "not-in-my-backyard" is growing stronger and is very prevalent in Asia. They want a strong U.S. military presence in the region, but off the coast, or in someone else's country, not theirs, and especially not permanently. It becomes an issue of access, of places, not bases. It is also an issue about where we can train and where we can conduct visits. The idea of permanency is not up for negotiation, except with a few regional partners.

A recent example is the current negotiation over moving the Marine Corps Air Station (MCAS) Futenma from Okinawa to a site off shore. Even this facility is viewed as temporary to reflect the temporary presence of U.S. forces in Japan. While the heinous rape cases of several years ago served as the catalyst for this effort, it is far more encompassing and reflects the requirement for unobtrusiveness of U.S. military forces in the region. Our departure from the Philippines is but another example.

Therefore, the Navy-Marine Corps team is the presence force of choice. Not only is the Blue-Green team the force of choice, but it brings to the equation the predominant capability to ensure stability and security in the region. We have done it in the past, we are doing it today, and we are positioning ourselves, through innovation and a coherent transformation process, to continue as a proven performer in this regard into the future. This includes looking beyond the status quo in the way we provide these enhanced capabilities and new technologies.

An example of this is sea basing. The Marine-Navy team is already the force with the smallest footprint and is sustainable from the sea, without large land depots in the region. As the Navy and Marine Corps continue to generate new innovations and move more combat power to sea, the ability to conduct presence operations and ensure security only increases. From the current capability provided by the maritime preposition ship program, we are moving toward ideas such as mobile sea bases. Expensive, yes, but unobtrusive. Also being examined are multipurpose ships, with the capability to support sea basing and to enhance the role of naval forces to influence events ashore in the twenty-first century.

Most important, though, is that in fulfilling this role in the region, naval forces are not independent. Naval forces will work as part of a joint force. They will link, not only with the unified commander in the region, but also with ambassadors. And this force will go beyond even those linkages, beyond even linking with an interagency process, to cooperation and coordination with, PVOs, NGOs, IOs, and all elements of national power. The advent of network-centric warfare, and the tremendous reach and power it will bring, including the prevention of such things as cyberwarfare or information warfare, will assist in insuring, and ensuring, the stability of the region for the future.

Conclusion

A brief summary of the challenges, current and future, in the Pacific demonstrates my initial premise that the region covers a lot of territory and reveals some big problems. The Asia and Pacific Rim economic, population, and security trends present real challenges. However, what makes the region vital is its increasing economic influence. This prosperity grows out of a foundation of security. The capability and presence of U.S. forces, especially naval forces, is the cornerstone of this security. Force is not the sum total of the structure, just the basis, for continued peace and prosperity. Maintaining stability and deterring aggression require all the elements of national power at our disposal. The military certainly cannot ameliorate all of the problems that growth in economic ties, population, and security issues may generate. Nevertheless, we must remain vigilant, innovative, and continuously prepared for the unexpected. If we remain engaged, with the Navy-Marine Corps team in the lead promoting stability, even potentially big problems can be minimized.

SOUTHWEST ASIA AND THE PERSIAN GULF

Fred Smith

Saddam Hussein has done a great job of introducing the topic of this chapter. While there has been a great deal of speculation as to what actions the United States should have taken in response to Saddam's eviction of Americans from the United Nations Special Commission (UNSCOM) and subsequently the curtailment of UNSCOM's inspectors in Iraq, we need to resist this urge and look to the future. Although how Saddam plays, or whether he plays in the future, is certainly one of the questions worth discussing.

I will focus on three main points about the Persian Gulf in the twenty-first century: U.S. interests in the Gulf will remain vital; this will also remain the most challenging region where we have vital interests; and our ability to operate in the Gulf will become more difficult.

Before explaining these three propositions, let me take a quick look at how our policy has evolved over the past thirty years. I do not want to dwell on the past and avoid looking at the future, but it is interesting to look at the trend that has developed. Also, it neatly breaks down by decades.

From 1970 to 1980, we were still in the cold war era, and our defense strategy was based primarily on arming Iran and maintaining close relations with Saudi Arabia, which was the so-called twin-pillar strategy. Our presence in the Gulf at that time consisted of two destroyers and the flagship *LaSalle*. We were there, but not really in a meaningful way. Despite the economic importance of the region, it clearly was backwater to the European Command and Pacific Command. There was, of course, no U.S. Central Command at that time.

The 1970s ended with the fall of the shah and, virtually on the last day of the decade, the Soviet invasion of Afghanistan. Much of the 1980s decade was dominated by the Iran-Iraq war. For the U.S. militarily, the defining moment was the reflagging of the eight Kuwaiti tankers and the inception of Operation Earnest Will in 1987. This caused a significant increase in U.S. naval presence, which approximately doubled to eight or nine ships. The United States had four AWACS conducting surveillance over the region. That was the Elf One operation. We were there, but we were still relegated to an over-the-horizon presence.

The 1990s decade started with the Iraqi invasion of Kuwait, and, in 1991, with a successful outcome of the Gulf War. Naval and marine forces, including aircraft carriers, were present inside the Gulf as never before. For about a year after that, the United States had unprecedented access and we signed several defense cooperation agreements.

We still maintain a robust presence throughout the region, ashore, and at sea. But slowly the Gulf states have slipped back into their prewar posture of not embracing Americans too closely. Our naval presence is approximately sixteen combatants, including a carrier battle group, an Amphibious Ready Group, and nine support vessels. Ashore, we have a considerable presence—over a hundred U.S., U.K., and French aircraft, and nearly two thousand soldiers.

That is the past and today. What about the future and the next decade? Unless there is a dramatic change in our dependence on imported oil, U.S. interests in the Gulf will remain vital for at least the next decade. There are probably economists and oil experts who can expound on this much greater. According to the *New York Times*, in 1996 the world consumed just over seventy million barrels of oil a day. That figure is projected to rise to nearly 105 million barrels by the year 2015, a 50 percent increase. The United States alone consumes 20 percent of that total. Oil imported to the United States has risen sharply and now accounts for just over half the oil the country uses. Given this continuing dependence on foreign oil, the United States has no choice but to stay engaged in this region.

There are a number of challenges of operating in the Gulf region. By comparison, operating in the two other major theaters—Europe and the Mediterranean, and Asia and the Pacific—is not nearly as difficult. Distance factors, lack of infrastructure, a host of logistic problems, the nature of the threat with short or virtually no warning time, and a harsh environment are but a few of the challenges we face.

By harsh environment, I mean both cultural and climatic conditions and the constant threat to our troops. This is the region that defined the requirements for force protection. In general, Western military presence is unpopular with indigenous people and serves as a target for criticism of the local regimes. It also serves as a target for terrorists.

These attitudes will not change; they will probably get stronger and more intense over the next decade. All future operations in the region will have to continue putting a premium on forced protection measures. This also puts a premium on sea-based forces.

Another factor that adds to the challenge of this region is the effects of the Middle East peace process on our military defense policy, strategy, and operations. Some would say that the peace process is mostly atmospherics in terms of the Gulf and military operations. I would say that it is more defining. If the process goes well, it will be easier for the Gulf states to cooperate with us. Conversely, periods in the peace process, such as we are experiencing now, make it more difficult to garner support. The 1997 summit meeting in

Doha serves as an example. Many states did not even attend the summit. If the peace process were in a more active and positive direction, it would have been easier and the mood would have been better to garner support for the current situation. The United States is closely associated with Israel. That is a reality and it will not change.

My third statement is that it will become increasingly difficult to operate in this region. I believe this is true for several reasons: the evolving threat, local domestic factors, and factors here at home in the United States. I forecast that the two protagonists, Iraq and Iran, will not change significantly. While it is extremely difficult to forecast what will happen in Iraq over the next ten years, I believe we must assume that, for at least the next five years, Saddam Hussein will be in power. Rather than speculate exactly what month or what year Saddam will pass from the scene, the issue of succession and how it will come about is more interesting.

First, we cannot assume that his successor will change Iraq's threatening posture. There will be an immediate urge in the Arab world, and by other countries, to accept the new Iraqi leader, which will also probably mean immediate lifting of the sanctions, if they still exist. How will succession occur? Who will it be? Frankly, I do not see too many Mohammed El Jeffersons running around Iraq. We need to think about this event and be prepared. It is not too difficult to imagine that some morning, or probably some Friday afternoon of a three-day weekend, or December 23d, or something like that, we will suddenly face the fact that Saddam has somehow passed from the scene. There will be, I predict, a certain amount of chaos in the country and there will be calls for help and assistance. How we should respond will be difficult to sort out, especially in the first few days, weeks, or even months.

I believe succession will occur in stages. Immediately after Saddam, we will probably have somebody, probably from the Takriti clan, who will assume power. But that person may not last more than six months or so, and then there will be a follow-on turnover.

I am a little more confident in predicting that Iran will not change its policies over the next decade. In fact, this is the threat that concerns the Gulf states the most and for good reason. Persian hegemonic aspirations have been constant for centuries. I contend that dealing with Iran will be the overall biggest challenge that we face in the region in the twenty-first century. By dealing with Iran, I mean a series of steps that we should take.

We, of course, need to stay prepared militarily to ensure the flow of oil and to provide assurances to our friends in the Gulf. Iran, as well as Iraq, will maintain large standing armed forces. But the greatest concern will be the development of weapons of mass destruction. Working with other countries—European countries, Russia, China, Japan—we need to prevent the proliferation of these weapons and associated technology. This will be essential. Diplomatic channels must stay open in case Iran decides to make sincere and legitimate overtures to the United States.

Associated with the weapons of mass destruction threat will be a growing need for theater missile defenses. I know this is one of General Anthony Zinni's highest priorities; also Dr. Jacqueline Davis and Dr. Charles Perry, of the Institute for Foreign Policy Analysis, have initiated work in this field. Theater missile defense is an area that begs for regional cooperation. Unfortunately, the Gulf Cooperation Council track record on cooperation is not exactly stellar. Promoting greater regional cooperation is definitely something we need to work on.

This region will also become increasingly difficult in which to operate because of a combination of economic, demographic, and political factors. Gulf economies will remain flat, unless they can develop their trade and income beyond virtually total reliance on oil. At the same time, high population growth rates will continue, adding to the strain on local governments to provide social services and infrastructure. Saudi Arabia's growth rate, for example, of 3.5 percent annually, is one of the highest in the world. And over 50 percent of the people in the Gulf region are under fifteen years old.

Politically, we must worry about regime stability of our Gulf partners. I am not—I repeat—I am not predicting the overthrow or downfall of any particular monarchy. I will only say that the local regimes need to accommodate greater popular participation of governance.

Unlike other regions of the world, religion in the Middle East and the Gulf is a dominant factor. Mainstream Islam is not antithetical to Western interests. It is, after all, the fastest growing religion in the United States. But it is no secret that the presence of Infidel forces is a source of discontent among conservative religious Islamic leaders and can foster radical opposition and possible terrorist acts. Religion in this region, and how it plays in their political thinking, is something about which we should be more conversant.

Two other local factors—Central Asia and Afghanistan—are important. While these may seem external to the Gulf itself, developments in Afghanistan already influence the environment. The great Jihad to expel Soviet occupiers in Afghanistan produced a number of radicalized Afghan Arabs who have returned home to the Gulf with both their weapons and the military skills to use them. Central Asia could turn out to be a major energy source, sufficient to effect the income of the Gulf economies. How the Gulf states, particularly Iran, interact with Central Asia will be an interesting development in the dynamics of this region.

Finally, there are U.S. factors that will affect our operations in the Gulf region. I am speaking primarily about our defense budget and force structure, as well as operating and maintenance funding. I am not sure how this really differs from the other regions and our operating forces elsewhere, but operating in the Gulf is not cheap. It wears on equipment and, more important, it wears on people. As a result of the 1997 *Quadrennial Defense Review*, the Navy's surface combatant fleet will be reduced from 1997's level of 128 ships to 116 in the year 2003. "Pers-tempo" will be a major factor in this region. I never met anyone who truly enjoyed a deployment to the Gulf, especially in July or August.

Despite the region's importance, there is the major question: How long is this nation willing to sustain the effort we must put forth to operate militarily there. To thwart this tendency to pull back, we need to strengthen international involvement in the Gulf. Not just militarily, although that will remain a key ingredient. The industrialized world depends on this region, and it is in everyone's interest to keep it secure and stable. We need a coalition strategy that calls on other countries in tackling these difficult problems.

I have raised some issues for discussion. I have probably asked more questions than I have answered. I come back to my three basic statements: Ten years from now, we will still have vital interests in the Gulf. It is the most challenging region in which we have vital interests. And it will become increasingly difficult to operate there. Given the factors that I have briefly discussed—the evolving threat, domestic issues in the local countries, logistic problems, lack of infrastructure, basing access, and the harsh environment—I will leave it to the reader to consider the role of naval and Marine forces in the Gulf in the twenty-first century. But, in my mind, many of these answers are clear.

LATIN AMERICA AND THE CARIBBEAN

Richard J. Quirk

The primary focus of this chapter is to share USSOUTHCOM's perceptions regarding the role of naval forces in the twenty-first century, with specific attention to the area of responsibility (AOR), the kinds of military or naval requirements that the AOR brings about, and how the AOR will deal with future challenges in Latin America and the Caribbean. Before addressing these issues, I will discuss the nature of this region and how we view our role as a unified command there.

Latin America and the Caribbean cover a vast area, comprising one-sixth of the Earth's land surface, which is only increased by the oceans surrounding that land. In the past two years, USSOUTHCOM gained responsibility for those oceans, and this has changed our unified command from being a land-locked entity—one which was very heavily ground and air organized and oriented—to a command in which the CINC has the ability to synchronize air, land, and sea forces in support of its particular mission.

What this means in USSOUTHCOM headquarters is a new period of learning and experimentation to determine how it is that the CINC's mission can be executed by all of those services. And it is, indeed, a time of learning for all of us. Fortunately, we have a commander in chief, a deputy commander in chief, and a J-5, all of whom are naval officers. It is a time of great change for USSOUTHCOM, which includes a recent move of our headquarters from Quarry Heights, Panama, to Miami, Florida.

I will now turn to the AOR itself. First of all, it is important to note that the term Latin America is a very deceptive one. Even if Latin America is considered to mean countries whose people speak a romance language, it is not so simple. There are thirty-two nations in the region, nineteen of them in what might be called Latin America, South America, and Central America, and thirteen others in the Caribbean.

All of these nations have histories and cultural heritages, which are, in some cases, as varied and dissimilar as those of the countries that range between Britain and the Urals. There are four principal languages—Spanish, Portuguese, English, and French—and yet the Organization of American States (OAS) recognizes seven official languages, and indeed, numerous other indigenous languages that are still used. Each one of these countries is very different. Homogeneity is not a characteristic of the region, and solutions to the challenges we face must be crafted to account for these differences.

Another aspect influencing our approach is the democratization process. Today all nations of the region, save one, refer to themselves as democracies. And it is extremely easy to get caught up in that move toward democracy and feel extremely optimistic that things are going well. In reality, we have to be careful not to try to accept a democratization process as some sort of fait accompli or an irresistible force that cannot be reversed. That is not the case and it is certainly not the case in history.

A better case for history might be to look back to about 1900 to see that democracy has gone through cycles, waxing and waning over that period. Our analysts say that in about 1900, democracy was at a low ebb; it then began to gain ground until the 1920s, when it declined. It turned the corner in 1940 and started to gain momentum as a popular movement. But by 1960 the support again fell off. It was not until 1976 that democracy again began to rear its head as a force in the region. We are quite concerned about trying to understand this cyclic nature. We need to determine if it is some sort of a pendulum and how to maintain the balance on the side of democracy.

The intervals between these cycles seem to demonstrate a fairly strong correlation between the U.S. forces' engagement in the region and the democratization trend. The more we are engaged, the more democracy seems to flourish. There is not necessarily a cause and effect relationship between them. The factors that involve these countries are far too complex to be able to make that kind of a correlation. However, it is fair to say that when we have worked in the region and were engaged there, democracy did well.

In view of the democratization process, our CINC has established and developed a strategy of cooperative peacetime engagement for the AOR. Engagement is the key word here. There are three goals to pursue with every activity that we undertake in the SOUTHCOM AOR: First, to promote and support democracy; second, to protect and promote U.S. interests through unilateral (when necessary) or multilateral actions against the threats we face; and third, to prepare for an uncertain future through modernization, innovation, and the development of interoperability among the forces of the region.

In the past we have seen an extremely important role for naval forces in support of these goals. Moreover, we have visualized that the importance may very well increase because we see nations of the region turning more and more to the sea. Many of the nations, as they established their democracies and traditionally looked inward (with armies serving as a strong dominating force) are now turning toward the sea as their future. This, of course, makes our naval engagement in that area very important.

I will now focus on the role of naval—particularly indigenous naval—forces in the region. It is important to note that although we think the strategic goals and aims of USSOUTHCOM in the region are fairly well advanced at this point, the specific events, actions, and operations we undertake in the future are still evolving. They are constantly undergoing review and change, as we develop a very important piece to our overall naval strategy. We are new at this. We are learning how to synchronize maritime activities within our overall plan. There is a long tradition of maritime naval engagement in the region, and it is our job to ensure that our activities are well integrated as we go into the future.

With that in mind, I would like to examine the issues we face, in particular those that will have an impact on the future of naval engagement in the region. First, within the region there is quite a mix of naval capabilities, subregion by subregion. Normally when we speak of the AOR, we would think of it in terms of four subregions. But from a naval point of view there are three. The first is the Southern Cone area. The nations of that region, especially Argentina, Brazil, and Chile, possess relatively advanced professional naval forces that are willing to operate outside of their territorial waters. These nations have a potential in the future to emerge with an international maritime role. The second group, the Andean, or Northern Tier countries, specifically Peru, Ecuador, Colombia, and Venezuela, have more limited capabilities. Although in the past some of them have had a blue water capability, we perceive that budget priorities in these countries will be directing them away from conventional navy activities in favor of riverine and Coast Guard activities, a part of which is clearly linked to the drug trafficking problem in that region. The third subregion is Central America and the Caribbean, the naval forces of which tend to be focused on brown water, Coast Guard types of functions. The variety of missions and capabilities in these three subregions requires a tailoring of our activities to meet their needs.

The second issue we must consider in defining naval roles in the twenty-first century is the range of threats we face in this particular theater. These threats are considered transnational, because they transcend national borders and make use of what we call borders as mere highways for their activities. They include illegal narcotics trafficking, illicit arms sales, terrorism, international organized crime, illegal migration, and various forms of environmental attack. These threats are not new in the region, nor are they new in the world. But advances in technology and in some cases increased financial capability, have made them much more potent. They are not necessarily traditional naval threats, but they are, nevertheless, serious threats to the nations of the region and can pose significant challenges to the United States. U.S. forward presence is required to effectively address these threats as we enter the new millennium. We envision U.S. naval forces continuing to play a lead role in CINC-level engagement activities across the AOR.

Yet, in the wake of our withdrawal from Panama in 1999, the U.S. military forward based presence in the AOR is going to diminish. This reduced presence, together with our recent assumption of responsibility for the Caribbean area and the reductions in engagement funding present a considerable challenge for USSOUTHCOM. Our loss of forward basing will call for other forms of presence in the AOR, most likely based on deployments as opposed to a formal basing. As new nations begin turning seaward, in an effort to continue their economic development and engage in or gain naval influence over territories they claim, naval presence will also become more important in this AOR.

Even now there is a growing requirement for USSOUTHCOM to increase its naval engagement activities to influence the evolving naval capabilities of this hemisphere. We need, for example, a mobile, flexible presence without the intrusiveness of "footprint." The term "footprint" in this region has a very negative connotation, and many of the nations of the region are very concerned about the number of U.S. military personnel who actually are standing on their soil at any given time. It is a political issue. In many ways naval forces have a way of being able to avoid that particular problem.

We must continue to develop a fast, capable response for massive relief operations and provide opportunities for reciprocal cultural exchange and professional military cooperation. Beyond the traditional approaches we have used in the past in our AOR, we need activities that build multilateral and interagency cooperation against transnational threats. In some cases, the only international actors seem to be the ones posing transnational threats. We must approach these problems in an international, multinational way ourselves. In sum, USSOUTHCOM naval forces must first and foremost maintain the ability to respond to crises and accomplish U.S. interests in the area. Second, it must serve as a model for the peaceful, orderly regional naval growth, as countries expand their own spheres of naval activity.

Our naval forces must also assist the nations in the AOR in modernizing and in increasing the interoperability of their forces, or their forces with our forces. With respect to the last point, it is important to make note of the regional military expenditures of today. To put it in perspective, consider, for example, that North Korea, a nation about the size of Honduras, has more submarines, has more personnel under arms, than do all Caribbean and Latin American democracies combined. It also has more tanks, as does Iraq, for that matter.

The point is that this is one of the least-militarized zones of the world. If current trends continue, it will remain so. All of these things being equal, there is no great drive there to militarize the region. However, that does not mean that these nations will remain static. They are modernizing and will continue to modernize where they can. In terms of naval forces, for example, the Center for Naval Analysis (CNA) envisions a movement toward consolidation of naval forces, made up of smaller numbers, of more modern and better supported vessels. The more capable navies are now largely frigate forces. The CNA also predicts that some nations will reach outward to protect shipping lanes. As such, a smaller force will be used, but its range will be extended.

How, then, should we address these events in this least militarized zone of the world? The staff at USSOUTHCOM is working hard to distinguish between the potential of an arms race and the prospect of appropriate force modernizations by sovereign democratic nations. It is encouraging the development of naval regional cooperative security and training arrangements between and among these countries—and including the United States—to reduce threat perception and to encourage restraint and transparency. In cases where modernization is taking place (as opposed to an arms race) USSOUTHCOM fosters recognition that Latin American naval forces have legitimate modernization requirements as they assume new roles and missions.

Our naval posture must take advantage of this great opportunity to influence their modernization programs. The ultimate goal of our naval strategy is the ability to conduct safely dispersed operations. The U.S. Navy achieved that goal long ago and is now exploiting the benefits of that favorable condition. Through the Navy, we can generate significant amounts of political and economic leverage with increased naval presence operating in the littoral of Latin America and the Caribbean. Now is an important time to use these dispersed operations to influence the modernizing navies of the region.

If we do not pay attention to their needs, these nations can easily meet their armament requirements through uncoordinated purchases on the international market or sponsorship in coordination with other navies. For example, I thought it was most interesting that several elements of the Chinese navy decided that it was important to steam across the Pacific and make port calls along the coast of South America. Although the wisdom of floating across the Pacific in one of those ships is questionable, there is something there that made the People's Republic of China decide that it was worth the risk.

There are considerable issues and challenges in this hemisphere that have an impact on how naval forces engage. First is the widespread social and economic inequalities that are exploited by insurgents, narcotics traffickers, and armed bands of criminals. Individually and collectively, they pose significant threats to cooperative security in the region and to the U.S. government as well. Second, Latin America has one of the world's most skewed income distributions, with a huge disparity between the very rich and the very poor and little in between. The pressures on the poor can drive significant illegal migration, which not only affects the United States, but also affects other nations of the region and is of great concern to them.

Third, nationalistic feelings have traditionally run very high in the nations of South America, Central America, and the Caribbean. In its own way, each political entity is extremely sensitive in matters that may threaten their view of national dignity, political sovereignty, or economic independence. Nationalism can become a potent force in the region. Therefore, naval engagement plans must be mindful of the fact that voices of the nationalist elite within these countries have expressed suspicions that U.S. security interests may ultimately limit their national sovereignty. Thus the more we tend to address security, the more the nationalist addresses sovereignty and independence from hegemony. The challenges presented by nationalist sentiment must be taken into account as we engage in the future. Our naval forces can reconcile security needs while taking into account existant nationalism in several ways.

First, we can enhance these nations' operational strategies for the security of their sovereign maritime and riverine territory by assisting or training them in exercising effective coastal control, maritime law enforcement, customs control, and control of their riverine frontiers. Training and cooperative programs cannot really be influenced too well by the nationalists. They serve extremely well in building a sense of sovereignty. Second, we can support coalition efforts organized primarily under the auspices of the UN and the OAS. Our multinational operation in Haiti is a recent example of this kind of effort. Third, we can assist in developing national capabilities to conduct multinational operations out of country and out of area, such as peacekeeping operations and humanitarian assistance. These kinds of activities are extremely important to the nations of the region. They are a great source of pride, and our naval and marine forces play a key role in developing these capabilities. Moreover, they do not threaten their nationalism.

Fourth, given our national strategy to wage war on illegal drugs, we can promote host nation participation in the testing and development of new naval doctrine and various tactics for sea and riverine counterdrug operations. Peru is one such example. But this effort must be expanded as we successfully close the air bridge, which is the current air route of transportation of drugs in and out of the region, and the drug traffickers rely more heavily on marine and riverine movement of drugs. Although this does not work for all nations, for some it is such a key issue that nationalist feelings can be tempered for this purpose. Even Brazil has recently made initiatives to work with the team, to come to the table, and to participate more cooperatively on this issue.

And lastly, we can train with the naval forces of the region as cooperative partners, while accommodating their individual needs and financial capabilities. Activities have to be scaled to the host-nation capacities, which vary greatly from nation to nation. This point is often misunderstood and overlooked. More important, we can overcome many nationalistic issues by approaching these nations as partners and our activities as cooperation rather than training and assistance. These words are extremely important in our AOR.

In summary, naval force presence will be essential in the future within the USSOUTHCOM AOR. It will have to be structured to actively engage within Latin America and the Caribbean, and it must be tailored to their unique circumstances. The states of the region are calling for U.S. naval and military cooperation, and it seems that no matter how much we can give, there is a very loud call for more. Basically, they like to work with us and this relationship is based on what appears to be nothing more than true professional respect. They are offering us a charter membership in the new clubs that are forming in this very dynamic part of the world. It will prove vital in the years to come that we continue to answer that call, not as Big Brother following only our own national agenda, but as a democratic partner nation, cooperating for the good of all.

PART III

NEW MISSIONS—NEW STRATEGIES

INTRODUCTION

Part three of this volume explores some of the fundamental challenges facing decisionmakers within naval operations today: What types of missions will naval forces have to prepare for in the twenty-first century? Will major theater warfare (MTW) or smaller-scale contingencies predominate or will both have to be prepared for simultaneously? Will traditional naval roles still apply in the next century or will new ones be needed to meet a changing and uncertain international environment? Will the challenges to naval forces occur on the high seas or in the littorals, and how will this affect the strategies and capabilities needed to respond in a timely and effective manner? What are the key strategic concepts that naval forces will require? These are among the questions addressed by the authors in this section.

Vice Admiral John Scott Redd and Admiral James O. Ellis Jr. ask whether traditional naval roles will apply in the next century or whether the Navy and Marine Corps will have to reinvent themselves. By traditional roles, Admiral Ellis, former deputy chief of naval operations and current commander in chief of U.S. Naval Forces in Europe and commander in chief of Allied Forces in Southern Europe, is referring to control of the seas for the purpose of projecting power and maintaining political influence, economic prosperity, and military superiority.

This traditional role will not change according to Ellis. The United States will remain dependent on the sea for economic prosperity. Thus maintaining control of the sea will be essential. Furthermore, as the world's population continues to increase, environmental and economic stress will contribute to competition over natural resources, including the seas. These developments, when coupled with an increase in threats such as terrorism, ecological and ethnic conflict, mass migration, and nationalism, suggest that naval forces will be engaged across the full spectrum of conflict: intrastate, interstate, and transstate.

In order for the United States to sustain its objectives of economic prosperity and democracy abroad, its military must have the flexibility and capability to meet a wide range of threats. They must be strategically agile, forward engaged, possess more precise strike capability, and remain highly mobile, sustainable, and survivable. Ellis views control of the seas by U.S. naval forces as the critical component of this flexibility. He asserts that naval forces will enable the United States to extend its forward presence and to develop a variety of options in the future, including the use of further advances in technology. Linking various platforms within an integrated operation will bring greater information and superiority, maximizing operational effectiveness. The sea can also be used, says Ellis, as a bastion, allowing greater security and maneuverability for critical support functions as well as fighting forces.

In sum, naval forces have a long tradition of developing solutions to emerging threats and problems. Admiral Ellis believes this will be no different in the twenty-first century. To this, Admiral Redd (ret.), former director for strategic plans and policy for the Joint Staff and current president and CEO of the NETSchools Corporation, adds that the Navy will have to be prepared for a number of traditional and nontraditional missions in a complex and uncertain future.

He notes that the National Military Strategy stipulates three fundamental tasks: one, shape the international environment to create conditions favorable to U.S. interests and security; two, respond to the full spectrum of crises; and three, prepare for an uncertain future. Redd argues that naval forces are playing and will continue to play a central role in achieving each of these objectives.

First, the Navy has been shaping the international environment for more than two hundred years, and its traditional roles have remained relatively constant. In the twenty-first century, sea power will continue to matter considerably and sea control will remain a foundation of national power. Second, with the end of the cold war, the challenges have become more complex, particularly at the lower end of the conflict spectrum, where crises have proliferated. While the armed forces have been able to respond effectively, they will need to improve their role in the interagency process and interaction with international and nongovernmental organizations. Third, the naval services are preparing now for an uncertain future through such important exercises as Joint Vision 2010.

To meet these challenges, naval forces will increasingly find themselves part of joint, interagency, and combined operations. Admiral Redd explains that within this context the Navy will continue to execute traditional roles and at the same time undertake new missions as required by an evolving operational landscape.

Where will the challenges to naval forces occur in the years ahead? Major General Edward Hanlon Jr., current commanding general of the Marine Corps Base at Camp Pendleton and former director of the Marine Corps's Expeditionary Warfare Division, believes it will be in the littorals of the world. He employs the term "chaos in the littorals" to describe the changing landscape of conflict and war. As the home to a vast portion of the world's population and wealth, these areas serve as major trade routes and bring together different cultures, all of which have potential security implications. Since the end of the cold war, we have seen the world's coastal areas become more chaotic. Conflicts in these areas generate a host of regional security problems, most significantly the fragmentation of nation-states. In addition to internal conflicts and state disintegration, the littorals also are home to several states that instigate other forms of instability.

As a result of these developments, a central strategic concept is power projection through expeditionary capabilities, according to General Hanlon. He notes that other industrialized nations, including France, the United Kingdom, Italy, and the Netherlands, are focusing their defense spending on expeditionary warfare and the need for smaller, highly trained mobile forces. The reason for this, in Hanlon's opinion, is that expeditionary forces give a nation forward presence and mobility without the vulnerability of land basing. He concludes by highlighting the value of balanced naval expeditionary forces and the need to possess the technological capabilities to stay ahead of the enemy.

Lieutenant General Carlton W. Fulford Jr., former commanding general of the 1st Marine Expeditionary Force (1 MEF) and current director of the Joint Staff of the U.S. Marine Corps, raises the question of whether major theater warfare like Desert Storm will be the primary mission or whether smaller-scale contingencies like Bosnia, Haiti, and Somalia will predominate. He suggests that the Marines will have to deal with both, noting that the stakes in MTW are greater, while the more likely employment of forces will be in small-scale contingency operations. This will complicate operational planning, training, and war fighting experimentation.

At both levels, training and educational programs to develop officers as operational thinkers have been critical to planning effectively for these contingencies. Conducting exercises to test and train staff members provides effective preparation for these situations and allows early identification and accurate assessment of threats that may present themselves in the littoral regions in the years ahead.

Fulford believes that refocusing naval forces to meet the needs of the twenty-first century should involve debate and experimentation in the development of future doctrine, tactics, procedures, and equipment. He notes that to this end Marines and sailors from 1 MEF and Third Fleet are engaged with the Marine Corps Warfighting Laboratory and the Fleet Battle Laboratory in developing innovations. He concludes by asserting that, faced with both MTW and small-scale contingencies, naval forces must continue to provide the basis for the strategic concept of power projection enabled by overseas presence. He sees 1 MEF as an ideal force for this mission, describing it as a key warfighting command that provides forces and support to CENTCOM and PACOM.

Brigadier General Wallace C. Gregson Jr., former director of the Marine Corps Strategy and Plans Division and current director for Asian and Pacific Affairs in the Office of the Assistant Secretary of Defense for International Ssecurity Affairs, points out that the end of the cold war has had an unsettling effect on policy, doctrine, and strategy. He cautions not to seek quick solutions and early resolution to these developments. Nevertheless, given the present and future international security environment, as described by the other authors in this volume, he proposes that power projection will remain a central strategic concept. Gregson notes that during the cold war, U.S. national and military strategies had to adapt and assume a more precise and controllable approach to the application of military power. Naval forces drafted maritime and amphibious strategies and began applying sea-based power with the goal of "taking the fight to the enemy." This capacity to project power from the sea remains essential in the post–cold war period, according to Gregson.

Under what conditions will the United States project naval power in this way? He argues that potential enemies will seek to avoid facing the conventional capabilities the United States employed so effectively in the Gulf War. This means they will seek to develop asymmetric and competitive strategies. Nuclear, chemical, and biological weapons, says Gregson, reveal a fatal weakness of our great strength—overwhelming force—and leave us vulnerable to attack against our massed forces and support structures. He proposes that minimizing this vulnerability requires close attention to the concepts of dispersion and mobility. We must change the overwhelming mass concept to avoid such exposure of our forces.

Furthermore, naval forces must be prepared to face long-term threats while simultaneously managing current short-term missions. The latter includes civil wars, ethnic conflict, and collapsed states that put diplomatic, political, and humanitarian efforts in the forefront. In these efforts, the military will continue to play an important supporting role by creating and maintaining security for other elements of national power. To respond to these short-term crises, Gregson proposes a new strategic approach he labels "complex contingency operations." Within this context, he seeks to show how military forces can support diplomatic and humanitarian efforts. Sea-based forces have much to contribute to these operations.

Finally, Rear Admiral Thomas F. Marfiak, former commandant of the National War College and current CEO/publisher of the U.S. Naval Institute, warns that naval power will not be sufficient alone in responding to MTW and non-MTW challenges. Alliances and coalitions will likewise play a key role. In his chapter, Marfiak provides a functional definition of alliances and coalitions; considers the political, diplomatic, and military implications each raises; and outlines their possibilities and limitations in application.

Alliances are based on the notion of collective defense and are typically characterized by some form of treaty, which defines specific force structure and uniform standards of operability. Coalitions are not governed by a formal treaty, but are formed to meet a specific need and are characterized by a wide range of capabilities in pursuit of national goals and coalition objectives. They are ad hoc, situation specific, and usually regionally based. Alliances and coalitions will be a necessary part of a response to security challenges in the twenty-first century.

Marfiak notes that a wide range of potential involvement exists in non-MTW contingencies. These include humanitarian assistance, peacekeeping, and disaster relief. In these situations, several nations may operate in concert but do not require the same coordination that is necessary in MTW operations. Nevertheless, Marfiak cautions that it is important for the United States to have a clear understanding of the conditions under which its forces are committed to achieve international objectives in operations other than war.

The authors in this section emphasize a variety of roles required of our naval forces, and they highlight complex challenges being faced today and likely to be faced in the future. There are many questions over roles and missions to be addressed, but it is clear that whatever form they ultimately take, the naval forces remain central as we move into a new era.

TRADITIONAL NAVAL ROLES

James O. Ellis Jr.

Today we are presented with a fundamental question—Will traditional naval roles still apply to twenty-first-century naval operations?

My view is that the traditional naval roles will not only remain relevant, but will become increasingly essential. To understand how those roles will be fulfilled in the future, we must understand the historical uses of the ocean.

Oceans have long served as a bridge between regions, a bountiful source of natural resources, a barrier from attack, and, more recently, a bastion from which to project power. In short, the oceans are a source of both prosperity and security for those nations able to control them. President John F. Kennedy was well aware of these uses, as well as how vital control of the seas is to the security of our republic, when he said, "Control of the seas means security. Control of the seas means peace. Control of the seas can mean victory. The United States must control the sea if it is to protect our security." That awareness has not been lost. The 1997 National Security Strategy echos the same message—"We can only preserve our security and well being at home by being entirely involved in the world beyond our borders." Implicit in these statements is the fact that American involvement in and leadership of the world is possible today and in the future only through control of the seas. That control grants political influence, economic well-being, and military superiority.

The importance of the sea is readily apparent when viewing world geography and population distribution. The greatest concentration of people, resources, transportation, and economic activity is in the littorals. Continuing expansion of international trade will only emphasize this fact. China, as an example of one of the world's fastest-growing economies, is forecast to become one of the world's major importers of oil early in the next century. Dual dependence on energy and international trade will tie the Chinese to the "great commons" as surely as are all modern nations.

This dependence of developed nations on the sea does not necessarily translate into weakness. As Sir Walter Raleigh stated in 1616, "Whosoever commands the sea commands the trade; whosoever commands the trade of the world commands the riches of the world, and consequently the world itself." The nation able to control the sea can turn that dependency into a decided advantage. Today and into the new century, that nation is the United States.

For example, in 1996 over five hundred billion dollars in trade moved to and from the United States via the oceans. This is not an anomaly in global trading patterns, but a constant. Though world markets are connected electronically, the physical goods they represent (oil, grain, and manufactured products) are transported over the oceans. Without that movement, international commerce simply does not exist. Oceans also provide a bridge to transport military might. In Desert Shield/Desert Storm, Military Sealift Command (MSC) moved 12 billion pounds of fuel and 2.4 million tons of cargo over 8,700 miles, a tonnage unachievable by any other means.

For those with maritime supremacy, the oceans can also act as a barrier. The British used their control of oceans to thwart the Spanish Armada, Napoleon, and Hitler. The Royal Navy's "wooden walls" were successful in defending that island nation, because they controlled a hostile maritime environment and took the fight forward to their enemies. We now possess a vastly greater advantage, because, unlike the British, our control of the sea is currently not contested. However, the sea is not the barrier it formerly was, but is more easily and safely crossed. While we have the luxury to adapt emerging technologies into innovative operational concepts, we must be vigilant in maintaining our forward-deployed forces to ensure that the sea remains a barrier to our adversaries and a shield for ourselves.

As the Earth's population continues to grow (a 25 percent increase is estimated by 2010), environmental and economic stress will increase competition for natural resources, which includes the bounty of the seas. Some well-known examples are the disputed Spratly Islands in the oil-laden South China Sea, fisheries disputes prevalent in the North Atlantic, and the attempts by some to extend their territorial seas beyond internationally recognized limits. This situation, coupled with images of relative wealth and freedom being disseminated through the electronic media to the most remote corners of the globe, will only aggravate tensions. The resultant threats will include terrorism, ecological and ethnic conflict, mass migration, and virulent nationalism.

These threats will span the full spectrum of conflict: intrastate, interstate, and transstate. They will challenge our National Security Strategy's core objectives of sustaining economic prosperity and promoting democracy abroad. To effectively meet these threats, our military must be strategically agile, forward engaged, capable of projecting precise and powerful strikes, and highly mobile, sustainable, and survivable. It must be able to span the spectrum of operations from humanitarian assistance to major theater war. All of these requirements are characteristics of the tasks required of the naval forces.

Strategic agility means being able to move, employ, and sustain our military forces entirely on our own initiative and our own timing. In today's uncertain world, we cannot afford the luxury of moving forces from the United

States or waiting for host-nation support for our actions. Unfortunately, those actions have often been constrained in the past: access and operational freedom for U.S. military forces has often been denied, restricted, or delayed. Fortunately, the United States has had the technological and operational capabilities to work around these obstacles—for example, the use of multiple tankings of British-based bombers during the 1986 strikes against Libya or the 1997 sea-based preparation for possible strikes against Iraq. However, the only diplomatically unconstrained force available has often been, and will continue to be, a naval force operating forward from the sea.

Naval forces, which are forward deployed and inherently self-sustaining, can independently carry out national tasking without being subject to the vagaries of the international climate. In the crisis over Iraq, we again witnessed that while diplomacy takes its measured pace to gain allied consensus, the response of naval forces is immediate and assured. Once on scene, they remain as long as necessary to reassure friends and deter adversaries, and if required, deliver precise firepower unhindered by political considerations.

Control of the seas will endure as a cornerstone of our national strategy, serving as the enabling mechanism of all other naval, military, and political roles. Yet, how we carry out our traditional missions must evolve as our capabilities advance. The Navy will strive to do more with fewer platforms, but there is a limit to how much we can accomplish without sufficient resources. Advanced equipment, streamlined organizations and process, and our sailors will accomplish the task only by being smarter and more capable. We must be committed to using our nation's dominant position and technological edge to our benefit, preempting aggression, and deterring conflicts before they escalate. And while we cannot *prevent* every crisis or conflict from occurring, we must be committed to being supremely well positioned and capable of driving crises and conflicts in the direction we desire.

Though we will not forfeit our traditional role of sea-borne ambassadors, extending the reassuring hand of the United States and serving as an ever-present symbol of American concern, we will be able to influence events from further away than ever before. Through naval forces, the United States will be able to extend its forward presence and call on a variety of options in response to the tumultuous decades to come.

Surface combatants will have longer range and more precise strike capability, submarines will be optimized to operate in the littorals, and aircraft will be more survivable and carry precision munitions further. Nonlethal technologies will also be at the nation's disposal, denying threatening actions without escalating tensions.

Advances in technology will fundamentally alter the way we employ and operate our forces. We have already departed from the stereotypical notion of escorts clustered protectively around the carrier in a ring of steel. Today, battle groups operate in far-flung fashion, as individual platforms carry out separate tasks. In the future, they will be dispersed in a similar fashion, yet will operate as a cohesive, integrated whole, coordinating actions to fulfill a variety of missions. This will be achieved through information superiority, which allows each individual component to have access to the data gathered by the whole.

This concept of linking various platforms into a connected whole is moving us from platform-centric warfare to network-centric warfare. Two capabilities that will operationalize this concept are theater ballistic missile defense (TBMD) and cooperative engagement capability (CEC), both of which will come on-line early in the twenty-first century. TBMD will shield U.S. and coalition forces from attack as well as provide security to potential partners without placing our defenses on their soil. CEC is a network that will instantly share detection and targeting information between sea, air, and land forces. This will enable widely separated platforms to "see" and react to events beyond their own sensors' horizons. Thus the best positioned platform can be directed to take action. This unprecedented integration of assets will maximize operational effectiveness while using all our assets to their fullest.

It must be recognized that our adversaries will employ not only military but commercial technology to their advantage. Overhead imagery, satellite communications, and precision targeting will become increasingly widespread. We must be prepared for potential challenges by reducing our vulnerability to both conventional and asymmetric threats. By using the sea as a bastion, a safe haven that allows both security and maneuverability, we can move easily targeted installations out of the enemy's range. Shifting our logistics to the sea and placing command centers afloat reduces their vulnerability to the inevitably increasing precision of modern weapon systems and the possibility of terrorist attack. In an uncertain strategic environment, our critical support functions will have the same advantages of mobility and self-protection enjoyed by our strike and amphibious power projection forces.

Not only will we be able to protect traditionally static installations with mobility, we will also use mobility and range to our advantage while transitioning forces ashore. Naval forces will no longer transition ashore through an array of mines under a hail of fire. We will employ our mobility to circumvent these static defenses and move forces directly to the critical nodes, making traditional littoral defenses obsolete, similar to that of the Maginot Line.

Naval forces have a long tradition of innovative solutions to emerging threats and problems. Whether creation of the convoy system for protection from submarines, optimization of carrier aviation and amphibious warfare capabilities, or the development of nuclear propulsion and submarine launched missiles, naval forces have led the way in adapting new technologies to operational concepts. Such innovation, founded on our enduring roles, will steer our course into the twenty-first century. It does not matter if our development is revolutionary (the revolution in military affairs) or merely evolutionary. What is important is that we choose the right transformation strategies to enable us to fulfill our national security objectives. Rather than scramble to absorb emerging technologies, we need to set guidelines for innovative solutions to our future security needs.

The geography of our planet is unlikely to undergo fundamental change in the years ahead and neither will the importance of the sea. The United States, as dominant nation of the Earth, will be able to exercise control over the seas to reap its rewards. Maritime supremacy will provide the ability to use the oceans as a bridge to its friends, a barrier to its enemies, a source of bountiful resources, and a bastion from which to wield power. From the tall ships of our beginning, to the ironclads of the Civil War, to the turn of the century's Great White Fleet, to the aircraft carriers in the Persian Gulf, the appearance and capabilities of our naval forces have evolved. However, their roles will remain constant. This consistency is not dictated by changing political environment or technological advances. Rather, exercise of these roles remains a steady characteristic of world powers. Twenty-first-century naval forces will provide the nation with valuable options, as they always have, to meet the threats of the future. Traditional roles are not just traditional, they are enduring and relevant two hundred years ago, today, and in the twenty-first century.

NAVAL FORCES AND *JOINT VISION 2010*:
TRADITIONAL AND EMERGING ROLES

John Scott Redd

With the end of the cold war and the dawning of a new century, the United States has entered an era of unparalleled promise, but one that also contains significant challenges. Strong military forces are necessary to restrain the forces of disorder that exist in many places in the world today. While forward presence and engagement can help to deter conflicts in the near term, they may not be enough to prevent the outbreak of another war involving the forces of the United States and its allies in the long term. Accordingly, the Armed Forces of the United States must be more than ambassadors of good-will; they must continually prepare for the ultimate challenge of fighting and winning the next war. History tells us that we will have to send young people into combat again sometime in the future. Although we do not know when or where the next war will take place, naval forces will be a major factor in the ultimate outcome.

What will be the roles and missions of naval forces in the twenty-first century? The answer to that question depends on two things: First, on defining the level of engagement required, that is, strategic, operational, or tactical; and second, and more fundamentally, on defining the perception of the emerging threat. Will there be a peer competitor to challenge the United States and its allies globally and conventionally in the next century? Or, alternatively, will traditional force-on-force conflict be largely replaced by asymmetric challenges, transnational dangers, or other unforeseen "wild card" scenarios that fundamentally change the paradigm of warfare? Whichever view of the future one ascribes to, the Navy undoubtedly will have to undertake a large number of traditional and nontraditional missions in the complex, dynamic, and uncertain strategic situation that confronts the United States today and in the years ahead.

At the strategic level, the primary purpose of our military forces in general—and the Navy in particular—will continue to be the fighting and winning of the nation's wars. That said, military forces will also continue to be employed at the lower end of the engagement spectrum in shaping the environment and responding to complex contingencies. In the future, these operations may be much more elaborate. They will likely involve working closely with a group of players with whom the Navy only had a passing acquaintance during the cold war. In virtually all cases, an ounce of shaping is worth a pound of responding.

At the operational and tactical levels, there will be significant changes in the way the Navy operates. Future operations will, for the most part, be joint operations. In this regard, the vision of the chairman of the Joint Chiefs of Staff, as articulated in *Joint Vision 2010*, provides a good concept for the next generation of operational art. By 2010 our joint forces will achieve dominance over a broad range of military activities through the use of dominant maneuver, precision engagement, focused logistics, and full-dimensional protection.

Despite the challenges ahead, the traditional roles of the Navy will remain valid for the foreseeable future. Although some analysts reject the notion of the United States facing a peer competitor in the next century, human nature and the fundamental workings of the international system have not changed with the end of the cold war. The biblical vision of the future—of wars and rumors of wars—may also be the most accurate. Until such dangers are gone forever, the United States and its allies had best be prepared to defend their vital interests when and where they are challenged and be prepared to do so at the highest level of the conflict spectrum.

The new National Military Strategy—drafted by J-5 in conjunction with the CINCs and services—lays out three fundamental elements that form the foundation of our military strategy: *shape* the international environment to create conditions favorable to U.S. interests and global security, *respond* to the full spectrum of crises to protect our national interests, and *prepare now* for an uncertain future. Shaping, where the United States remains globally engaged for the foreseeable future to mold the international environment and deter current threats, stands in stark contrast to a retreat into isolationism, which would be counterproductive. Responding is the ability of our armed forces to meet the full spectrum of crises, from smaller-scale contingencies such as Haiti and Bosnia to the ability to deter or defeat nearly simultaneous large-scale, cross-border aggression in two distant theaters in overlapping time frames. Preparing now means that we need to take immediate steps to prepare for an uncertain future, not just in terms of technology, but also in terms of organization, doctrine, tactics, techniques, and procedures.

Although the concepts have been packaged under new names, the Navy has been shaping the international environment and responding to crises since its birth over two centuries ago. Whether fighting the Barbary Pirates in the early nineteenth century, showing the flag with the Great White Fleet in the early twentieth century, dispatching carrier battle groups to the Taiwan Straits in 1996, or sending the *George Washington* Battle Group racing to the Arabian Gulf in November 1997, the Navy's traditional roles have remained fairly constant. By virtue of continuous overseas presence and the ability to steam quickly and relatively unencumbered to an area in crisis, the Navy remains perhaps the nation's premier service in shaping the international environment and responding to crises. But it would be a mistake to think the Navy is the only service involved in this regard. The other services are intimately engaged in shaping and responding in places such as Bosnia and Haiti. In fact, a lot of ink has been devoted in recent years to the discussion of appropriate missions and tasks for military forces involved in peacekeeping operations, a topic that will no doubt continue to be hotly debated in the years ahead.

A historical viewpoint helps to put the Navy's future in perspective. Alfred Thayer Mahan wrote extensively at the turn of the century about how naval power could be used to advance national interests in a situation not unlike our own: a world at peace but in competition for economic resources, with multiple centers of power; a world in which democracy was largely ascendant if not dominant. In fundamental terms, very little will happen in the twenty-first century that will invalidate what Mahan wrote at the end of the nineteenth century. In fact, two simple statements by Mahan capture much of what will remain true of sea power in the twenty-first century.

First, sea power will continue to matter considerably as a determinant of national power. Mahan equated sea power with trade and wealth, both crucial to the accumulation of national power—then and now. Naval power protects seaborne commerce, projects power across the seas, influences events ashore, and guards resources drawn from the sea itself. In short, while Mahan would be amazed and astounded by the technology of today, he would nod knowingly at the strategy—same song, second verse.

Second, sea control will remain the foundation of sea power. To defend our national security interests overseas, we depend on our ability to cross what Mahan called "the great commons." We need not only ensure our own access, but also to be able to deny that access to our enemies. While it is true that today the United States has the unchallenged ability to control the world's blue water, there are no guarantees that this will endure. Even if it does, the Navy has no promise of complete freedom of action. Opponents can and will challenge the United States in the littoral regions of the Earth and will attempt to drive us back to the blue water, thereby establishing a measure of regional sea control.

Tough as these traditional challenges are, they are relatively comfortable territory to us. The Navy has a reasonably good record of innovation in adapting technology and tactics to warfare at sea. That comfort zone does not extend, however, to all the tasks the nation faces. The end of the cold war, the lack of a superpower competitor, the increasing economic interdependence of states, and the emergence of "transnational" threats have made the world a more complex place.

That complexity translates into operations at the lower end of the spectrum, especially to what can be broadly termed "interagency operations." These operations include noncombatant evacuations, natural disaster response, humanitarian relief, sanctions enforcement, counterdrug activity, counterterrorism, peacekeeping, and the control of migrants—missions that loosely fall under the rubric of "smaller-scale contingencies." Rapid reaction in these missions will help to prevent, contain, or resolve conflict; alleviate suffering; demonstrate leadership; and encourage commensurate contributions from the international community.

In these operations, the armed forces are victims of their own success. Their organizational abilities enable a swift reaction in crisis, which produces results. They can move large numbers of people and vast amounts of equipment around the globe virtually on call and, by interagency standards, the Department of Defense has a big budget. These factors make DOD attractive for the assignment of tasks—but not all the tasks fit.

One of the critical challenges for the future is improving the interagency process. Today, we are adept at deploying military joint task forces to a crisis. We now need to explore the concept of a joint *interagency* task force that incorporates the strengths of a wide array of national agencies. Indeed, National Security Council meetings today typically include the attorney general and the secretary of commerce, as well as the secretaries of state and defense. The question of command and control in these operations needs to be carefully considered. If there is a need for a second level of jointness, it is in the area of interagency operations.

Moreover, the Navy and other armed services must also be prepared to work with international organizations, such as the United Nations, nongovernmental organizations like the International Organization for Migration, and private voluntary organizations, including the American Red Cross or Doctors Without Borders. Operations with these nonstate actors will be challenged by differing outlooks, doctrine, terminology, and organizational cultures. However, they are a necessity if we are to achieve our objectives when faced with complex contingencies in the future.

Although most of these missions will require naval presence and power, they do not establish a new core competency for the naval services. In the broad sense, the Navy has undertaken these types of missions for over two hundred years. They are not necessarily either new or unique. It would be a mistake to be seduced by the allure of low-end missions at the expense of the Navy's primary purpose—to fight and win our nation's wars on and from the sea. Modernization of our equipment, reengineering of our organizations, and the training and education of our personnel are all necessary to ensure the Navy is prepared to meet the challenges of the next war in a new century.

The third element of the National Military Strategy, *preparing now* for an uncertain future, is necessary to maintain the military superiority essential for continued global leadership. One of the key signposts in this effort is *Joint Vision 2010 (JV 2010)*, a document produced by J-5. This document, signed by the chairman of the Joint Chiefs of Staff in 1996, lays out an operationally based template for the evolution of the armed forces as we approach the twenty-first century. It is intended to provide, for the first time, both a template and an azimuth for individual service visions within a joint framework of doctrine and programs.

It may be helpful to review the purpose behind *JV 2010*. First, *JV 2010* is not a strategy, but rather a document that lays out a vision of future operational capabilities. It is designed to guide our future military requirements, procurement, and research and development. Second, *JV 2010* is, as the title suggests, a *vision*—not a detailed plan. Third, *JV 2010* is not a look at the world of 2020 or beyond. It is not a blueprint for the next Army/Navy/Marine Corps/Air Force, although it anticipates the next generation of these services. Long-range planning is still necessary to complement *JV 2010*, which, after all, extends only two programmed objective memorandums into the future. Finally, *JV 2010* is not just about war fighting. The concept of "full spectrum dominance" envisions the ability to operate effectively at all levels of the spectrum, from peacetime presence to global conflict.

In nautical terms, *Joint Vision 2010* is not unlike the charts of the earliest seagoing explorers, who plotted their courses across little-known seas toward a hopeful destination, supported by the science of the time—but touched by uncertainty. *Joint Vision 2010* is based on informed analysis, backed by intelligent conjecture, and grounded in the best-available technological assessments. But, like the nautical charts of the early explorers, it is designed to get the navigator to landfall, not tied up to the pier.

At the center of *Joint Vision 2010* are four emerging operational concepts: dominant maneuver, precision engagement, focused logistics, and full-dimensional protection. Taken together, the implementation of these four concepts will give the United States and its allies full spectrum dominance over the broad range of military operations, from smaller-scale contingencies to major-theater wars.

The first operational concept, "dominant maneuver," most clearly fits traditional naval warfare. The essence of naval forces is maneuver and the ability to move quickly and shift forces to attack the enemy's center of gravity. This traditional employment will continue into the next century. Successfully executed, it will give the Navy control of the seas, give it the ability to project power over great distances and ashore, and enable strategic deterrence in the support of vital national interests.

The second operational concept, "precision engagement," is equally familiar. The service that delivered Harpoon and Tomahawk on target is comfortable with "precision engagement," both afloat and ashore. It is not a great stretch to say our history of naval bombardment, strategic blockade, and amphibious assault were precision engagements to the limit of contemporary technology—especially when applied accurately to the enemy's center of gravity. As we approach 2010, the possibilities for naval precision engagement will be enhanced by such new technologies as hypersonic cruise missiles, extended-range guided munitions, and unmanned aerial vehicles, along with doctrinal innovations such as operational maneuver from the sea.

The third operational concept is "full-dimensional protection," the multilayered protection of forces and facilities from enemy attack. Navies will continue to protect forces, both at sea and ashore, against familiar and new threats, such as land-attack cruise and ballistic missiles. The fundamental imperative is to control the battlespace to maintain freedom of action for our forces in all phases of an operation. The Navy is on the cutting edge of this concept with the continuing development of area and theater missile defense.

"Focused logistics," the fourth operational concept, is a fundamental part of the Navy's raison d'être. In the modern day version of Mahan's navy the USN plans to be free to go anywhere with everything, when and as needed. The initial movement and critical resupply of equipment, warriors, and materiels to a theater of war is an enduring mission the Navy will continue to undertake in 2010 and beyond. But naval transport and logistics will be undertaken in technologically advanced ways, including high-speed sealift, netted logistic support, and globally transparent inventory control to produce increased efficiencies. Naval power enables movement on a vast scale, such as occurred before the Gulf War, when the United States moved personnel and materiel equivalent to the city of Atlanta half-way across the globe in less than six months—over 95 percent of which was transported by sealift. Strategic sealift and mobile prepositioned materiel create tremendous leverage for decisionmakers in a crisis.

Tying all of these emerging concepts together will be information superiority: dispersed, netted formations of naval forces, using a multimedia network to achieve the full integration of all components. Information technology will also improve the processing of all-source intelligence to enable quicker and better decisions by commanders. The fog of war may not be eliminated, but it will become more transparent.

Does all of this sound like technology is steering the ship? To some degree, this is the inevitable by-product of the advance of science and technology. As we all know, history is filled with examples of improvements that have been resisted by those who would benefit from them. The key is to remain open to the march of technology, incorporating improvements where possible, while never forgetting that technology is no substitute for quality people who are trained and motivated to accomplish the mission at hand. We also know that technology cannot make up for bad policy, flawed doctrine, or unworkable tactics.

As *JV 2010* states, naval missions in the future will usually be undertaken in the form of joint operations. Faced with flat budgets and increasingly costly modernization, the armed services must operate more effectively in the future to leverage their unique capabilities and eliminate redundancy. For better or worse—mostly better—the ability to operate jointly has become a key priority in our military structure today, and it is an essential quality for a service to claim a relevant role in our national defense. But what are the important qualities that drive "jointness"?

First, the major platforms operated by each service—as well as the broader organization—must be able to operate in conjunction with those from other services. Interoperability is crucial as we leverage technology to take advantage of the power of the microprocessor. We must, for instance, strive to create a common software architecture to bind the services and our allies into a common command, control, and intelligence network. This is perhaps the largest challenge ahead in jointness as the services seek to realize the goals loosely associated with the expression "revolution in military affairs."

Second, each service's contribution must be synergistic with all other contributors to the overall campaign. We will normally not execute separate sea, land, or air campaigns. This applies to interagency operations as well. Indeed, we must move forward beyond simple jointness—defined as interoperability with other U.S. military services—into the rapidly accelerating world of interagency and combined operations. All of this must be captured in appropriate operational art, tactics, techniques, and procedures, and must be bounded by appropriate joint doctrine.

As an aside, this is an interesting time for jointness to be a priority. A move toward greater interoperability is rare for our armed forces and is virtually nonexistent in a time of potentially declining and at best constrained defense budgets. During past interwar periods, the individual services have concentrated on protecting their own roles and resources, rather than focusing on the joint functions of the armed forces. But our political and military leadership have recognized, in a way that is fundamentally different from the past, that a military second to none is essential to our national interests in the present security environment—and the only avenue to achieve that goal is through jointness. It should be noted that there are limits to jointness. Each service possesses a unique core competency that it brings into the joint arena, and it should be recognized that there are times when an operation is best conducted by a single service. The escorting of reflagged Kuwaiti oil tankers in 1987 and the withdrawal of United Nations forces from Somalia in 1995, both naval missions, come to mind as examples.

When the National Military Strategy is written in 2015, I suspect the Navy will be reasonably comfortable with the result. While a return to isolationism is possible, there are too many factors that militate toward continued forward engagement to allow the United States to turn inward. At the same time, barring the transformation of humankind, there will continue to be wars and rumors of wars. We will need a strategy to deal with them, as well as to prepare for the world of the next generation. In short, the Navy will continue to execute "traditional" roles—naval presence and engagement, sea control, power projection, strategic sealift, and strategic deterrence. At the same time, the operational landscape will have some new features, which will force the Navy to undertake an evolving basket of "new" missions—land and sea defense against cruise and ballistic missiles, interagency operations, sea-based information operations, and sea-based command and control for the joint task force commander.

In my view as a sailor, we must sail and not just drift. To reach our goal of a balanced and effective naval force for the twenty-first century, we must likewise sail, using *Joint Vision 2010* as our chart, as we undertake an exciting and challenging voyage into an uncertain but promising future.

TAKING THE LONG VIEW:
LITTORAL WARFARE CHALLENGES

Edward Hanlon Jr.

Throughout the industrialized world, many governments are paying increased attention to their expeditionary capabilities. These governments seek the ability to deploy a military force to a place far away, to quickly and decisively influence events ashore, and to bring the force home with a minimum of delay. This trend is most evident in Europe, where the continental armies and blue-water navies of the cold war era are being replaced by smaller, highly trained, and extraordinarily mobile intervention forces.

France, for example, is making the most radical change in its defense structure since the mid-nineteenth century. By the year 2002, the French armed forces will be smaller and far more deployable than they are today. To take these leaner, all volunteer forces where they need to go, the French Navy is building four amphibious ships that will be among the most advanced warships in the world.

The British armed forces, which can build on a strong, centuries-old tradition of expeditionary warfare, are moving in the same direction. While British forces on the continent of Europe are shrinking, the United Kingdom is beefing up its expeditionary capabilities. New amphibious ships are being built, nuclear-powered submarines are being equipped with the land-attack version of the Tomahawk cruise missile, and the Army is being reconfigured into formations optimized for rapid deployment.

Spain and Italy have come together to form the Spanish-Italian Amphibious Force (SIAF), a standing, self-contained, and self-transporting expeditionary formation that includes the light carrier *Garibaldi* and the amphibious ship *Galicia*. The Netherlands, which has long linked its amphibious capabilities to the NATO mission of defending Norway, now has, thanks to the amphibious ship *Rotterdam*, the option of conducting a wider variety of expeditionary operations.

I do not presume to know all of the motives behind this trend. I would argue, nonetheless, that a common thread runs through all of these developments. The governments devoting more and more of their shrinking defense budgets to expeditionary capabilities are doing so for good reason. They are, in fact, making a rational response to one of the major international developments of our time, a phenomenon that can best be described as "chaos in the littorals."

The term "chaos in the littorals" was coined by Major General Mike Myatt, former director of expeditionary warfare. As early as 1992, General Myatt argued that the collapse of public order in places like Lebanon, Afghanistan, Somalia, and the former Yugoslavia was the harbinger of things to come. The breakdown of existing states, struggles for limited resources, the rise of nonstate actors like Hezbollah and the Medellin Cartel, and the revival of old hatreds and the invention of new ones—all pointed to a world in which war between states would give way to war within states, war between states and nonstate actors, and, in extreme cases, war in places where states used to exist. General Myatt added that the most important of these conflicts would take place in the littorals, the places where land and sea meet. The littorals provide a home to most of the world's population, wealth, and industrial capacity. The great conduits of trade and culture pass through coastal areas to the great metropolises of the world. These conurbations—Lagos, Capetown, Karachi, and Manila—to name but a few, also tend to lie at the juncture of dry land and salt water. As a result, chaos in the littorals has greater implications for the world as a whole than chaos in landlocked regions. Put more bluntly, a civil war in a remote area is a local tragedy, a civil war along one of the world's major trade routes both is a local tragedy and can become a global emergency.

Since General Myatt started talking about chaos in the littorals, his prediction that the world's coastal areas would become more chaotic has, unfortunately, come true. The place where this is most obvious is sub-Saharan Africa. In many parts of that region, the normally deplorable situation of familiar elements, such as decaying infrastructure, sharp declines in standards of living, and ill-disciplined armed forces, has given way to something worse—the collapse of transportation networks, outright famine, and banditry as a way of life.

Less obvious to us, but of great concern to our European friends, is the situation along the coasts of the Mediterranean Sea. To many observers, the wave of anarchy that swept over Albania, and the refugee crises that followed, was a dress rehearsal for what might soon happen on a somewhat larger scale in Algeria. The good news is that, thanks largely to the expeditionary capabilities of France, Italy, Greece, and the United States, Albania was quickly stabilized. The bad news is that the situation in Algeria shows little sign of getting better. What had started as a struggle between groups with very different visions of Algeria's future has now degenerated into aimless violence. Those who kill, rape, and loot still claim allegiance to a particular cause. Yet it seems increasingly apparent that much of the savagery has become an end in itself.

The result can be seen in places like Somalia and Afghanistan, where armed conflict has become endemic. While the poverty of the belligerents prevents warfare from being waged on a large scale, so that week-long artillery bombardments are out of the question, fighting is constant. For a small minority, this return to a "state of nature" brings prestige, power, and profits. For the vast majority, the fruit of the "forever war" is perpetual misery, punctuated frequently by pain, sorrow, and moments of sheer terror. It is no wonder, then, that the major by-product of chaos in the littorals is large numbers of refugees.

In many cases, the refugees, invisible to the outside world, suffer in silence. This is particularly true when the breakdown of order takes place far from the developed world, bringing to mind Afghanistan, Rwanda, and Somalia. In other cases— such as the crisis in Albania and its predecessor in the former Yugoslavia—the refugees are neither silent nor invisible. Borders are porous. Narrow seas are easily crossed. Thus, where geography obliges, refugees will seek not merely to escape the anarchy in their home countries, but also to rebuild their shattered lives in the best environment they can find. For those on the shores of the Mediterranean, this means Western Europe.

For those who live next to or across the water from a country that is falling apart, the implications of chaos in the littorals are clear. The price of failing to contain anarchy close to home may result in a portion of that anarchy moving into one's own backyard. This is, in part, why European reaction to the crisis in Albania was so swift. It also explains why Europeans whose countries border on the western Mediterranean—France, Spain, and Italy—are so concerned about what is going on in Algeria.

Even though I have discussed a great deal about sub-Saharan Africa, Albania, and Algeria, I want to make it clear that chaos in the littorals is much more than a local or regional problem. It is a worldwide phenomenon, the product of a larger trend in the history of our planet and the relative decline of the nation-state. For most of the twentieth century, the nation-state has been the most important institution in the world. Nation-states have provided many essential services—from keeping the peace and managing the economy to coining money and delivering the mail—so that nearly every human being, and every square inch of inhabitable land, has had to be closely associated with one of them.

This is no longer the case. Even the most powerful of nation-states have abandoned any notion that they can manage an increasingly global economy. Both "money" and "mail delivery" have evolved to the point where they comprise a multitude of very different services provided by a bewildering array of private and public organizations. Even the maintenance of public order, once the definitive service of the state, is a function shared with the private sector. In many parts of the world, private security guards outnumber members of the armed services.

The counterpart of private-sector security is private-sector insecurity. War is no longer exclusive to relations between states. Rather, a glance at the news stories dealing with ongoing conflicts suggests that military operations are chiefly the business of "militias," armed groups with little or no direct connection to a recognized government. If we expand the definition of war to include terrorism, we find that nonstate actors are responsible for much, perhaps even most, of the organized violence taking place today.

At present, the military activities of most nonstate actors is largely restricted to their own neighborhoods. The armed forces of Hezbollah, for example, do not range far beyond their bases in southern Lebanon. The clans in Somalia are currently limited to their little corner of the Horn of Africa. This situation, I fear, is likely to change. One of these days, a nonstate actor is going to get hold of a weapon of mass destruction, and chaos in the littorals is going to become chaos close to home.

Though the possibility of the use of old-fashioned weapons of mass destruction cannot be ruled out—war is, after all, the realm of the unexpected—the concern is not with atomic explosives, chemical weapons, or even biological weapons of the traditional type, because nonstate actors lack the facilities to build, store, or deliver them. Rather, the greatest worry is weapons of mass destruction that are easy to make, transport, and employ. At present, these fall into two basic categories. The first consists of devices that distribute highly poisonous materials directly into the atmosphere or water supply. The 1996 incident in which Chechen rebels hid four canisters of radioactive cesium around Moscow is a forewarning that this sort of weapon is on its way. The second category of these "new weapons of mass destruction" consists of what might be called "biotechnicals," which are biological agents custom-tailored at the genetic level. While these weapons have yet to be invented, the phenomenal growth of the biotechnology industry is quickly spreading the means of building these weapons to the far corners of the earth.

Terrifying as they are, weapons of mass destruction are not the only means that nonstate actors have of disturbing the peace. The fragility of modern life, our dependence on the complex networks that provide us with food, water, energy, transportation, and information, provides both the nonstate actor and the state-sponsored terrorist with lucrative targets. For those with a will to destroy, attacks on power grids, water supplies, the banking system, and even the global economy are relatively easy to engineer. The days when Sherman's men had to twist steel rails into pretzels to interrupt the Confederate transportation system are long gone. These days, breaking into the computer that controls traffic signals can create a comparable degree of havoc.

The decline of the state is not absolute. In addition to the nonstate actor, we will still have to deal with "rogue states," strongman governments so dissatisfied with the global status quo that they are willing to break most of the rules of international behavior. During the cold war, these states could often count on the Soviet Union for aid and advice. Now they rely chiefly on each other.

Prior to the Gulf War, "rogue states" appeared to be trying to beat the West at its own game. Standards of living were ruthlessly sacrificed to amass huge tank armies, fleets of high-performance aircraft, and even rudimentary navies. The rapid defeat of Iraq's armed forces in the course of Desert Storm, however, sent a signal to rogue states that their attempts to create military might on the Western pattern were doomed to failure. In its place, they started investing in "asymmetrical" capabilities, military forces designed to counter, rather than imitate, Western capabilities.

The most significant of these asymmetrical responses to Western military power is the "antiaccess" strategy, which involves a combination of long-range sensors, naval mines, cruise missiles, speedboats, and diesel submarines designed to prevent Western navies from navigating in coastal waters. At first glance, the antiaccess strategy is defensive in nature. Indeed, it is sometimes referred to as the "antiaccess defense." A look at the map, however, tells a somewhat different story. In places, like the Strait of Hormuz, where major international trade routes lie close to the shore, the deployment of "antiaccess" weapons can have a profoundly offensive effect.

Just as chaos in the littorals is closely related to the decline of the nation-state, the antiaccess strategy is part of something larger, a phenomenon that might be called "strategic diversity." Before the collapse of the Soviet Union, there were essentially two approaches to the building of military forces: those who, for reasons of ideology or alliance politics, aligned themselves with the Communist Bloc and tended to copy Soviet methods and those who oriented themselves toward the West and imitated Western models.

These days, however, the Soviet approach has been discredited and, in the absence of generous aid packages, the Western model is proving far too expensive. As a result, a lot of military leaders around the world have been looking for new models. In some cases, they are drawing on indigenous traditions. In others, they are taking bits and pieces from various nations and joining them together to create the military equivalent of a crazy quilt. The Iranian antiaccess strategy, for example, combines Chinese cruise missiles with Russian diesel submarines, mines of local manufacture, and speedboats from around the world.

As a rule, strategic diversification makes things more difficult for Western military forces for the simple reason that opponents are less predictable. Had he remained faithful to his Soviet training, Mohammed Farah Aideed would have been little more than a nuisance. As a warlord who developed his own style of strategy and tactics, Aideed turned out to be a formidable adversary.

Having described the problem of chaos in the littorals, it is necessary to consider what we can do about it. Before doing so, it is important to emphasize that chaos in the littorals is not a minor phenomenon, a flesh wound in the international body politic that can be cured with a bandage and a dab of antibiotic ointment. Indeed, chaos in the littorals is a symptom of one of the great developments of our age, something that is happening nearly everywhere on the planet and is likely to remain a problem for the foreseeable future.

It is also important to make the distinction between solutions and responses. Solutions to the problem of the breakdown of order lie in the realm of diplomacy, not military operations. The best that the military can do is respond and stabilize a situation, putting an end to the shooting long enough for the diplomats to do their job.

One possible response to chaos in the littorals is the establishment of permanent overseas bases. Such bases were of great use during the cold war, when they served to remind allies of America's commitment to the common defense. In today's world, however, overseas bases suffer from a number of disadvantages. The greatest of these is the simple fact that people are often uncomfortable having somebody else's military base permanently within their territorial jurisdiction.

In the aftermath of World War II and the Korean War, countries ravaged by invasion put up with American bases because they realized that, with an aggressive Soviet Union around the corner, such bases were essential to their survival. These days, however, the threat is far less obvious. Governments that tolerate existing U.S. bases or invite new ones are hard pressed to explain, in clear and simple terms, why they put up with so much inconvenience in order to gain an added measure of security.

This is not to say that many governments are unhappy with the proximity of military forces from the United States or another Western country. Many realize that these forces add greatly to their own security, both by inhibiting potential enemies and by preventing local arms races. In most cases, however, they would like to have the troops close to their territory, but not on it. In other words, they want an American presence without the presence of Americans.

Secondly, as we saw in the recent attacks on the Khobar Towers in Saudi Arabia, overseas bases are vulnerable to terrorism. There are, of course, measures we can take to protect our troops. Barbed wire, concrete obstacles, and well-armed guards will do much to deter would-be terrorists. Unfortunately, these measures give a base the appearance of a fortress, creating an exaggerated sense of separation between American forces and the people of the host nation.

The third great disadvantage of permanent bases is that they are immobile. As we discovered in 1979, when the relatively friendly shah of Iran was replaced by a hostile government, regimes fall. When they do, alliances shift. Bases that once served a useful purpose can become irrelevant, or, what is worse, they can become the property of a new enemy. Either way, the huge amounts of both money and political capital invested in the base are lost.

This leads us back to where we started, with the general trend toward the building of expeditionary capabilities. Like our European friends, we in the United States are rediscovering the value of balanced naval expeditionary forces, capable of service in peace, war, and the enormous gray area between the two. These include aircraft carriers, surface combatants, amphibious vessels with their complements of marines and special operations forces, submarines, mine countermeasures ships, and the full panoply of auxiliary vessels.

The organization and equipment of these expeditionary forces is, of course, very much a function of the times in which we live. Modern technology, both that which we possess ourselves and that in the hands of our potential enemies, does much to determine the size, shape, and texture of America's expeditionary capability. The need to possess that capability, however, is as old as the United States itself.

American history suggests that the employment of flexible expeditionary forces is a perennial feature of American foreign policy. This has certainly been true in periods when the United States sought an active role in world affairs. Most nonspecialists would be surprised to discover, however, that American expeditionary forces have been both strong and active in eras when the United States, as a whole, sought disengagement. It was during the administration of Thomas Jefferson, for example, that an American seagoing expeditionary force, working with local allies, put a stop to the depredations of the Barbary pirates. Despite his desire to insulate the United States from the turmoil of global politics, Jefferson recognized the fact that America was a maritime nation, with an economy dependent on international trade. Thus, when faced by the nineteenth century version of chaos in the littorals, President Jefferson called on the Navy-Marine Corps team to set things right.

Suggesting changes in U.S. policy and predicting the future go far beyond the scope of this essay. I am, however, convinced, that whether the United States chooses to be more active in world affairs or less—and whether the defense budget goes up or down—there will be a need for strong, flexible, and up-to-date expeditionary force. In a world where permanent bases have a high political cost, a good portion of these must be based at sea, out of sight but close at hand.

My optimistic nature is no match for the problems we face. I must therefore conclude by offering a prognosis that is far from rosy and a prescription that may be hard to fill.

Chaos in the littorals is a symptom of one of the major developments of our time. Like nationalism in the nineteenth century or totalitarianism in the twentieth, the decline of the state is an extraordinarily powerful force. On a local level, it can be suppressed, curbed, or even redirected. On a global level, however, we have no other choice but to wait until it has run its course. The example of the Barbary pirates is instructive in this regard. The effect of the American expedition that ended with the capture of Tripoli was to put a damper on piracy for a few years. Within a decade, however, the pirates were back to their old tricks.

Even temporary suppression of chaos in the littorals, enough to prevent economic disaster for millions or to buy time for diplomats, does not come cheaply. In an era when many states and even a few nonstate actors possess cruise and ballistic missiles, we need to get forces off their transports and onto the land in record time. This means we will have to make a considerable investment to improve our means of ship-to-shore movement—landing craft, aircraft, and assault amphibious vehicles. In a period when both the naval mine and the diesel submarine are enjoying a renaissance, we need to improve our means of locating and countering these relatively primitive, but still very potent, antiaccess weapons. Finally, we can never forget that success in expeditionary operations requires the combined efforts of well-trained, talented people. We must therefore continue to call on some of our most promising young people to dedicate the best years of their lives to mastering, and, if need be, practicing, the art of expeditionary warfare.

MTW PLANNING AND SMALL-SCALE CONTINGENCIES: ENDURING UTILITY OF NAVAL FORCES

Carlton W. Fulford Jr.

Today, the United States faces many different challenges to its security, interests, and way of life. In an era characterized by diverse threats, our national security strategy increasingly relies on forward-deployed naval expeditionary forces to meet these challenges, most of which are likely to occur in the littorals and the adjacent sea lines of communication. These regions lie within direct reach of and are extremely vulnerable to the striking power of U.S. forces.

Our Naval Forces bring a unique operational flexibility and synergy to the National Command Authority (NCA) and the joint force commander. Whether it is a large-scale amphibious operation projecting combat power ashore or support for humanitarian assistance, U. S. Naval Forces provide a credible forward presence, ready to influence events by operating throughout the spectrum of potential conflict. My purpose is to discuss an operational perspective on the relevant utility of Naval Forces in meeting the significant challenges of major theater war (MTW) and small-scale contingencies (SSC). The focus will be on MTW and SSC operational planning, training, and experimentation and will address the following areas:

➤ past and present employment of U. S. Naval Forces
➤ operational planning for MTW and SSC
➤ training and support for MTW and SSC
➤ warfighting experimentation

This operational perspective should begin with a brief discussion of the Marine Corps's role as the nation's premier crisis response force, one which has been validated repeatedly. For example, during the cold war (1946–89), the Marine Corps responded to 139 taskings from the NCA. These responses, an average of one every fifteen weeks, included blunting military attacks against our nation or our allies, stopping actions of political violence against Americans abroad, and conducting small-scale contingencies such as disaster relief and evacuation of American citizens.

Since the end of the cold war, contingency employment of Naval Forces has been greater than at any other time in our history. Tasking from the NCA has increased by a factor of three, resulting in responses by the Marines and Navy shipmates in the protection of our nation's interests on an average of once every five weeks. Operations such as Provide Relief, Provide Comfort, Uphold Democracy, Pacific Haven, and Desert Storm provide an idea of the breadth and scope of the NCA's tasking. These operations accomplished a myriad of missions, including: providing relief to famine victims, providing comfort to peoples oppressed by their government, upholding democracy where threatened, providing sanctuary to displaced peoples, and fighting to repel aggression. These complex operations could not have been conducted in such a successful manner without detailed, thorough operational planning.

Our ability to think and plan at an operational level both in MTW and SSC is a direct result of the time, effort, and dollars invested in training and educational programs to develop our officers as operational thinkers. A flexible, yet consistent, approach to operational planning allows us to plan effectively for contingencies. Our decision-making process has never been better. Operational planning teams at the Marine expeditionary force (MEF) level spearhead the planning effort for every possible contingency we currently face with respect to MTW.

Our planning-decision-execution (PDE) cycle is streamlined to provide the commander the best courses of action in the shortest possible time, while fully integrating our subordinate commands' staffs to maximize their planning effectiveness as well. This allows us to thoroughly plan, decide, and execute well within the decision cycle of any potential adversary. Planning for a wide variety of contingencies while concurrently conducting exercises to test and train our staffs prepares us for the real-world missions we are ultimately called on to perform.

Our exercises reflect the naval character of our operational planning. This contributes to an integrated effort, assuring that we train our battle staffs, and, in turn, our major subordinate commands, as realistically as possible and at the correct operational focus. Continued emphasis on operational planning prepares us for contingencies through early identification and accurate assessment of the threats we may face in the littoral regions.

An example of a threat, which is identified continually through our integrated planning process, is the use of underwater mines in the littoral regions. Recent history has shown us the potentially devastating effect mines could have on naval operations and provides a foreboding snapshot of the particular danger they will pose on amphibious operations in the future. If we are to project power and maneuver from the sea, we must plan for and develop solutions to the threats we will face in the littorals, particularly underwater mines.

Naval Forces provide the joint force commander support through training and exercises that are conducted to maintain operational flexibility and readiness. This support and training spans the warfighting spectrum in both MTW and SSC.

The 1 MEF is a combined arms Marine air ground task force (MAGTF) consisting of more than forty-five thousand Marines and sailors with world-wide commitments. On any day, approximately eight thousand Marines and sailors are forward deployed in naval expeditionary areas or the Arabian Gulf region. The 1MEF mission is to deploy and employ ready naval, expeditionary air-ground task forces in response to commander in chief (CINC) and component commander tasking, operate in joint and combined operations, conduct military operations in small-scale contingencies, and win in combat. This mission requires that the MEF train, organize, and equip forces to operate across the spectrum of conflict. To maintain combat readiness, 1 MEF has an exercise program that is focused on maritime prepositioning force (MPF) and amphibious proficiency, small-scale contingency operations, CINC-directed MTW exercises, and the development of joint task force and consequence management proficiency. Exercises provide the best vehicle to hone and refine war plans, tactics, techniques, and procedures. The 1 MEF supports the Pacific Command (USCINCPAC) in the following major exercises: reception, staging, onward movement, and integration (RSOI) and Ulchi Focus Lens (UFL).

RSOI is a joint and combined exercise in the Republic of Korea (ROK), which centers on the reception, staging, onward movement, and integration of U.S. Forces into the Korean Peninsula. Additionally, the exercise focuses on rear-area operations, command and control, force protection, force tracking, and sustainment of forces. It provides naval forces an excellent opportunity to participate in combined and joint planning. The centerpiece of this exercise is a combined seminar, where U.S. and ROK leaders discuss issues associated with RSOI, noncombatant evacuation operations, and warfighting.

The UFL exercise provides state-of-the-art simulation training for Korean Theater warfighters to test current OPLANs and evolving warfighting concepts. Serving as a Corps-equivalent headquarters, UFL provides the framework for 1 MEF to focus on sustained operations ashore. In this role, the MEF has operational control of such diverse forces as the 1st ROK Marine Division, the 22d ROK Infantry Division, and the U.S. Army's 101st Air Assault Division, in addition to organic Marine forces. UFL provides the opportunity to validate operational procedures in a combined and joint environment and to examine current amphibious doctrine in a mature theater with the associated challenges of integrating naval air and operational fires.

In the USCENTCOM geographic area, 1 MEF is actively involved in two major exercises: Internal Look and Native Fury. Internal Look is a computer simulation wargame that provides naval forces the opportunity to play a major role in securing the CINC's strategic and operational objectives. The framework of the exercise provides the opportunity to develop, validate, and refine amphibious doctrine, tactics, techniques, and procedures along with our naval counterparts. Additionally, the exercise provides the operational context to contrast our present amphibious doctrine with those capabilities found in our evolving concept of operational maneuver from the sea. There is a striking difference between these two operations. Our current capability "ship to shore" often involves an intermediate objective, which might limit tactical surprise; our future capability will allow us to go directly from "ship to objective." Far from becoming obsolete, these new capabilities will demonstrate the viability of continued planning for amphibious operations for future conflicts well into the twenty-first century.

Another exercise in support of CENTCOM is Native Fury, which provides us the opportunity to exercise one of our most important naval capabilities in support of any CINC—maritime preposition force operations. In addition to focusing on off load, throughput, force stand-up, and regeneration, this exercise allows us to test our Marine Expeditionary Force (Forward) concept and the inherent challenges in communication connectivity that are associated with command and control of a mechanized combined arms task force.

While the stakes in an MTW are certainly greater, the more likely employment of our forces will be support for SSCs. I will cover four areas that complement our preparations for these contingencies. The first is joint task force consequence management, or JTF CM.

The 1 MEF has been designated by one CINC as the JTF Headquarters for CM operations. These operations are in response to incidents involving nuclear, biological, and chemical weapons and conventional and improvised high-explosive weapons. We are working with both the joint and civilian community to develop a credible JTF CM capability.

The second area is humanitarian assistance and peace operations (HA/PO). The year 1997 marked the fifth time 1 MEF hosted Emerald Express, a CINCCENT- and CINCPAC-sponsored exercise. Emerald Express has provided us the opportunity to prepare for humanitarian assistance and peace operations. The target audience included 1 MEF commanders and principal staff members; CINCCENT and CINCPAC staffs; component staffs; senior U.S. and international officials from government, diplomatic, and military organizations; nongovernmental organizations; and potential coalition partners. The theme "Integration and Education" focused on cultures, mission planning, execution, and refugees. A triad focus for the working groups covered areas of interest to CINCCENT and CINCPAC, while developing approaches toward handling HA/PO challenges.

The third area is the Marine Expeditionary Unit (Special Operations Capable) (MEUSOC) program. Our bread and butter force is the forward-deployed MEU(SOC). It is a self-sustained, amphibious, combined arms, air-ground task force capable of conventional and selected maritime special operations. Mission capabilities include amphibious raids, noncombatant evacuation operations, and humanitarian and civic assistance. MEU(SOC) units, embarked in amphibious ready group ships, form a unique naval force specially trained to operate in the SSC environment. Additionally, MEU(SOC) units are on the leading edge in the employment of nonlethal weapons. Each

MEU(SOC) has been equipped with a nonlethal equipment suite, which allows our Marines to defuse situations without resorting to deadly force.

Refocusing Naval Forces to meet the needs of the next century will, as in all successful military innovation, involve a great deal of debate and experimentation. The rates of change are accelerating, and the future is unpredictable. Experimentation is the key to developing our future doctrine, tactics, techniques, procedures, and equipment. Marines and sailors from 1 MEF and Third Fleet are fully engaged with the Marine Corps Warfighting Laboratory and the Fleet Battle Laboratory in warfighting innovation. Together, we have spent the last years experimenting with new tactical concepts and emerging technologies.

This essay will now provide a brief focus on five programs that are key to our sustained engagement in the twenty-first century. The first is Hunter Warrior, an eighteen-month advanced warfighting experiment that ended in 1998. It examined how modest, forward-afloat Marine forces could use new concepts and emerging technologies to improve their warfighting capabilities. Five limited objective experiments, which examined specific tactics, techniques or technologies, were conducted. Information gained in these limited experiments was used in a ten-day advanced warfighting experiment. Over seven thousand Marines participated in this free-play, force-on-force experiment that covered a 1,287 square mile battlefield in southern California. Hunter Warrior has provided us a prototype ability for forward-afloat expeditionary forces to significantly affect a capable foe on the extended battlefield. We can expand the area of influence of a modest forward-afloat expeditionary force and significantly increase its effectiveness within that area of influence.

Another program is Urban Warrior, having the goal to develop new capabilities for Marines as they prepare for combat in an urban environment. Developing tactics and techniques for individual Marines and communications, mobility and fire support concepts are some of the major areas being examined in Urban Warrior. Urban Warrior was conducted during the spring of 1999.

Our third program is Dragon Drone, which is an experiment that involves the use of unmanned aerial vehicles (UAV). We are testing a UAV called "Dragon Drone," which is a concept that emerged from our Hunter Warrior program. The Dragon Drone UAV provides commanders with an organic point reconnaissance asset capable of either being deployed aboard ship or operating from shore. Equipped with a video camera and data link, the UAV provides a commander with a means of conducting point reconnaissance before the start of an operation. Dragon Drone will be deployed with one of our MEU(SOC) units to test its compatibility in a realistic operational environment.

Although somewhat less glamorous than these other initiatives, our focus on logistics is another extremely important area within the Marine Corps that has benefited from experimentation and innovative thinking.

Our Commandant's Planning Guidance challenged Marines to identify opportunities for streamlining, eliminating, duplicating, and improving efficiency through organizational change to provide fully integrated logistics support to the Marine Corps. This guidance led to the development of the concept of "Precision Logistics."

Precision Logistics targets critical vulnerabilities that prevent us from being flexible, responsive, and adaptive and identifies factors that inhibit our ability to anticipate and rapidly deliver our logistics requirements. Precision Logistics replaces mass and footprint with speed and information. The goal is to adopt the best commercial practices and standards and apply these to our logistics processes. Precision Logistics is more than a fancy name; it reflects a new attitude. Already, we have seen significant improvements in ordering and shipping repair parts and in equipment repair times. These kinds of changes translate into increased readiness and reduced costs.

The final experimental program is Admin Warrior. Since 1 MEF is the Marine Corps's active duty test bed for centralized personnel administration, Admin Warrior will experiment with ways to make personnel administration more effective and efficient with significantly fewer personnel resources than we currently devote to administration. Concurrently, the test will attempt to integrate new technology into the office environment by outsourcing from the civilian marketplace and developing automated service records and smart card and travel reengineering applications. We are aggressively pursuing concepts and ideas that will create a paperless environment, thereby reducing the need for office personnel and allowing Marines to return to the field.

In summary, from major theater war to small-scale contingencies, Naval Forces continue to support the national security objectives and JCS/DOD *Joint Vision 2010* strategic concept of "power projection enabled by overseas presence." Our complementary Navy-Marine Corps strategic direction of "forward from the sea" and capstone operational concept "operational maneuver from the sea" are synchronized with *Joint Vision 2010*. These documents provide the framework for Naval Services to be "ready, relevant, and capable" for the twenty-first century. Power projection from the sea is and will remain a fundamental strength of our nation's military capability.

SEA-BASING: PROJECTING POWER AND INFLUENCE FROM THE SEA

Wallace C. Gregson Jr. and R. V. Dutil

"Not a single principle in the management of our foreign affairs, accepted by all statesmen for guidance up to six months ago, any longer exists. There is not a diplomatic tradition which has not been swept away. You have a new world, new influences at work, new unknown objects and dangers with which to cope, at present involved in that obscurity incident to novelty in foreign affairs."[1]

Wars create change. The end of the cold war is causing profound changes in the world's political and military condition. The factors affecting this condition change in an unpredictable manner at varying speeds. It is a distinctly nonlinear, non-step-function phenomenon. Our tendency to explain what we observe through chaos theory is eloquent testimony to our attitude. We prefer order. We assume the current period of "big change" is unique in world history. However, as the quote above indicates, history bears witness to many periods of such big change.

Our planned organizational responses to the political and military condition are called policy, strategy, and doctrine. Changes to policy, strategy and doctrine are step functions. It is a dominant American tendency to make an assessment of a situation, immediately prescribe a solution, and then expand that solution into an overarching, universal principle. Thus, our ad hoc responses to an unanticipated condition or event tend to become a pillar of our policy, strategy, or doctrine. We are Americans—we prefer certainty and want to examine a problem, settle it quickly, and move on to the next issue.

The currently unsettled nature of our policy, strategy, and doctrine—after nearly fifty years of certainty brought about by "containment"—is the source of much angst in official and academic communities. Uncomfortable though we may be, "unsettled" is our best course for the near-term future. It is the key to maintaining our balance and agility, and it is our tradition of rigorous intellectual inquiry and challenge. Our past experience with quick solutions and early resolution of policy, strategy, and doctrine reveals unfortunate results.

End of World War II to Korea

"To maintain a five-ocean Navy to fight a no-ocean opponent . . . is a foolish waste of time, men, and resources."[2] The climactic end of World War II led many to conclude that "the Bomb" was the answer to our national security. Our preferred concept was to use our technological superiority to dominate the East-West competition from a distance. How could any leader, faced with the destructive power of the atom bomb, commit suicide by challenging the United States? According to many, this technological-dominance approach to the application of military power was all that should have been needed as the United States uncomfortably settled into its role as a world leader.

This approach proved impractical within a very short time. At the height of the Berlin Crisis, when President Harry Truman wanted to "give the Russians hell," General George Marshall told him that he thought that one U.S. Army division in Europe was insufficient for even the *threat* of hell. As for U.S. naval and amphibious forces, although they proved a vital component in the war-winning, power-projecting strategies of both the Pacific and European Theaters, they were thought to have been rendered obsolete by this new weapon. As one of the most notable generals to emerge from World War II stated, "I predict that large-scale amphibious operations will never occur again."[3] Moreover, there was no navy for our Navy to fight! "Why should we have a navy at all? There are no enemies for it to fight except apparently the Army Air Force."[4]

This preferred solution lasted less than five years, as we learned that there were strategic, political, and moral restrictions to using the Bomb. After the Soviet Union exploded its own atomic device in August 1949, we were no longer the sole nuclear power. We realized our technological dominance was short-lived. China fell to Mao Tse-Tung's forces despite our dominance in the field of nuclear weapons technology. The world's political and military-technological conditions had changed to accommodate, and in many ways render moot, the American military-technological advantage. On 25 June 1950, the forces of Kim Il Sung crossed the 38th Parallel and challenged a vastly out-manned and unready coalition of American and Republic of Korea soldiers. Our first "hot" campaign of the cold war rendered our preferred strategy impotent.

Korea

"The first six to eight months of the Korean War were primarily naval in character. Naval forces, with their inherent mobility, self-contained logistics, and relative invulnerability, ranged up and down both coasts during the initial movement phase of the war, providing the foundation for successes and repeated salvation against disasters."[5]

The initial stages of Korea were disastrous for U.S. Forces. We narrowly avoided our own Dunkirk. Nor were we permitted the luxury of a single problem. We suspected Korea was a diversion and that the hot embers of

Europe would reignite. Just south of the Korean Peninsula, Nationalist and Communist Chinese threatened a wider conflict across the Taiwan Straits. We quickly learned that our forces were insufficient to garrison the ramparts of Europe and to maintain sentinels in the Taiwan Straits.

From the very beginning of the Korean War, we realized that a strategy based on technological dominance is not always appropriate. There are political, diplomatic, moral, and military restrictions and limits to waging war. Unless we were willing to wage total war, we needed a more focused, precise, adjustable, and flexible approach to the application of military power.

There may have been no navy for our Navy to fight, but fleet-based combat power and logistics projected over the shore from a mobile, secure sea base, kept us in Korea during the initial months. The moratorium on amphibious operations voiced by General Bradley ended with the brilliant action at Inchon, which executed General Douglas MacArthur's great turning movement. As he remarked, "The Navy and Marines have never shone more brightly than this morning."[6] This and the amphibious operation along the eastern coast were the types of operations that the nation required of our naval forces during the opening stages of the war.

After Chinese forces entered the war, the 1st Marine Division executed a breakout from encirclement and a fighting withdrawal *to* the sea, supported by sea-based combat power and logistics, and demonstrating the ability of sea-based combat power to be a salvation from disaster as well as the foundation for all our successes. Once the UN had significant land-based combat power available, the U.S. Navy effortlessly evolved to a more appropriate role of support for operations ashore.

Unfortunately, the later, static warfare phases of this war dominated the policy, strategy, and doctrinal lessons we drew from Korea. We thought that, with sufficient military and economic support, we could keep almost any anti-Communist regime afloat, regardless of its intrinsic viability. "The fact that Syngman Rhee was the unpopular leader of a thoroughly corrupt regime, whose army was incapable of effective self-defense on the battlefield, did not prove a fatal disadvantage to sustaining the South Korean cause."[7] In addition, "The American Army emerged from Korea convinced that its vastly superior firepower and equipment could always defeat a poorly equipped Asian army if it was provided with the opportunity to deploy them. Shrewd commanders were well aware of historic weaknesses in American infantry. But most senior officers continued to believe that the historic American military virtues, centering upon the massive concentration of scientific and technical expertise, could more than compensate for these."[8] We quickly forgot the lessons of the early, mobile phase of the war. Meanwhile, our enemies also learned. They realized they could not face a Western army on our terms and that democracies are notoriously impatient. We would not have long to wait to test these respective lessons.

Vietnam

We employed our political and military power, relentlessly fitting a new, Far Eastern war to our preferred concept of fighting. We failed! Political and diplomatic restrictions over fighting on the Korean Peninsula paled in comparison to those of the war in Vietnam. The enemy army refused, for the most part, to present itself for destruction by our superior technology. The North Vietnamese leadership was tone deaf to our repeated signals.

During that time of great political and social turmoil, progress in the development and advancement of military art, as opposed to military science, languished in evolutionary purgatory. The U.S. Navy supported our forces ashore as we pursued a continental strategy. The Marine Corps, out of necessity, concentrated on its mission to conduct sustained operations ashore. The political lessons learned in places such as Haiti, the Dominican Republic, Panama, and the Philippines during the early part of this century were ignored.

Our application of a massive, firepower-based, continental military strategy to a profoundly political dispute unsettled our forces for years. We rushed to reembrace the type of warfare that might be conducted on the European continent as our true military cornerstone. Many perceived an identity crisis for U.S. Naval Forces. "Is the continuing preoccupation of the Marine Corps with amphibious warfare founded upon a realistic appraisal of future U.S. requirements for such a capability? To what extent will amphibious assault remain a technologically feasible military operation?"[9] The post-Vietnam renaissance in American military art awaited our recovery from this collective identity-crisis hangover.

Development of Maritime Strategy

Throughout the cold war, the Soviet Union challenged the United States in all areas, and it was even considered to be superior in some capabilities. As the global strategic situation continued to change and assume a rather ominous posture, the countervalue doctrine of "mutually assured destruction" required our national and military strategies to adapt. The application of brute strength was no longer practical—it was mutually suicidal. The concept of fighting a war under conditions that precluded the use of nuclear weapons emerged. The capability to create unlimited destruction put limits on warfare. Our nation needed a more focused application of its power, and we needed to be able to shape our strategic environment: We needed a more precise and controllable approach to the application of diplomatic and military power.

U.S. Naval Forces then drafted maritime and amphibious strategies. While taking battle to enemy naval forces—at times and places of our choice—our forces could bring battle to the homeland of the Soviet Union, preventing it from being able to concentrate its significant capabilities on our outnumbered ground forces. The mission of the old 4th Marine Brigade epitomized this stratagem. Airlifted to Norway to join with prepositioned equipment stored there for this contingency, the brigade's mission was to protect the air bases and the aircraft that would prosecute the Norwegian Sea Antisubmarine Warfare (ASW) campaign. This ASW campaign, in turn, enabled the fleet to steam north and carry the battle to the enemy homeland. With this, we were applying sea-based power onto the far shore as we never had before. This meant sea-based national power could bypass enemy land-based might to attack its national source of authority directly, that is, its "center of gravity."

Sea-based forces affected the battle for central Europe. On the European land mass, this meant operations in the frigid climate of Norway and the Barents Sea. In the Far East, our enemy faced a threat along the region's vast coastline anywhere from Vladivostok to Kamchatka. When the Soviet Union imploded, U.S. Naval Forces sought to refine this "rheostatically controllable" approach.

With a renewed focus on the littorals, U.S. Naval Forces developed . . . *From the Sea* and *Forward . . . From the Sea.* These documents reinforced the ultimate goal of taking the fight to the enemy. They were—and are—the articulation of the political and military value of naval forces, in conflicts and operations, both major and minor, when there is no fleet to fight. It is a dominant, asymmetric strategy at the national level and applies our strengths directly to the critical nodes required for victory from a position of relative invulnerability.

Operations Desert Shield/Storm

As our armed forces celebrated a full recovery from the damage wrought by the Vietnam era, we observed other momentous changes. We saw the iron curtain raised, an "evil empire" come to an end, and the first hints of a "new world order." However, this optimistic intoxication faded when we realized that there were still tyrants who had power but who wanted more power for their despotic regimes. In addition, technology continued to change the face of battle. Our approach needed even more refinement. What the modern-day artisans of diplomacy and war needed was a "scalpel" approach to the application of military power.

One foreign leader perceived a strategic opportunity and challenged our interests in the Persian Gulf. Quite by happy accident, we found that one continuous action over the period of the cold war provided us the political and military means to respond effectively.

Our road to Desert Shield and Desert Storm—our ability to react to this challenge both militarily and politically—was paved by fleet-based action, beginning with the inception of the Middle East Force in 1948. Political conditions following the recognition of the State of Israel greatly restricted our presence in the Persian Gulf. The only possible tangible military evidence of our interest and our intentions in the region during that time was the small naval force established in 1948, which was maintained despite enormous fiscal and military pressures to move these ships elsewhere. After the fall of the shah of Iran in 1979, U.S. Naval Forces were even more important. They were the only base for our national presence and power projection in the area. These forces allowed us to contain the Iran-Iraq War, to wage the "tanker war," to keep the Persian Gulf oil commerce flowing, and, most important, to keep diplomatic ties open with the nations and key leaders of the region. Without the continuous presence of naval forces in the Gulf since 1948, which signals our interest and our intentions to allies, neutrals, and potential foes, it would have been much more difficult, and perhaps not possible at all, to gain the access agreements for our forces when we encountered a despotic leader who would not be deterred.

Desert Shield demonstrated well how forward-deployed naval forces can quickly project influence and power ashore. Without firing a shot in a fleet-to-fleet engagement, our navy won the sea control battle in a manner that the ancient Chinese military strategist Sun Tzu would have envied: convincing your opponent that engaging you in battle is futile. Sea-based combat power was the first to arrive on the scene with heavy armored, mechanized, air-ground combined arms combat capability and sustainment inherent to naval and Marine maritime prepositioning forces.

Had Saddam Hussein decided to continue south into Saudi Arabia after consolidating his position in Kuwait, he would have faced a combined air-land-sea force that would have prevented him from going further. Also, had he taken this course of action, he would have exposed his operational flank to amphibious operations. The evidence is overwhelming that he was indeed concerned about an assault from the sea, given the level of effort he expended in defending against an amphibious assault. Instead, the CINC was able to play on Saddam's fears and the Marines, already ashore, assaulted through the littoral to liberate Kuwait.

Given that both we and our potential enemies seek to learn from history, the early lessons of Desert Shield/Desert Storm should still be actively challenged. However, one significant lesson we may garner is that the type of political and military access we were presented with then, and our critical ability to establish the bases that enabled all that followed, was not an accident. It was the result of the measured, appropriate, tailored application of power and influence by U.S. Naval Forces on the scene since 1948. This lesson is *not* new, just routinely forgotten. What the future will bring may indeed be uncertain, but we can reduce our risk of being wrong by examining continuities from the past.

Our potential enemies have undoubtedly learned, again, to avoid facing a Western army on our terms. The news reports about the tragedy of Gulf War Syndrome will surely convince potential enemies that a regional power can effectively checkmate U.S. conventional power with weapons of mass destruction. Our resounding high-intensity, mechanized-combat success in the Gulf War convincingly demonstrated a conventional capability impossible for any power or plausible combination of powers to match. This virtually guarantees the development of asymmetric, competitive strategies by others. As one Indian government official is reported to have said in summing up a lesson learned from the Gulf War, "don't take on the U.S. unless you have nuclear weapons."

Our preferred end-of-twentieth-century strategy of "overwhelming force" requires overwhelming industrial-age mass. If we examine pictures of the Desert Shield/Desert Storm base areas and command posts, it becomes obvious that nuclear, chemical, and biological weapons make a fatal weakness of our greatest strength. When one Scud missile hit a barracks in Dhahran near the end of the Gulf War, it destroyed the barracks and caused many casualties among the members of a reserve unit from Greensburg, Pennsylvania. If it had been a mass destruction weapon—of any type—instead of a relatively unsophisticated high-explosive warhead, the destruction would have been crippling and catastrophic. This means that antimissile defenses, which are supposedly impregnable, are not an answer. Delivery means can vary from ballistic missiles to old trucks. Indeed, perhaps the most precise and most stealthy weapon is a dedicated terrorist, hiding among the civilian population. A used Chevy truck driven by someone who embraces suicide is a very effective stealth bomber, one not hindered by adverse weather conditions or requiring extraordinary maintenance efforts. Furthermore, used Chevy "stealth bombers" cost a lot less than our Stealth bombers. It becomes obvious that overwhelming force and overwhelming mass are now an overwhelming vulnerability.

With only a few nuclear, chemical, or biological weapons, an aggressor can avoid our strengths and attack our weaknesses in our massive support structures. Minimizing vulnerability to both nuclear, chemical, or biological weapons and terrorists with the ubiquitous truck bomb requires dispersion and high mobility. The massive base areas and logistics installations so necessary to our current continental concept of warfare are immobile and require strong antimissile defenses and strong local security forces. The choice to mass as an aid to security or disperse as a hedge against the big weapons is one that cedes initiative to the enemy. Either way we turn, we expose a flank. We must fundamentally change this continental-warfare, overwhelming-mass concept. The threat is clear and present. Remember how the North Koreans mixed soldiers with refugees in 1950? The potential refugee population of the Republic of Korea is much greater now. Moreover, finding enemy launch platforms may be very difficult. We will not be able to "see" everything on the modern battlefield. Recall that it required eighteen days to find an A-10 aircraft in the United States when we knew where to look. And remember our rear-area security problems in Vietnam. Those rockets that disrupted our operations were man portable and were launched from rude earthen ramps.

What do these conditions imply for the role of U.S. Naval Forces in twenty-first-century operations? What lessons can we draw from the past, considering both the elements of continuity and those of change?

The Future

A. Political Challenges

The promise of the twenty-first century has been extensively documented. It is achieving near-Clausewitzian status: more discussed than understood. However, we can wonder how accurate twentieth-century predictions were as we celebrated a one-sided victory in the Spanish-American War. As with other periods of global political change, as described by Benjamin Disraeli, this period will include unforeseen geopolitical permutations, increasingly rapid technological advances, a paucity of U.S. and allied funding, highly nebulous threats, the rise of nonstate actors, chaos writ large, and, in all likelihood, a return to Great Power competition. History offers little hope that the current period of remission will become a permanent cure. As with other periods when Great Power competition was in remission, the requirement for forces to perform the demanding duties of what have come to be known as operations other than war will continue to increase.

This time is not a strategic "pause" or "holiday," but an inflection point. Those entrusted with the defense of the nation must prepare for countering the long-term threat while being able to complete a plethora of assigned missions in the near term. Having no crystal ball to the future to make perfect decisions and take flawless courses of action, the best we can hope for is to be able to reduce risk to a minimum—and that minimum, in some cases, may indeed pose a significant risk.

If this is a period free from Great Power competition, our actions will help determine its length. Our postwar decisions in 1919 and 1946 decisively affected world events. Surely, the prospects for peace looked as good in 1919 and 1946 as they do now. Our decisions are likely to shape the world again, and shaping the world we want will require, more than ever, a much higher level of sophistication in the use of our armed forces as a political instrument. The civilian leadership needs to recognize military utility as an instrument of policy. In return, military leadership must step away from the use-only-in-crisis-or-war mind-set and incorporate the nuances of persuasive and coercive diplomacy. Immediate and compelling world conditions make this military-diplomatic function, accomplished largely through our overseas presence programs, our most important mission and our nation's most important contribution to shaping the world.

As one example, consider the difficult and important political issue of counterproliferation. Rogue nations are pursuing fledging nuclear programs and many possess chemical and biological weapons. Our demonstrated national character is such that we are not willing to violate another nation's sovereignty to eliminate their weapons of mass destruction programs with preemptive strikes. We are not likely to replicate the Israeli attack on Iraq's Osirak reactor, nor would that likely be practical. Since Osirak, rogue nuclear programs have literally gone underground. At present, the risks simply do not substantiate that type of action. However, our presence nearby in international waters assures other nations of the region that we, in effect, are extending our protective umbrella over them. With our presence and engagement, they understand that they do not have to build their own weapons of mass destruction in response to those being built by others. If some form of action is required, U.S. Naval Forces are there and do not have to await any clearance other than that issued by our own National Command Authorities.

As with other periods of remission of Great Power competition, the collapse of cold war discipline has created an era of ethnic conflict and collapsing states. We can stand by and do nothing, or we can act to prevent the spread of atrocities and genocide. Doing nothing will hasten a return to conflict. Refugee camps are a productive terrorist recruiting ground. Civil wars, ethnic conflict, collapsed states, and other calamities reduce world business opportunities, create tremendous population migration pressures, encourage terrorism, and hasten the reappearance of totalitarian regimes.

The administration has created a new doctrine to arrest and ameliorate this spreading anarchy and chaos. The term for these operations is Complex Contingencies. It puts the diplomatic, political, and humanitarian efforts in the forefront, with the military acting in a supporting role, creating and maintaining the security environment necessary for the other facets of national influence. It rests on the assumption that the military can indeed become a deft instrument when used to complement the other elements of national power.

A complementary military doctrine for Complex Contingencies is also emerging. It rests on twenty rules articulated by General Anthony Zinni following his experiences in northern Iraq, the former Soviet Union, Turkey, and Somalia.

Table 1:
General Zinni's Twenty Rules

1.	The earlier the involvement, the better the chances for success.
2.	Start planning as early as possible, and include everyone in the planning process.
3.	If possible, make a thorough assessment before deployment.
4.	In the planning, do a thorough assessment before deployment. Determine the center of gravity, end state, commander's intent, measures of effectiveness, exit strategy, cost-capturing procedures, and estimated duration.
5.	Stay focused on the mission and keep the mission focused. Line up military tasks with political objectives. Avoid mission creep; allow for mission shift.
6.	Centralize planning and decentralize execution during the operation.
7.	Coordinate everything with everybody. Set up coordination mechanisms.
8.	Know the culture and the issues.

Table 1. *continued*

---

9. Start or restart the key institutions early.
10. Do not lose the initiative or momentum.
11. Do not make enemies. If you do, do not treat them gently. Avoid mind-sets.
12. Seek unity of effort and command. Create the fewest possible seams.
13. Open a dialogue with everyone. Establish a forum for each individual or group involved.
14. Encourage innovation and nontraditional approaches.
15. Personalities are often more important than process.
16. Be careful whom you empower.
17. Decide on the image you want to portray and stay focused on it.
18. Centralize information management.
19. Seek compatibility in all coalition operations. Political compatibility, cultural compatibility, and military interoperability are crucial to success.
20. Senior commanders and their staffs need the most education and training for non traditional roles. The troops need awareness and understanding.

This emergent doctrine traces its heritage to the era between the world wars, when our forces were employed extensively in the Caribbean, China, and the Philippines. It contains principles first articulated in the *Marine Corps Small Wars Manual* of 1940 and our experience with the Combined Action Platoon [CAP] Program in Vietnam, the only unqualified success of that war. As one author wrote, "Even though only a small percentage of the total Marine force in South Vietnam was utilized in these operations (a mere ten companies were involved in the CAP program during 1967), the results were impressive."[10] Another stated, "the use of CAPs is quite the best idea I have seen in Vietnam, and it worked superbly."[11]

Reduced to its simplest terms, this emergent doctrine seeks to show how military forces can support diplomatic and humanitarian efforts in these Complex Contingency operations. It must reveal how we can avoid making a lucrative target of our support areas and infrastructure, sites of unbelievable wealth and largess to these benighted societies. It must show how to avoid obtrusive presence with no purpose and the inevitable adverse cultural impact that follows.

Sea-based forces are ideally suited to pursue these Complex Contingency operations. Forces operating from a sea base can carefully and precisely introduce military forces into the situation ashore and, just as quickly can withdraw when the mission is complete. No prolonged, purposeless, static presence occurs. There is no creation of "Little America" islands of unimaginable wealth-support areas that become targets for terrorism, theft, and resentment. No complicating logistics or command-and-control establishments are necessary. Using sea-based naval forces has the opportunity to offer the nation a new course and new opportunities to resolve these old challenges.

B. Technology Challenges

Technology provides both benefits and challenges for future military operations. It can be a significant force multiplier that can assist young American men and women when we ask them to underwrite our foreign policy. However, this same technology, misused, can be our modern-day Maginot Line. The U.S. military must be well able to deal with a number of factors—ubiquitous weapons of mass destruction and their delivery means; long-range precision weapons; access versus antiaccess, both military and political; information warfare consisting of readily available weapons, such as the Internet, cell phones, faxes, and satellite imagery available to anyone willing to pay for it—against an enemy who is as ruthless as he is innovative and in a chaotic, challenging environment.

Our enemies can be expected to take advantage of this "era of precision." Rockets are getting less expensive, while satellite technology increases their precision. Any country or armed element capable of producing fertilizer or pharmaceuticals can create highly lethal chemical and biological agents. An armed terrorist is the ultimate, and easily affordable, stealthy precision weapon. This inexorable march of militarily adaptable technology, combined with complex and confusing political imperatives, threatens to make hostages of our overseas bases. As shore-based activities and massive logistic stockpiles become targets, we must come to think of our overseas bases as liabilities.

The only way to prevent a catastrophic attack is to avoid presenting a highly lucrative target. Antimissile defenses or perfect antiterrorist screens are not the solution. Only forces capable of operating in a highly mobile fashion from a widely dispersed posture, and supported by a widely dispersed and mobile base, will be able to survive. To be effective, we must reduce the target. Naval forces operating from a highly mobile sea base are the solution.

C. Naval Forces—Their Time Has Dawned

The continued decline around the world described earlier will lead to increases in the problem of terrorism, refugees, and international crime, all exacerbated by a global trend of increased urbanization. If we, as a nation, wish to prevent the problem from getting worse and shape the world, we have to remain engaged. If we are to be engaged in this day and age, we must be sea based and able to conduct dispersed operations. This is the venue of U.S. Naval Forces that have an ultimate utility, regardless of where a contingency may fall on the spectrum of operations—from the high end, including weapons of mass destruction to the low end, involving humanitarian assistance and disaster relief. Dispersed, mobile, and secure bases are no longer a luxury, they are a prerequisite.

Where weapons of mass destruction will threaten, damage, or destroy a ground-based force, sea-based forces are inherently mobile regardless of weather and, for most opponents, are impossible to target. In situations requiring humanitarian assistance and disaster relief, where an already overstressed or nonexistent infrastructure is saturated, naval forces remain off shore as part of the solution and not part of the problem, while projecting ashore precise application of power and influence for the time required. From alliance maintenance and reassurance to persuasive influencing, to preventing, suppressing, or deterring international disturbances short of war, the age of the "laserlike" application of power and influence by naval forces has dawned.

One thoughtful commentator predicts that our future military forces will have to fight in greatly dispersed, small—but relatively much more capable—organizations, over very large areas, in order to survive and to be effective against the range of possible threats. Professor Bracken calls it "The Military after Next."[12] World events, technological possibilities, and doctrinal efforts are bringing that future into the present much faster than anticipated. The danger is clear and present. The strategic concept is here. The technology is nearly here. The doctrine is emerging. *Forward . . . From the Sea*, and *Operational Maneuver from the Sea* are the answer to this future. Reaching this future requires safe navigation through the near term. It requires real overseas presence—forward from the sea. Success when we get there requires the full range of possibilities within *Forward . . . From the Sea* and *Operational Maneuver from the Sea*.

Epilogue

A deadly trinity is at work against us. Weapons are gaining in range, becoming more precise and more deadly. From major conflict against an enemy willing to threaten or use the most terrible weapons, to relatively normal deterrence and reassurance operations, to complex contingency operations in response to man-made and natural disasters, world political and military conditions mandate that we change our industrial age ways of waging war and preserving peace. Large base areas inhibit mission accomplishment at the lower conflict levels and will be deadly at the higher levels.

Naval forces, operating *Forward . . . From the Sea*, coupled with *Operational Maneuver From the Sea* and our emerging naval operational concepts, provide the only viable method to reduce the fixed, vulnerable infrastructure targets still within enemy reach. These integrated concepts will keep our logistics, command and control, and fire support at sea, aboard high-speed, mobile, defensible, hard-to-find, hard-to-target, hard-to-attack, fighting bases. The only elements ashore will be those that are highly agile, highly mobile, kind to our friends, and dangerously hostile to the enemy. These concepts also provide the only method of entry into a fight when the threat causes neighboring countries to refuse U.S. access for fear of suffering "countervalue" nuclear, chemical, or biological attacks from a regional predator. As we look beyond the lessons of our most recent experience, it should become clear that the role of U.S. Naval Forces in twenty-first-century operations is to be the foundation for the application of national power and influence across the globe and across the spectrum of conflict levels, operating forward from a secure, dispersed, and highly mobile fighting base.

Notes

1. Attributed to Benjamin Disraeli, 1871, speaking about the birth of the first German Reich.

2. Major General H. J. Knerr, USAF, "If We Should Fight Again," *Military Review*, December 1947, p. 24.

3. Chairman of the Joint Chiefs of Staff General Omar N. Bradley's 1949 testimony before the House Armed Services Committee as quoted in "Inchon 1950" by Colonel Robert D. Heinl Jr., USMC (Ret.), *Assault for the Sea: Essays on the History of Amphibious Warfare* by Lieutenant Colonel Merrill L. Bartlett, USMC (Ret.), ed., Naval Institute Press, Annapolis, MD, 1983.

4. General Carl Spaatz, Army Air Corps, as quoted in Samuel P. Huntington, *The Common Defense*, New York, 1961, p. 368.

5. James A. Field, *United States Naval Operations, Korea*, U.S. Government Printing Office, Washington, D.C., 1962, p. v.

6. William Manchester, *American Caesar: Douglas MacArthur 1880–1964*, Little, Brown, and Company, Boston, 1978.

7. Max Hastings, *The Korean War*, Simon and Schuster, NY, 1987, pp. 333–4.

8. Ibid.

9. Martin Binken and Jeffrey Record, *Where Does the Marine Corps Go From Here*, Brookings Institution, Washington D.C., 1976.

10. Andrew F. Krepinevich, *The Army and Vietnam*, The Johns Hopkins University Press, Baltimore, MD., 1986, p. 174.

11. Sir Robert Thompson, *Lessons of the Vietnam War*, RUSI, Whitehall U.K., 12 Feb 1969, p 19.

12. Paul Bracken, "The Military after Next," *The Washington Quarterly*, Autumn, 1993, pp. 157–174, 16:4.

THE ROLE OF ALLIANCES AND COALITIONS IN MTW AND NON-MTW CONTINGENCIES

Thomas F. Marfiak

Let us begin by clearly defining alliances and coalitions, by understanding the political, diplomatic, and military implications of each, then applying those definitions in both major threat warfare (MTW) and non-MTW operations. At this same time, let us seek to understand the possibilities and limitations of both. It is work that is necessary—so much of what we read today in policy documents and in the press at large fails to make a distinction between these two definitions.

Alliances are based on the concept of collective defense, a continuing need that transcends a temporary emergency or passing confrontation. They are, or have been, characterized by some form of structural treaty—NATO is the primary example—defining specific members, obligations, and objectives in the event the alliance is challenged on the field. They give rise to specific force structure, trained to uniform standards of interoperability.

Coalitions, conversely, are not governed by a structural treaty. They are formed to meet a specific need, are joined by a more or less shared set of goals, and, to the extent forces are dedicated to achieve those objectives, are characterized by a wide range of capabilities, some complementary, others supportive, each seeking to accomplish national goals in support of the coalition objectives.

In both cases, the conditions under which they are formed are predetermining, that is the political will demonstrated by respective governments, operating as sovereign states or as members of an international organization, such as the United Nations, is likely to govern the pace with which forces are committed to action, the resources allocated to support those forces, and, from a commander's perspective, the rules of engagement under which those forces will be committed to operate under combined command.

Two examples can be cited here. First, in his book, *In Eye of the Storm*, General Frederick Franks describes the U.K. forces in direct support of his operations as he swept around the Iraqi line of battle. Second, in my own experience, there was an occasion involving multiple ships from eight nations. The U.K. ships were completely associated, as were the Canadians, Dutch, and Australian/New Zealand ships. Others were constrained by their own national guidance to support operations somewhat removed from the field of battle.

At this point it is important to note that a coalition or alliance-based force, properly deployed, at an early point in crisis generation, can play a deterrent role. Should these conditions not occur, maritime forces deployed unilaterally may be the only means of generating a timely response. They, in turn, may subsequently become the nexus about which a substantial and sustaining force can be built.

Whatever the origins of combined forces, they are likely to be confronted with a charged and ambiguous situation. Charged, because in most instances it is possible that the pace of crisis maturation will outdistance their ability to insert themselves in sufficient time, and with sufficient power, to prevent a hostile power from taking initial action. This may precipitate an even higher state of crisis, and, in today's media-rich environment, arouse international sensitivities, affect markets, and give rise to conflicting advice to national decisionmakers. Ambiguous, because initial commanders may arrive on scene with guidance still in process, lines of command needing articulation, personal relationships requiring establishment, and the intent of the hostile power still unclear.

As a consequence, the genesis of the force and of its military components, whether born of coalition or alliance, can be expected to have real consequences for the commander and could very well, to the extent problems of interoperability can be resolved, influence the effectiveness of the operation to which he is committed. Further complicating the matter is the decision as to how and when, or even if the force is to be used, and toward what end. We are all well aware of the ongoing debate regarding the end of Desert Storm—did we stop too soon? Were our objectives achieved? If democracies are, as the common wisdom would have it, not adept at defining the conditions under which conflict should be terminated, how much more difficult is it for a coalition, whose members may each have regional concerns, to decide where or when, and under what circumstances, the participation of their forces will be brought to a conclusion?

To this point, I have sought to highlight the difference between coalitions (ad hoc, situation specific, and regionally based) and alliances (mission oriented; framed by formal agreement; and in the case of NATO forces, generally enjoying a higher degree of interoperability). What we have seen since the demise of the Soviet Union, via a variety of contingencies in several cases, and in the case of the Gulf War in particular, is a blending of both, a coalition led by alliance-based forces, which form its effective core, augmented by a variety of coalition partners, each bringing to the operation those forces that each nation can afford to dispatch and often supported by one or more members of the alliance that have at their disposal lift, communications, or logistics support.

In addition, regional partners may be able to participate to a limited but key extent, providing airfields, stevedores, port facilities, fuel, and water—the necessities for force generation and support without which no armed force can remain effective for long. Although not always visible, these national commitments are important and should not be underestimated.

Let us now turn to the question of non-MTW contingencies. Whether referred to as operations other than war or any other name, they cover the great majority of operations—including peacekeeping, humanitarian assistance, and disaster relief. In both humanitarian assistance and disaster relief operations, the question of adequate force protection may be held to be neutral. We are concerned here with the application of the basic exercise of humanitarian relief—people are in need, and it has been judged to be in the best interests of the United States to assist in giving them an upper hand in restoring their lives. These sorts of operations may involve several nations operating in concert, but do not connote the same degree of force coordination necessary to achieve air and maritime supremacy.

Conversely, operations in support of Chapters Six and Seven of the United Nations Charter may very well involve sufficient force, with adequate rules of engagement, and run the risk those forces may be involved, to some degree, in conflict. Indeed, even such operations as withdrawing peacekeeping forces in the face of local resistance, as General Anthony Zinni experienced in Somalia, can involve themselves in the delicate exercise of national power while attempting to preserve coalition partners from harm.

It should be apparent from the foregoing development that it is crucial to have a clear understanding from the beginning of the conditions under which U.S. forces are committed to achieve international objectives. It should be equally clear that some idea of the end goal toward which those forces are dedicated is desirable, if not necessary. Only the National Command Authority can provide such guidance.

We should also note that coalitions, like alliances, are maintenance intensive. Coalitions are organized around shared interests that are only intermittently threatened and therefore only intermittently perceived to be important. Consequently, governments must consistently devote considerable national resources to maintain the cohesion necessary to a successful coalition operation. Moreover, they must pay particular attention to the central issues that define their cooperation. Are the objectives clear? Are their goals semipermanent or ad hoc? However, it is likely that, over time, objectives will change. This only reinforces the notion that cooperation must be shared and must be sufficiently flexible to accommodate those changing objectives.

In the case of the Persian Gulf region, we must recognize that a coalition, be it political, military, or both, is at once more fragile and more robust than we realize. It is more fragile because of its connection to the Middle East peace process. It is more robust because the media is inclined to emphasize the differences and sensitivities that divide it, while understating the solid cooperation and progressive engagement that have increasingly united the United States and the Gulf region states.

So, we are faced with an apparent dilemma. On the one hand, prospects for a collective defense in the Gulf region appear slim. On the other hand, there is a fair degree of unanimity in favor of some sort of security arrangement that would favor economic growth, the creation of internal opportunities, and the maintenance of regional and international trade.

In the Gulf region, therefore, and in other areas as well, we need to place some intellectual capital next to such questions as: what might be the consequences if Iraq or Iran were to emerge from this decade as a less-than-completely-hostile state? What if changes should occur in the Korean Peninsula without conflict? (That is, our policy of deterring aggression and maintaining the truce over four decades succeeds.) Consensus among the potential partners in either case is vital to the proper and prompt deployment of military force. Lack of consensus could result in increased risk, both to the region and to the viability of U.S. policy.

Perhaps under these circumstances it is time to advance a new concept, one of cooperative security, wherein nations or even regions might be bound by the desire for continued economic prosperity and might also be characterized by the need to contain aggression. Such cooperation might be dedicated to the objective of ensuring that aggression cannot commence, or be prosecuted successfully, on any scale without unacceptable costs to the perpetrator. Focussed on arms control, verification, and the limitation of aggressive weapons, collective defense is aimed at the universally held advantages of promoting peace while deterring war.

Ultimately, collective defense would depend, for its successful exercise, on the merits of preserving peace by deterring aggression—and here we are face to face with the limits of coalition power. Confidence and security building exercises, in the absence of conflict, may be sufficient. In the presence of a determined adversary, only international solidarity and the willingness to commit force may make a difference. In short, coalition building requires continuous dialogue at the governmental level and a shared sense of values that transcends the crisis of the moment.

If we accept that coalitions, as opposed to alliances, are more situation specific, with objectives tailored to a specific conflict rather than to widely held norms of international behavior, then we must also agree that it is necessary for us to exercise a superior degree of leadership, serving to define coalition objectives while seeking to incorporate our partners' perceptions.

In many ways it is an art form. Motivation and self-interest must counterweigh those forces that might conspire to divide the coalition. The repeated events in Iraq underscore these observations, but they are not limited to the Gulf region. The Adriatic, Africa, and South Asia are also regions where the exercise of coalition leadership is crucial to the maintenance of peace.

In the military sphere, CINCs and their staff are keenly aware of these unique aspects of coalition peacekeeping and coalition warfare. They are aware that insensitivity and national arrogance have no place in the coalition manager's book. We must recognize the unique contributions of which each nation is capable, accept them at face value, and expect each to shoulder whatever share of the burden world peace may assign.

Let me suggest that there is one area of cooperation that transcends conventional alliances and coalitions, where capabilities are not shared uniformly by several members: tactical missile defense. Should the present system of coalition deterrence lose its coherence, either because of a major shift in relationships relative to a change in regime via a key ally, or because of the unforeseen change of a significant national initiative, we might be confronted with the need to deploy an effective missile defense without regard to sovereign borders or defendable airspace.

We are confronted today by forces that aim at a sudden and irrevocable reversal of U.S. presence in more than one region of the globe. Whether because of ideological or even theological incompatibilities, there are those who would look on our retreat as sufficient cause to advance their own interests, spawning yet more occasions when hard decisions may be required in the future.

The existence of a credible deterrent is even more vital in those circumstances. National means of providing a credible and forward deployed theatre missile defenses counter are likely to be crucial in the next decade. Moreover, collective defense could be enhanced by advancing the notion of a nonspecific threat defense, characterized by an area net, information sharing and U.S.-led forces capable of countering potentially hostile IRBM or MRBM threats.

Such a security system would require a degree of coordination and intelligence sharing that transcends present arrangements and the existing capabilities of potential partners. Its creation would require the expenditure of resources toward a rational goal—in short, a reversal of what we often see, which is the pursuit of national pride or the creation of possible national allies by the distribution of arms purchases. Nevertheless, creating information networks sufficient for real-time decision making in a ballistic missile engagement might be sufficiently interesting to engage the support of potential partners in Europe, Asia, and the Gulf region.

All of the foregoing suggests that the conventional application of coalition or even alliance forces in MTW operations may very well be different in the future from what we have known in the past. It also suggests that, absent effective counterproliferation efforts and shared concerns as to the containment of the growth of ballistic missile or cruise missile capability by would-be regional hegemons, we may very well have no other resource than to develop an effective autonomous interdiction capability. This would be as a precondition for being able to provide a credible deterrent by other means, including the successful development of ground forces, the protection of fixed air bases, or the generation of credible combat power through timely logistics support.

It is recognized that TBM defenses are a special case—they require advanced technology, C4ISR systems, including space-based systems, and highly trained people. However, there is a wide range of capabilities necessary for effective TBM operations in today's environment that allows sufficient latitude for diverse nations to participate in those operations to the extent of their capabilities. As we proceed into the information age, the relative capabilities of our forces compared to those of our actual and potential allies are a matter of concern to them, and should be to us as well. From basic voice communications to the electronic exchange of data, future commanders will need to give these matters close attention, assuming that national decisions regarding degree and intensity of participation have been reached with some degree of convergence.

This too brief discussion is not meant to exhaust the possibilities of this issue—adequacy of cooperation, effectiveness or cohesion of forces, or potential for future development. However, it does aim to point out the pitfalls, for active policy participants or interested academic participants, of failing to think through the implications and limitations of combined arms in an age when speed of reaction and the technologies potentially available to an opponent are both increasing. In the final analysis, we are rapidly approaching the advent of a new type of warfare. This is one in which conventional concepts of force coordination and the application of high technology to achieve strategic objectives will need to be blended with effective land, air, and sea power, and one in which the forces of willing allies will be incorporated to preserve the peace and prosperity on which the world so much depends.

PART IV

MODERNIZATION/INNOVATION/
SOCIETAL CHALLENGES

INTRODUCTION

The final section of this volume focuses on additional challenges that naval forces will face in preparing for twenty-first-century operations. Here these challenges are divided into two categories: first, innovation and modernization; and second, societal concerns.

Dr. Andrew F. Krepinevich Jr., Mr. William D. O'Neil, and Vice Admiral Conrad C. Lautenbacher Jr. examine the modernization and innovation requirements of naval forces for the next century. As executive director of the Center for Strategy and Budgetary Assessments, Krepinevich notes that the Navy's strike capabilities are not likely to be sustained at even today's level of effectiveness unless it can meet the challenges presented by increasingly capable third world military systems. To do this, the Navy will have to expand its emphasis on conducting long-range precision strikes and defending the fleet from the threat of submarines, mines, and antiship missiles.

If the Navy assumes that future armed conflict at sea will be similar to what it was during the cold war, this will result in very little operational flexibility. It seems prudent, argues Krepinevich, for the Navy to begin the transition to a more "distributed fleet" made up of carriers, arsenal ships, and Trident submarines. Vigorous experimentation and innovation must take place to determine the optimal mix of these forces. If the Navy is unwilling or unable to invest in a "distributed capital ship strike architecture," and carriers become progressively more vulnerable, Krepinevich warns that the worst-case scenario could be catastrophic.

Vice Admiral Lautenbacher, deputy chief of naval operations for resources, warfare requirements, and assessments, believes America's Navy is in a period of rapid intellectual and technological evolution. As a result, many new concepts have emerged over the last five years. New programs have been funded to implement these concepts. The objective, according to Lautenbacher, has been twofold: first, to maintain a force that will excel across the spectrum of operations; and second, to leverage technological capabilities to achieve this level of engagement with a smaller number of affordable units, all of which can perform multiple tasks and transition from one mission to another.

Future investments in modernization by the Navy must focus on what the chairman of the Joint Chiefs of Staff calls "full-spectrum dominance." This means that every combatant ship must be part of a "distributed network of firepower." Furthermore, central to how the Navy plans to fight in the future will be the ability to pass ever-expanding volumes of information rapidly to all levels, to use this information to make well-informed, effective command decisions, and to act faster than any opponent can react. This level of connectivity will move the Navy, asserts Lautenbacher, from its platform-centric past to its network-centric future.

The Navy knows where it needs to go in the twenty-first century. Its speed in achieving the objectives set out by Lautenbacher will only be limited, he believes, by the availability of resources. It is precisely this issue that is of concern to William D. O'Neil, vice president of the Center for Naval Analyses. He notes that workforces in industrialized nations are projected to remain at existing levels or to decrease (except for the United States, which will have a moderate increase) over the period to 2050. Productivity growth in these nations has been low for twenty-five years, and the data do not suggest that it will improve in the near term. Consequently, with good policies well applied, China and others with moderate population growth could close much of the labor productivity gap.

O'Neil explores the implications of these projections. With large workforces and growing productivity, China and other Asian nations are likely to grow much richer relative to the industrialized nations, including the United States and its major allies. Consequently, the twenty-first century will see a great deal of wealth created, but an increasing portion of it will lie outside the United States. As increasingly powerful destabilizing forces emerge and seek to dominate key regions of the world, O'Neil warns that this has important ramifications for U.S. military modernization and innovation initiatives.

The final three chapters examine societal challenges that may affect the development of naval forces for twenty-first-century operations. Dr. Harvey M. Sapolsky, director of the Security Studies Program at MIT, examines an important societal issue—casualty intolerance in distant conflicts. He observes that America is the most powerful nation on Earth but that it also is the most constrained. It cannot be outspent, outproduced, or outresearched when it comes to military might. It has the best equipment and the best-trained and the best-led forces. And yet, it is easy to thwart. Why?

According to Sapolsky, because no opponent really challenges the United States as the Soviet Union once did, the threats today are so distant from our national survival that we demand very clean fights. In other words, we want no American casualties, no civilian casualties, and hardly any dead enemy soldiers. We want to "neutralize" the leaders, not the followers. There cannot be any sunk ships, lost battles, or unintended results. The cameras are always rolling when we fight.

These constraints and how to take advantage of them through asymmetrical means are understood by potential opponents. The effectiveness of their strategy has already been demonstrated and we can anticipate future actions to include: surrounding themselves with innocents, preferably in a city; showing the horror of cluster weapons and phosphorous shells to as many film crews as possible; killing a few American service personnel, but not too many at one time; making the United States think it will be a long, nasty fight requiring a vast, sustained response; suggesting they have more willing eighteen-year-olds than we do; and making the United States wonder why this is its fight and not someone else's.

These and other asymmetrical tactics described earlier in this volume by Peters, Dunlap, Shultz, and Coll, and highlighted here by Sapolsky, point to the kinds of unconventional challenges the United States will increasingly face in twenty-first-century conflicts. In this environment, will our troops be prepared for adversaries who have no intention of fighting on our terms but will select means we find both perplexing and abhorrent? Furthermore, in these situations, should our combat forces include women? This question is addressed by Captain Rosemary Bryant Mariner, the first woman to command an operational aviation squadron and the first to be selected for major aviation shore command.

Captain Mariner begins by raising several questions. What does it mean to be an American warrior? What is the operative warrior ethic of our armed forces and how is it taught? Are American women "warriors" in the same category as men are, or are women and warriors mutually exclusive terms? What does this all have to do with the common defense of the United States and twenty-first-century conflicts? Mariner makes clear at the beginning that she is not attempting to destroy the warrior spirit, but is trying to examine the issue of women in the military through the lens of that warrior ethic.

In terms of an American warrior, she makes the point that a crucial element of the American warrior ethic is the principle of absolute primacy of civilian control. The American military is not just a warrior, it is a guardian class of citizen defenders and one that holds allegiance to a set of principles that are designed to prevent tyranny.

Turning to women in the military, Mariner points out that women have always "been in combat" and that the repeal of the combat aviation exclusion laws for the Air Force and the Navy occurred as a result of women's service in the Gulf War and not as a result of the Tailhook scandal. The arguments by proponents and opponents of women in combat are ultimately irrelevant because the fundamental issue is this: "are men and women equal human beings first and thus participate in society as individuals, or does gender override individual accountability and thus participation is predicated by group membership?" Mariner asserts that it is the former and that participation extends to the defense of the American polity against adversaries in combat.

She contends that acknowledgment of women as full citizens is an affirmation that men and women are equal human beings first with the same individual rights. Therefore, this should also apply to women's participation in the military, and women should be judged on individual ability and aptitude just as men are—all of which is consistent with the principles laid out in the Constitution and the tradition of citizen armies, and enhances common defense. This is the American basis for civil-military relations.

In the final essay, Mr. Thomas E. Ricks, former Pentagon correspondent for the *Wall Street Journal* and currently writing for the *Washington Post*, believes he detects a breakdown—a growing rift—between citizens and soldiers. What is causing this divide? Ricks asserts it has to do with the growing political views of those in the armed services. Relying on some survey data, he finds important changes in outlook between 1976 and 1996. In this earlier period, over half of those in uniform who were interviewed saw themselves as independent or nonpartisan. Today, only one in four claims to hold neutral political views. In other words, only 25 percent now identify themselves as neither Democrat nor Republican, liberal nor conservative.

This is not all that the survey data reveals, cautions Ricks. Partisanship has become highly skewed. In 1976 the conservative-liberal ratio was four to one, but now it is twenty-three to one. In other words, those in the military increasingly identify themselves as conservative in political outlook. He also finds that many in the military see weaknesses in aspects of American society, such as a breakdown in values. As institutions, the armed services are rejecting these weaknesses.

Ricks sees danger in these trends and worries that the shift from a nonpartisan outlook to one in which soldiers express political preferences will lead to the "politicization of the officer corps" and to "military ineffectiveness." Furthermore, promotion up the chain of command could come to be based on political preference rather than merit and skill. Officers will oppose policy by using improper modes and styles of dissent. All of this might turn the American armed services into a "banana republic military." They will no longer be responsive to civilian control but will act as their own interest group.

In sum, Ricks raises worrisome questions about the endurance of American civil-military relations. However, to date, the fact that soldiers express political preferences (not unlike those of many of the civilians they have taken an oath to defend until death) does not seem to have undermined civilian control of the armed services. Our constitutional principles remain firm. Still, Ricks cautions that the growing rift may widen as the military becomes smaller and separated from society. What impact will this have on policy and operations, he wonders.

The differing views on innovation, modernization, and societal challenges put forward in this section touch on some of the complex questions and debates over naval operations in the twenty-first century. Each adds another dimension to the issues at hand and further highlights the need for an integrated effort on the part of civilian and military leaders to most effectively meet the challenges that lie ahead.

THE IMPACT OF PRECISION WEAPONRY

Andrew F. Krepinevich Jr.

Crisis: The Strait of Hormuz

Consider the following scenario, set some fifteen years in the future. The president of the United States is meeting with her National Security Council to consider military options aimed at stabilizing the escalating crisis in the Persian Gulf. The crisis began in November 2014, when the Iranian government executed a plan to confront the West by blocking the Strait of Hormuz and holding Saudi and other Gulf oil state production facilities at risk.

Washington's long-time suspicions regarding the Iranian nuclear weapons program were not without foundation. By the fall of 2014, the U.S. intelligence community suspects that Iran possessed a clandestine inventory of up to eight nuclear weapons and nearly fourteen hundred ballistic missiles. The Iranian military also boasted over twelve hundred cruise missile systems (including several hundred low-observable missiles), over eight hundred precision-guided munitions (PGMs) (for example, laser and optically guided bombs), and wide access to commercial and national satellite networks. Iran also possessed significant chemical munitions stocks, nearly seven thousand antiship mines (some quite advanced), and substantial quantities of late-generation legacy systems (for example, tanks, aircraft, surface warships), including five diesel submarines capable of conducting clandestine mine-seeding operations.

On 6 November 2014, Iranian ballistic and cruise missile forces were dispersed. Mine seeding of the Strait of Hormuz commenced. Iranian submarines began their "underwatch" patrols of the mine fields and antiship cruise missile batteries were positioned along the approaches to the strait. Iran's small air force, equipped primarily with PGMs and antiship missiles, also was dispersed.

The Iranian leadership moved to deep underground shelters for its protection. Essential communications and data flows were handled by fiber-optic landlines or through satellite "subscriber" services on systems like Iridium and Teledesic. Overhead reconnaissance was provided by commercial satellite services augmented by Russian satellites. Global positioning data were available both from the U.S. Global Positioning System (GPS) and the Russian Glonass system.

On 9 November, having deployed its forces to their wartime positions, the Iranian leadership announced the conditions that must be met before the straits would be reopened and the flow of oil resumed: All Western forces must depart from the region (that is, the U.S. support forces in Kuwait and Saudi Arabia); Saudi Arabia and the other Gulf states must substantially curtail their oil and gas production; and tankers transiting the Strait of Hormuz must pay a transit fee to Iran.

The Iranian leadership believed that, if they could achieve these objectives, the key, enduring effect would be to make the Saudi Kingdom and the Gulf Cooperation Council states wards of Tehran. Recalling the Gulf War, Tehran issued a warning to all states in the region: cooperation with any powers "external to the region" will lead to "dire consequences" being visited on the cooperating state. Several options were open to Iran in making good on this threat: it might employ weapons of mass destruction or conduct precision strikes on oil and gas fields in the region. Iran's hope was that these threats would deter potential U.S. allies, especially those within the region.

Back in Washington, the president is concerned about the risks posed to deploying U.S. ground and tactical air forces because all major in-theater ports and airfields are well within range of the Iranian military's distributed force of ballistic and low-observable cruise missiles. Tehran's access to third-party commercial satellites enables its military to plot the movement of U.S. forces in and around the strait. Washington faces the dilemma of allowing its forces to be observed in this manner or of attempting to deny this information to the Iranians. This would require convincing the governments of national satellite systems and the multinational corporations that control commercial satellite constellations to cease providing satellite information to Iran. Additionally Washington would have to shut down certain portions of its Global Positioning System data links, which have become indispensable for a variety of commercial activities. Other options involve employing electronic warfare against the satellites. The United States possesses no specific capability for attacking the satellites themselves.

The scenario described above illustrates the very different kind of challenge U.S. power-projection forces may face in the future from what they experienced during the Gulf War and that animated planning in the Defense Department's *Quadrennial Defense Review*. In particular, this scenario represents an Iran that has taken a very different path than that chosen by Iraq in 1990.

This chapter examines the potential impact the emerging military revolution could have on the character of naval warfare and on the potential challenges the U.S. Navy will face in light of its shift toward operations in the littoral. The chapter begins with a discussion of the changing character of conflict. Next, a description of the emerging antiaccess challenge is provided, with particular emphasis on important enabling technologies. The chapter then concludes with an assessment of the implications of the foregoing for U.S. Navy operations and suggests directions for future research.

The Military Revolution and the Emerging Threat Environment

Throughout the cold war, the U.S. Navy was an important instrument of American foreign policy. The Navy projected presence away from home shores, serving to deter prospective enemies while reassuring alliance partners. The frequent deployments of carrier task force groups also provided rapid response in times of crisis.

In the assessment that took place after the 1991 collapse of the Soviet Union, the Navy accorded primary focus in the post–cold war period to littoral operations. This stems from its recognition that there simply is no "blue-water" enemy fleet to sink, nor is there any naval competitor on the horizon that could be envisioned as possessing the ambition and the capability to challenge the U.S. Navy directly for command of the sea. It also reflects the Navy's rapidly increasing potential to influence the land battle.

The recognition of U.S. naval preeminence has not, however, eliminated any prospect of competition with emerging regional powers. Although potential third world aggressors have little capability to challenge the U.S. Navy on the open seas, they will increasingly have the potential to deny U.S. forces access to in-theater bases and littoral waters.

The Emerging Antiaccess Challenge

The international postmortem that occurred in the aftermath of the Gulf War indicates that many states believe that the measures of military power have changed. A number of regional powers have channeled a growing percentage of their resources toward a few critical areas (such as precision-guided munitions; increasingly cheap command, control, communications, computers, intelligence, surveillance, and reconnaissance assets; and advanced surface-to-surface missiles), rather than revamping their military capabilities across the board along traditional cold war lines. Potential U.S. competitors seem inclined to adopt asymmetrical counters to the "American" style of warfare. Chinese military theorists are now writing about a future antiaccess environment, dominated by subsurface forces, to include submarines, undersea mine-laying robots, and seabed military bases, while the Iranian government appears to be focusing on weapons of mass destruction, ballistic missiles, and long-range aircraft for power projection in the region, and improved air defenses.[1]

Missiles. Third world rogue states are acquiring the means to strike targets at far greater distances and with greater precision than they could just a few years ago. The relatively primitive Scud ballistic missiles employed by the Iraqis during the Gulf War are being supplanted by missiles of greater range and accuracy. For example, North Korea possesses a growing number of such systems, which it not only produces but exports as well. Iran has provided financial support for Pyongyang's missile programs since the mid-1980s, and both Iran and Syria have test-fired North Korean-made ballistic missiles in recent years.[2]

But this is just the tip of the iceberg. More than twenty nations (including Iran, Iraq, Syria, North Korea, and Libya) have ballistic missiles. Moreover, more than a score of countries possess or are developing weapons of mass destruction (WMD)—nuclear, chemical, or biological weapons.[3]

Over forty third world militaries now possess antiship cruise missiles (ASCMs), which can be launched from land, aircraft, ships, or submarines. While not cheap, these missiles have been used to devastating effect in recent years. For instance, during the 1982 Falklands War, Argentine Exocet missiles caused substantial damage to the Royal Navy. In 1987, when the U.S. Navy escorted reflagged Kuwaiti oil tankers in the Persian Gulf during the Iran-Iraq War, another Exocet, fired by Iraq, severely damaged the USS *Stark*, killing thirty-seven members of her crew.[4]

Iran seems particularly enamored of ASCMs. One commander of U.S. naval forces in the region has expressed concern that, over time, Iran's acquisition of an increasingly capable inventory of ASCMs, when combined with its attack submarines, ballistic missiles, and antiship mines, could make the fleet's job "a lot tougher."[5]

If they can be detected by the enemy, surface combatants will likely exhibit greater vulnerability to the high-velocity, sea-skimming weapons increasingly available on the international arms market. This is especially true for those surface combatants operating in littoral areas, where warning times are likely to be far shorter than for those combatants operating far out at sea. Over time, as the stockpiles of these weapons increase, the fleet will confront the problem of defending against saturation attacks of ASCMs.

Mines.   Mines have long posed a vexing challenge for the Navy. Of the eighteen Navy ships seriously damaged in operations since 1950, fourteen were stricken by mines. According to Navy lore, after enemy mines stalled the amphibious assault at Wonson during the Korean War, a disgruntled U.S. admiral observed that "we lost control of the seas to an enemy without a navy, using World War I weapons deployed from vessels that were built before the time of Christ."[6]

Things have not changed significantly since then. Antiship mines in the Persian Gulf during Operation Desert Storm hampered sealift, fire support, and other operations and were an important factor in preventing an amphibious landing of Kuwait. Three U.S. ships struck mines in the open waters of the Persian Gulf. The combined damage to the USS *Princeton* and the USS *Tripoli* was about $21.6 million, while the cost of the two mines that sunk them was $11,500. The effectiveness of antiship mines in the Gulf War has not gone unnoticed. Since 1991, worldwide production of sea mines has increased about 50 percent. Today, there are nearly fifty navies capable of laying mines, over thirty nations manufacturing mines, and more than twenty nations exporting mines.[7]

Most of the world's mines are tethered contact mines of a kind that has been in existence since the beginning of the century. During its 1980–88 war with Iraq, Iran deployed Russian-made mines (some purchased through North Korea) using pre–World War I technology. These types of mines were also used by Iraq during the Gulf War. Now, however, about 30 percent of the world's mine stockpile is composed of so-called "smart" mines. These mines are remotely activated by sensing the target's acoustic, magnetic, pressure, underwater electrical potential (UEP) or extremely low-frequency electromagnetic (ELFE) signatures, either singly or in combination. These mines can distinguish decoys and can be set to respond to the signatures of specific types of ships or submarines, and, theoretically, even individual vessels. The Russians are developing underwater rocket-powered torpedoes and continental-shelf mines for use against submarines in 60–300m of water. These mines can be deployed from ships, helicopters, airplanes, and submarines.

Submarines. Conventional submarine sales are expected to double over the next decade, with an estimated sixty submarines being bought by twenty countries from shipbuilding firms in the former Soviet Union, Sweden, Germany, Australia, and Italy. The Navy has voiced concerns over the Russian military's continued emphasis on submarines, despite its obvious resource difficulties. These concerns center, in part, on Russia's willingness to sell its sophisticated submarines to any country with the money to pay for them. At 8 percent of total military exports, Russian naval equipment might not seem a significant proliferation problem, unless one considers the fact that the newest generation of Russian Kilo-class diesel submarines STET are ostensibly some of the quietest in the world.

Although SSKs are relatively slow and easily spotted during long voyages, they are well-suited to operations in the littoral. Indeed, until recently, U.S. sonar designs for submarine detection were optimized for blue-water environments. The proliferation of submarine technology and the reorientation of Naval operations to the littoral have highlighted the limitations of traditional deep-water active and passive antisubmarine sonar. Used in the littoral, sonar effectiveness is hampered both by extensive background noise levels and by the contours of the sea floor. As a result of this technological shortfall, diesel submarines could provide important stealthy mine-laying capabilities and serve as antisurface vessel warfare platforms.

Implications for U.S. Strategy

As competitors erect antiaccess barriers, U.S. forces, as currently constituted, will find themselves increasingly at risk, whether they are forward deployed or attempting to deploy into theater. Although the U.S. Navy views its forward-presence forces both as a means to deter would-be enemies and to reassure allies and friends, this could change, perhaps markedly. As both great powers and regional "rogue" states acquire ever-greater numbers of long-range strike capabilities, dramatically more effective munitions, and far more sophisticated C4ISR assets, ships operating in the littoral may well become increasingly vulnerable. Eventually, barring dramatic improvements in missile defenses, the ever-increasing engagement envelopes and strike capabilities of major powers and rogue states alike will put at risk the access of U.S. ground and land-based air forces to major ports and airfields within a theater of operations. As former U.S. Air Force Chief of Staff General Ronald Fogleman observed, "Saturation ballistic missile attacks against littoral forces, ports, airfields, storage facilities, and staging areas could make it extremely costly to project U.S. forces into a disputed theater, much less carry out operations to defeat a well-armed aggressor. Simply the threat of such enemy missile attacks might deter the U.S. and coalition partners from responding to aggression in the first instance."[8]

Preparing For The Future Threat Environment

How might the Navy meet the antiaccess challenge? One option might be to surround U.S. carrier task forces with ever-thicker arrays of defenses. This might prove an effective short-term solution. However, eventually the fleet will encounter the problem of large numbers of missiles and the need for fleet defenses under these conditions. Over the longer term, a solution may be found along a different path, one that relies less on marginal improvements to existing capabilities, and, instead, exploits rapidly emerging technologies and capabilities to develop a dramatically different solution to this prospective operational challenge. Given existing resource constraints and the opportunities offered by an emerging military revolution, the Navy has both fiscal and warfighting reasons to begin reducing its emphasis on carriers and increasing its emphasis on distributing its warfighting among all of the platforms in the U.S. defense arsenal. Fortunately, the service has positioned itself to do exactly that, should it choose to proceed with a strategy for transforming the battle fleet.

Network-Centric Warfare.   An outgrowth of the Cooperative Engagement Capability (CEC) program, network-centric warfare emphasizes the integration of information processes on all Naval platforms to facilitate the timely exchange of data among them. All combat systems and major sensors on surface, aerial, space, and subsurface platforms will be integrated into a single architecture for C4ISR. Not only would shore-based or sea-based forces be able to move large volumes of data over great distances, but this capability would give commanders a dramatically improved picture of the extended battle area and would greatly improve their ability to engage targets successfully at extended ranges. Sensor grids of satellites, unmanned aerial vehicles (UAVs), and ground and undersea sensors would generate battlespace awareness, synchronize battlespace awareness with combat operations, and increase the speed of information dispersal throughout the force. At the same time, shooter grids would exploit this enhanced battlespace awareness to generate increased combat power, enable the massing of combat effects as compared to a massing of forces and platforms, and thereby maximize joint combat power.

Instead of relying principally on aircraft carriers whose strike range is being exceeded by missiles and whose survival may be increasingly at risk from antiaccess forces, the Navy should migrate toward a "distributed" capital ship. Two important platforms can help realize this vision of the future: the arsenal ship and the converted Trident submarine, or SSGN.

The Arsenal Ship. The concept for an arsenal ship dates back at least to the late 1980s, when Vice Admiral Joseph Metcalf published a paper in the U.S. Naval Institute *Proceedings* challenging traditional surface combatant designs and laying out the basic characteristics of the "strike cruiser": a stealthy, sturdy warship that could deliver a devastating amount of ordnance at great range. Envisioned as a highly automated, semisubmersible combatant with a very low profile incorporating stealth design and composites, the arsenal ship would operate with a crew of fewer than a hundred, as compared to the five thousand to six thousand crew of a carrier. It also would have active-point defenses and a mine- and missile-resistant double-ballasting hull. The arsenal ship would have some five hundred vertical launch systems (VLS) capable of launching a wide variety of extended-range precision munitions like the Tomahawk Land-Attack Missile (TLAM), the Naval Tactical Missile (NTACMS), and the Evolved Sea Sparrow Missile, as well as UAVs. It would be nothing less than the battleship of the twenty-first century.[9]

Even though the prestigious Chief of Naval Operations (CNO) Executive Panel (composed of distinguished defense experts whose advice on the Navy's future is frequently sought by CNOs) recommended the arsenal ship be built and incorporated directly into the fleet, the Navy canceled the program. Although the Navy cited a shortage of funds, it has vigorously pursued funding for yet another Nimitz-class carrier and a new class of carriers.

The Trident "Stealth Battleship." Submarines have a proven track record as "capital ships" in their own right. For example, during World War II, with only 2 percent of naval personnel, the Navy's submarine force accounted for 55 percent of Japanese losses at sea. The Navy's submarines sunk over thirteen hundred Japanese ships, including a battleship, eight aircraft carriers, and eleven cruisers. Today the Navy has the opportunity to convert four Trident ballistic missile submarines to "stealthy, general purpose" warships, each having a total capacity of 154 missiles. The Trident also could be configured to support embarked special operations forces (SOF).

Battle for the Strait of Hormuz

How will the U.S. military conduct joint operations to meet the challenge posed in the scenario above? And, given the problems associated with deploying Army and Air Force units without the assurance of safe access to forward bases, how will the Navy shoulder what would likely be increased responsibilities early in the conflict? Definitive answers to these questions cannot be divined at present. However, it is possible to at least offer a "first-cut" concept for how the battle fleet might operate under such conditions.

Maritime forces might come to rely heavily on the "network-centric" operations of a "distributed" battle fleet comprising a strike element of converted Trident submarines, arsenal ships, land-attack destroyers, carriers (employing both tactical aviation, and reconnaissance and strike UAVs), attack submarines, and other surface combatants. Operations might be conducted along the following lines:

The battle fleet is led by a screen of attack submarines, whose mission is twofold: to conduct antisubmarine warfare against enemy submarine forces, and to employ underwater unmanned vehicles that can clear the antiship minefields blocking chokepoints in the littoral. Behind the screen are Trident "stealth battleships" (each equipped with over 150 precision-guided strike missiles, or several teams of special operations force troops), followed by the semisubmersible arsenal ships. The arsenal ships each have some five hundred VLS tubes capable of launching a variety of missile types.

Once lanes have been cleared in the mine belts, other multipurpose Trident boats move close to shore and begin to deploy Marine "Hunter Warrior" teams and Army special operations forces. The Trident "stealth battleships" and arsenal ships, along with small, dispersed forward-deployed Army units and long-range Air Force elements, launch UAVs with missiles capable of deploying remote sensors. This action is intended to "flesh out" the U.S. precision-strike architecture, composed of an upper tier of satellites, a UAV "grid," remote sensors, and special operations forces (those deployed by the Navy, Marine Hunter-Warrior "infestation" forces, and Army special operations forces based ashore).

Even before the architecture is in place, the "stealth battleships" and arsenal ships, in combination with long-range Air Force bombers, commence an extended-range precision-strike campaign designed to neutralize enemy fixed-strategic targets, and, if necessary, to arrest the advance of enemy ground forces. These strikes are supplemented by similar (although likely far less effective) attacks on those critical mobile targets—especially enemy missile forces—which can be identified and tracked by the U.S. deep-strike architecture. A key objective is to establish "information dominance." If necessary, forward-deployed, highly dispersed Army forces use their extended-range precision strike capabilities (for example, attack helicopters and rocket artillery) against advancing enemy ground forces.

United States forces attempt to deal with enemy missile attack barrages through a combination of attacks on enemy command and control architecture, direct strikes on its missile forces, and land- and sea-based missile defenses.

If the missile threat, at some point, begins to subside, the full range of U.S. forces can be brought to bear within acceptable risk levels. Navy carriers can move closer to shore, allowing them to increase aircraft and UAV sortie rates. Tactical land-based air forces might deploy in small numbers to forward air bases. Ground forces could be reinforced through "over-the-beach" resupply operations, and perhaps through airlift operations as well. Landings (and over-the-beach operations) might best be accomplished during periods of intense U.S. attacks on suspected enemy mobile missile force locations. Airfields chosen for resupply operations might be protected by preferential missile defenses.

Once enemy missile forces and weapons of mass destruction have been reduced to relatively low levels, operations may be undertaken to reverse the aggression, either through continued strategic bombardment of the enemy homeland or operations designed to reoccupy friendly terrain (for example, urban eviction operations).

A major benefit of considering operational concepts such as the one presented above is to explore alternatives to the "default" Desert Storm operational paradigm ("halt-pound-counterattack") as a far more relevant point of departure for a Navy transformation effort, both in terms of exploiting the potential of emerging technologies and in preparing to meet the very different operational challenges that will likely emerge over the next decade.

Conclusion

The Navy's strike capabilities are not likely to be sustained even at today's level of effectiveness unless the Navy can meet the challenge of increasingly lethal third world military systems. As shown in the contingency scenario above, to do this, the service will have to increase its emphasis on conducting long-range precision strikes and on defending the fleet from the threat of submarines, mines and antiship missiles.

Much as the carriers of an earlier era held a range advantage in strike operations over the battleship, so today these latter-day "battleships"—the arsenal ship and converted Trident submarine—can "outrange" the carriers. They do so by virtue of their missiles and their reduced vulnerability, which will allow them to operate more closely to shore than do carriers at a comparable level of risk. The "stealth battleships" can also undertake offensive mining and countermine operations, and still operate with less detection—and less protection—in the littoral areas than can the carriers.

In summary, it seems prudent for the U.S. Navy to begin the transition toward a more distributed fleet, composed perhaps of eight to ten carriers (the number that can be sustained within projected Navy budgets), while experimenting with several arsenal ships and Trident "stealth battleships." A vigorous level of experimentation and innovation can help to determine the optimal mix of ships that will compose the "distributed capital ship." If the Navy undertakes to exploit emerging technologies in this manner, the worst case would be that the new systems prove relatively ineffective. But the consequences would not likely be dire. The Navy would still have eight to ten carriers to cover at least one major regional conflict, and probably two, while maintaining adequate forward presence in this period of relatively low danger to the national security.

However, if the Navy fails to invest in a distributed capital ship strike architecture, and carriers do become progressively more vulnerable, the worst-case scenario could be catastrophic. The Navy would have bet everything that the future conflict environment at sea will be very similar to what it was during the cold war or the Gulf War, leaving it with very little operational flexibility. The Navy has wisely given itself the opportunity to create a fleet that will meet the very different geopolitical and military-technical challenges of a new era. But it must seize on that opportunity, for as Francis Bacon once observed, "He who will not apply new remedies must expect new evils."

Notes

1. Shen Zhongchang, Zhang Haiyin, and Zhu Xinsheng, "21st-Century Naval Warfare," *Chinese Views of Future Warfare,* ed. Michael Pillsbury (Washington, D.C.: National Defense University Press, 1997), pp. 262–63; Garrity, pp. 97–99.
2. For an overview of the North Korean program, see Greg Gerardi and Joseph Bermudez Jr., "An Analysis of North Korean Ballistic Missile Testing," *Jane's Intelligence Review* (April 1995) and Joseph S Bermudez Jr., "N. Korea Set For More Ballistic Missile Tests," *Jane's Defense Weekly* (October 23, 1996), p. 5. It is believed that North Korea tested a production version of its Nodong 1 intermediate-range ballistic missile in 1996. The Nodong 1 is believed to have a range of 1,000 kilometers. More sophisticated missiles, the Taepodong 1 and Taepodong 2 missiles (with ranges of 2,000 km and 3,500 km, respectively) are in development.
3. William S. Cohen, *Annual Report to the President and the Congress* (Washington, D.C.: GPO, 1997), p. 213.
4. K. Scott McMahon and Dennis M. Gormley, *Controlling the Spread of Land-Attack Cruise Missiles* (Marina del Ray, Calif.: American Institute for Strategic Cooperation, 1995), p. 12; Tim Weiner, "Cruise Missile is Test-Fired from a Ship by Iran's Navy," *New York Times* (January 31, 1996), p. 5.
5. Weiner, "Cruise Missile is Test-Fired," p. 5. The missile is the Chinese-made C802, which has a 15–120 kilometer range, and a 700 kilogram warhead.
6. David Wood, "Navy Tries to Handle Mines," *Cleveland Plain Dealer* (September 23, 1995), p. B-11.
7. Robert Holzer, "U.S. Navy Seeks Ways to Counter Threat of Mines," *Defense News* (November 10–16, 1997), p. 12.
8. Bill Gertz, "The Air Force and Missile Defense," *Air Force* (February 1996), p. 72.
9. Indeed, Admiral Michael Boorda himself once referred to the arsenal ship as "a modern equivalent to the battleship."

OPTIMIZING NAVAL FORCES FOR TWENTY-FIRST-CENTURY CHALLENGES: MODERNIZATION PRIORITIES AND CONSIDERATIONS

Conrad C. Lautenbacher Jr.

This chapter provides a broad brush stroke to a very wide canvas in its discussion of Navy modernization, its larger programs, and how these fit into our overall conceptual framework.

A number of concepts, including forward from the sea, Joint Vision 2010, and network-centric warfare are key concepts relevant to Navy modernization, which are pertinent in today's post–cold war world and in the future. There is also a group of programs that is matched to those concepts being developed and fielded in Information Technology 21. When we develop and combine these concepts, our purpose is to build naval forces that make a difference across the full spectrum of warfare, from peacetime presence to full-scale war, wherever needed.

The platforms through which these concepts are brought together in the battlefield today and of the future represent a revolution in capability. The word "revolution" is used in terms of what can be implemented from state-of-the-art technology today, as well as what can be developed and transformed in the future. These platforms will have to deal with theater, air, and missile dominance. They will also deal with power projection ashore, all of which encompass network-centric warfare principles.

Our force is composed of AEGIS CG 47s, 52s, and the DDG 51, which will continue to come off the line for the next decade. We will be phasing into the DD 21, or the Land Attack Destroyer. This is a surface ship that will be able to make a meaningful difference in a battlefield situation. It is a revolution in technology, with a very small crew (of ninety-five people); it is a total ship system, combat systems integration; and a strong missile launching platform, fire support platform, and theater air and missile defense platform. DD 21 is what fills the gap for the surface combatants in the future.

For aviation, the Navy is developing a smaller but more powerful airwing. It will be more flexible as the transition to an airwing, which will be F/A-18C/Ds in the near term, and then F/A-18E/Fs, takes place. As we move into the next century, beyond 2010, JSF (Joint Strike Fighter) will be completed and our airwings will be composed of F/A-18E/F and JSF. The F/A-18E/F is on track, on budget, on target, meeting test milestones, and a model program to this point. The JSF is in its initial stages of development and will bring to bear all of the power of the future in terms of stealth, advanced capability, and engine technology.

The Navy is also interested in unmanned air vehicles, as there is clearly a place for these in the future. A spectrum of capability already exists that is represented by long-term endurance or long-range type platforms, which are national assets. In the next few years, Navy capital ships will be outfitted with ways to control and receive information from these assets. In addition, we are developing ways to use tactical platforms at sea as well. All of this represents a significant capability for the future, as we will be connected with the national surveillance assets and all battlefield assets that are available for reconnaissance, surveillance, and intelligence.

The last Los Angeles class submarine was delivered. At present, we are producing three Seawolf submarines, which are viewed as the bridge to the next century. The submarine for the future is the New Attack Submarine (NSSN), which is optimized for littoral warfare. However, we have not forgotten our need to maintain blue-water maritime dominance as well. NSSNs will have Seawolf level stealth and will be capable in all roles that we foresee for undersea dominance into the near and far future.

It is now important to consider integration and how this relates to these platforms. The Navy is in the process of transferring to an area defense and a theater defense in the littoral, which will include an umbrella over land and important maritime portions of our littoral theater. Without this capability, there is no land-based attack, there are no ports of entry, and there will be no friends. The U.S. Navy has to protect its allies. To do so, it must have an entry point for joint forces. Naval forces are the ideal platform to bring into the theater to provide what I would call air dominance against tactical ballistic missiles, cruise missiles, and air attack.

A number of new precision weapons across a wide spectrum of delivery means and techniques are used for land attack, including precision engagement guns such as the Extended Range Guided Munitions (ERGM) projectile, which will be a 155MM-type system with a range of a hundred miles or more. The Navy will still have the venerable Tomahawk in its system, which is being updated to the Tactical Tomahawk, as well as some others. The Fasthawk will be a supersonic missile. Joint Direct Attack Munition (JDAM), Joint Standoff Weapon (JSOW), and Standoff Land Attack Missile Extended Range (SLAM ER) are all employable from our air platforms. Thus we have a wide variety of precision weapons that cover the full range of targets. It is very important to the naval services to build these weapons and to field them.

The Navy is still focused on our "bread and butter" of undersea warfare, including the diesel submarine threat and the mine warfare threat. We are in the process of looking at the mine warfare problem as one of transitioning from the old World War II mentality of mine warfare to an organic capability. Accessibility and integration are key elements of the way we are going to do business on the battlefield of the future.

The object of network-centric warfare is that we will have networks in which all of these platforms, including surveillance sensors, intelligence sensors, and reconnaissance sensors, are nodes that are connected at various levels with various systems. For example, they include the Cooperative Engagement Capability (CEC) concept and its joint counterpart, the Joint Composite Tracking Network. CEC would be just a part of that network in which the entire battlefield would be able to trade fire-control-quality information. The Global Command and Control System (GCCS) is a top-level command and control system. It is used for passing information valuable to the commanders. Within the overall operation of the theater Tactical Digital Information Link (TADIL J) is a link system for tactical data that will give all of our platforms situational awareness and Identification of Friend and Foe (IFF), just as a start. Information Technology for the Twenty-First Century (IT 21) is a system of pipes that allows us to hook together the entire Navy into a large internet. It is a set of standards that ensures compatibility. Using IT 21 as synergistic backbone, the idea is to reengineer the process of warfare to become more efficient, to move data faster, to self-synchronize our operations, and to improve what is called the "speed of command."

The area covered by our naval forces is worthy of consideration. For example, when applied to Asia, with two battle group coverage, it extends to the northeast, southeast, and southwest parts of the continent. Although some of those arcs overlap, others reach out a great deal of distance into land-based territory. The ability to either individually control those ships from a large network or to mass fire from those ships, submarines, and air platforms in the area will bring us a revolutionary capability in the future.

Finally, I want to discuss the fleet battle experiments. As the Third Fleet commander, I spent a great deal of time trying to analyze the problem of bringing technology to the user and allowing the user to figure out how to work with the equipment and at the same time build the tactics and doctrine of the future. It is important to build those things together to be more efficient. A key element is the ability to accelerate the acquisition cycle. If technology can be brought to the fleet, applied in a realistic situation, and used by fleet operators who can figure out its strengths and weaknesses, it will be possible to more efficiently discard a lot of ideas that are not worth pursuing. Moreover, for ideas that are good, this would shorten the time required for implementation in the field and simultaneously keep our forces up to date. Additionally, we have the ability to affect the technology that is being developed by the operator. This would generate a direct feedback into the system and could lead to a doctrinal revolution. For instance, thirty years elapsed between the invention of the tank and the ability to use it in World War II, as demonstrated by the Germans. We will be able to work these things out much, much more rapidly as part of the Chief of Naval Operation's goal of "operational primacy." The Navy has two fleet battle experiments: the first was designed to work in consonance with Hunter Warrior, the Marine Corps battle lab experiment, and the second, "Ring of Fire," which was completed the summer of 1997, is the latest technology. It enables distribution of fires from a centralized, or network-centric manner, in which information from sensors and the shooters were allocated in a way that made sense, were coordinated and integrated, and occurred within a matter of seconds to allow a response to targets.

I would like to sum up this chapter with three main concepts critical to the Navy's plans for the future: more firepower for overland operation, strike dominance, and air dominance. This is where the Navy is going and that is what can be seen in the programs we have today. We are looking for revolutionary increases in capability and efficiency and to being able to do the mission better with smaller numbers of platforms, smaller numbers of people, and in networked command. We believe there is a great deal to be derived from these concepts. By way of comparison, if you consider the way the business revolution has taken off with information in the corporate structure and the resulting corporate efficiencies, there are many things for the military to gain.

We believe in maintaining maritime dominance: This is not just about land attack. It is about the traditional missions of the navies of the world in maintaining freedom of the seas and our strategic interest as a nation in the oceans of the world. We are the nation's on-scene expeditionary response force, and we have to be fully capable in that role now and in the future.

INNOVATING FOR TWENTY-FIRST-CENTURY NAVAL OPERATIONS

William D. O'Neil

In this chapter, I address some of the challenges the Navy and Marine Corps will face in the twenty-first century, and how the naval services are shaping their operations to meet them. The principal points made are:

➤ Dramatic and unprecedented aging trends in the world's population will severely strain public finances, and will tend to limit military expenditure as one consequence. This will come soonest and most severely in the industrialized economies—the United States and the nations we count as our closest and most valuable allies—although other nations also will feel these trends.

➤ At the same time, populations of people in their most productive years will rise very significantly for decades to come in most of Asia, while remaining level or declining in most of the industrialized world. If Asian nations make good use of their opportunities, they will become a great deal richer and the world's economic "center of gravity" will shift decisively toward Asia, notwithstanding the region's current financial difficulties. Will the United States continue to be able to exert a strong stabilizing influence on Asia in these circumstances, as it has over the past century? Will Asian nations develop their own institutions for peaceful cooperation and conflict resolution? Or will Asia become a cockpit of internecine conflict, on an even greater and more destructive scale than was Europe in the first half of this century?

➤ The world's supplies of petroleum will be largely exhausted before the new century's close, and probably will not last far beyond its halfway mark. The world will turn to other sources of liquid fuels, but the process could result in major economic and political dislocations, depending on the path taken. While petroleum lasts, the Persian Gulf region will become even more critical to the world's economy, and as a result will continue to be a critical security interest. By some estimates, a supply crisis could come before 2010.

➤ The climate will change in the twenty-first century, at least in part because of mankind's activities. It is most likely that the dislocations resulting from this change will not be severe on a global scale, painful though they may be for those most directly affected. But there is some risk of sudden and catastrophic climate change, perhaps a miniature ice age involving significant reductions in temperature and moisture worldwide, developing swiftly over a period of a decade or less and lasting somewhere between decades or centuries. Responding to such a climatic excursion would involve enormous and unprecedented security challenges for the United States, in addition to internal economic and social challenges.

➤ Technological progress, at least over the first half of the twenty-first century, is likely to focus primarily on processes for manipulation of matter and energy at very small scales. These processes will continue to be applied to computing devices, although the results in terms of increases of computing power are not very predictable beyond about fifteen to twenty years in the future. Increasingly, they will also yield new biological products (for industrial as well as medical applications) and materials with wholly new properties. But the direct military impacts of new technologies are likely to be relatively marginal—revolutions in military affairs may well come in the new century, as a result of new concepts and new problems, but technology will be an aid, not the principal driver.

➤ The offshore shift in the economic balance, as well as sharply increasing dependence on imported oil, will dictate that the naval services remain rotationally deployed and expeditionary. But the real threats to U.S. interests will lie ashore, not at sea, making power to affect events ashore critical.

➤ The naval services have taken the initiative in preparing for this future with the Marine Corps Warfighting Lab and the Navy's series of fleet battle experiments. Only the first few experiments have been conducted, but a great deal has been learned concerning potentials and constraints. The focus so far has been on unconventional means to counter conventional threats in littoral regions, but future experimental programs are planned to address a wide variety of issues. Results to date show that sea-based forces can gain considerable leverage over stronger forces ashore and have revealed a number of areas that must be worked on to improve this leverage.

➤ The fundamental methodology for exploring new concepts is simulation, involving physical, imaginary, and virtual elements. Operational elements are conceptualized and integrated, modeling is used to predict results and select key parameters, simulation is used to explore and measure, and the data form the basis for reconstruction of the action and assessment. The key is close integration of military planners, operations scientists, and technologists in all phases of the conceptualization and simulation process. All need to have broad knowledge of the entire process in addition to their special competencies.

➤ Promising as this beginning has been, it remains only a beginning. Many important challenges have not yet been addressed.

The World of the Twenty-First Century

There are widespread expectations that the world of the twenty-first century will be one of breathtaking technological advance, of disruptive gulfs between rich and poor, of soaring economic advance alongside persistent economic stagnation, of passionate crusader beliefs and hatreds, of intense international competition, of excitement and chaos. In short, a world with plenty of material for conflict. But it is also widely prophesied to be a world in which the freedom of action of nation-states will diminish, in which their competition will be largely economic and social rather than military. Thus this chain of reasoning goes, major wars will become very unlikely, while nonstate violence could well grow to epidemic proportions.

Perhaps so—but then again, perhaps not. Before going on to talk about innovation to meet the naval challenges of the first half of the twenty-first century, I want to investigate some other aspects of what they might be. Briefly, they include:

Aging Populations and Financial Stringency

There are some things that we know about the twenty-first century with a great deal more certainty than we know many of the "trends" frequently cited. One thing we can be quite sure of is that the population of the industrialized world will grow significantly older and that the ratio of people in their prime working years to those in what are today considered retirement years will fall sharply.[1] Absent some very dramatic offsetting changes, this will mean declining proportions of the population in the workforce, increased expenditure for pensions and medical care—and thus reduced potential for saving, investment, or public expenditure. These effects will be very visible within two decades and will persist at least through the first half of the century. The demographic problem is actually a bit less severe in the United States than in many other places, but the economic difficulties this country will face depend critically on how successful we are in slowing the rate of medical cost growth.[2] One implication is that many of the developed countries are going to feel harsh economic pressures and will be able to increase defense expenditure only at the cost of significant disruption elsewhere in their economies and societies.[3] Indeed, without the emergence of some serious external threats, it seems very likely that in general the industrialized nations will cut their defense budgets over the first half of the twenty-first century.

It is not only the industrialized nations that will see a rising proportion of elderly to those in the prime working years.[4] China's proportion of people sixty-five and over will climb sharply over the second quarter of the new century, and will converge with that of the United States by about 2040. Even India and Southeast Asia will see rising proportions of older people, by midcentury reaching levels that are today found only in industrial nations. Because these nations for the most part have no established and politically sanctioned "right" to public support for the aged, these trends may not have quite the same impact on government finances as in the industrialized world, but it is hard to imagine that they will have no impact, or that these will not act in some ways to constrain government fiscal freedom.[5]

Productivity

The proportion of elderly will rise in part because people are living longer, but also in large measure because in many areas the numbers of those in the twenty-five to sixty-four age band will grow only slowly, or actually decline. The population in this band is projected to grow modestly in the United States—largely because of continued immigration as well as fairly high birth rates among the less wealthy portions of our population—but will actually sink a bit in most other industrialized regions, reflecting birth rates that have remained steady or declined over the past quarter century. If this is indeed the part of an industrialized state's population that holds the greatest potential for productivity, then it seems these trends must put limits on the production and wealth of the nations that are today highly industrialized.

China experienced a vast increase in population during the Mao Tse-Tung years, notwithstanding the disastrous famine his policies brought on. But then the regime, fearing the consequences of continued unrestrained population growth, adopted a rather draconian "one-child" policy. As these "sole children" themselves reach reproductive age the growth in population is slowing sharply. Within twenty-five years the Chinese population in the twenty-five to sixty-four age band will have peaked, and it will decline rather sharply for several decades thereafter. Thus we can anticipate a sharp deceleration in the growth of China's national product after 2015 or so. With sound policies, however, China may by then have the foundations for strong productivity-led growth in per capita production.

In Southeast Asia and particularly in India (and the rest of South Asia as well), we can foresee a continued rapid rise in population in general, including in the twenty-five to sixty-four group. These nations will face challenges in finding the resources to prepare and equip these increasing numbers of people for productive work, notwithstanding their high savings rates.[6]

A very rough indication of how productive twenty-five to sixty-four year-olds are, on average, in all these nations today can be assessed by dividing total national production by the number of people in this age range. The tremendous advantage of workers in the United States over those in less-developed economies reflects not only superior skills and more favorable social conditions, as well as some important technological advantages, but also more favorable market and natural circumstances. The rate at which these gaps can be closed or offset will determine how rapidly Russia, China, India, the countries of Southeast Asia, and other nations can expand output per worker.

There has been some debate about Asian economic performance. The conventional view has been that the high growth rates achieved by many Asian economies have been driven to a significant extent by productivity growth reflecting "Asian cultural values." This has come under some challenge, however.[7] Naturally, there are differences among Asian economies; a recent examination of China's growth suggests a significant productivity contribution.[8] There are many conceptual, methodological, and empirical obstacles to accurate measurement of productivity trends, which have clouded the debate. Much of Asia has gone through significant monetary and financial turmoil, which has prompted some to express more pessimism concerning long-term prospects. On the whole, it seems most likely that, with prudent policies, Asian economic growth should be strong for decades to come, if not so buoyant as some had supposed.[9]

The United States and other highly industrialized nations face limits on growth that differ from those of the developing nations. We have already seen that growth will not come through increases in the productive population (except perhaps to a limited extent in the United States). Moreover, the rapid increase in the numbers of the elderly may tend to depress savings rates and divert resources, therefore limiting amounts available for capital investment. Thus technology-driven productivity growth will be a very prominent factor in determining overall economic growth.

It is very widely believed that we live in an age of great and unprecedented technological advance, in which wonders abound. It is certainly not difficult to find specific examples of truly remarkable technological growth trends, particularly in the fields of computing and communications. A great many people believe quite firmly that this technological advance is leading directly to significant advances in productivity, and there are many well-attested individual examples at the firm or activity level. But broader measurements of productivity are fraught with very complex conceptual, data, and methodological issues, which are probably not susceptible of complete resolution, even in principle. The findings of careful studies of the productivity effects of information technology are mixed, to say the least, however.[10]

At the level of the nation as a whole, and of industrialized economies in general, it is clear that productivity grew at very high rates for a quarter of a century following the end of World War II. But the evidence all seems to point to a significant and persistent slowing of productivity in the early 1970s, a slowing from which we have yet to recover. More precisely, in the United States, output per labor hour grew at an average of more than 2.5 percent a year from 1945 to 1973, and has grown less than 1 percent a year, on average, ever since. Many explanations have been offered, but most can easily be disproved (although of course this has not affected their popularity very much).[11] Some commentators have attacked the methodological and empirical foundations of the system for measuring productivity, claiming that it systematically underestimates growth of the kinds supposed to have occurred in recent years.[12] At present, however, it is difficult to see how a case can be made for strong economic growth having resulted from recent technological advances, even making the fullest possible allowances for possible under-measurements. It has been suggested that the effects of the information technology revolution simply have not yet worked their way through the economic system and that we can expect strong growth from them in the future.[13] Perhaps growth in the United States and other industrial economies will once again accelerate in the first half of the twenty-first century—but for now we can only speculate and hope.

Thus there are uncertainties about economic growth for both developing nations like China and Indonesia and for industrialized nations like the United States and Japan—but of different kinds. For the developing nations, the challenge is to bring productivity up to the levels already achieved elsewhere, and they may learn a good deal about how to do this by studying and adapting the experiences of others. In particular, it is clear that well-allocated investment and application of best-existing practice in employing the physical and knowledge capital it buys can be expected to yield returns that can be estimated with reasonable certainty in these economies. Moreover, much is known about the kinds of economic institutions that tend to promote better allocations and applications. For the United States, Japan, and other industrialized nations, where productivity in most sectors is already high by world standards, the challenge is largely to invent and apply entirely new ways to produce still more value. If China, the Republic of Korea, the more advanced of Southeast Asian nations, and some others, consistently pursue wise policies, they have the potential to reach the labor productivity levels of today's most advanced nations within the first half of the twenty-first century. If productivity in the industrial nations continues to grow very slowly, the nations of Asia, with relatively high labor productivity and very large labor forces, could exceed the United States and other present industrial nations in gross production and wealth well before 2050. Such a vast enrichment of Asia would no doubt be a very good thing in most ways and would surely bring economic benefits to us as well, but it would unquestionably result in a significant realignment of strategic relationships.

The data illustrates two different labor-productivity trajectories. In scenario one, industrialized economy "I-1" experiences productivity growth of 0.8 percent a year—about the rate the U.S. economy has achieved over the past quarter century. Developing economy "D-1," starting at only 15 percent of I-1's productivity, manages to achieve 5 percent yearly productivity growth, bringing it to 115 percent of I-1's level within half a century. Of course, 5 percent is a very high rate of labor productivity growth.[14] The second scenario has the industrial economy experiencing 2 percent annual growth in output per labor-hour, while the developing economy achieves 3.5 percent. The 2 percent figure is less than the United States achieved over the first three-quarters of this century, but, of course, a good deal better than our current rate. The figure of 3.5 percent is representative of the results achieved over extended periods in many "catch-up" economies. Here the developing economy moves from producing 15 percent as much per labor-hour, relative to the industrial economy, to about 31 percent as much.

Growth in GNPs

The population data discussed earlier can be combined with some speculative but not unreasonable rates of productivity growth to build hypothetical trajectories for the GNPs of some major nations and groups of nations. It assumes that productivity growth rates in the United States and other major industrialized nations will improve somewhat from present values, while China and other developing nations will experience steady growth at rates that are less than they have recently been achieving. That is to say, it shows somewhat greater growth for the United States and other industrial nations than the trends of the past quarter century might suggest, and rather less for China and other developing nations.

This is not intended as a "prediction" of what will happen, but I want to take it as one example of what might very well happen, at least in general terms. That is, we might very well see a world in which:

➤ The major industrial nations that are our closest allies today will experience growth in individual income, but little in national product—because the numbers of people in the most productive age ranges will grow little or even will decline in these nations;

➤ The developing nations of East Asia, and perhaps in other regions as well, will grow quite strongly in both individual and national product, and will collectively far outpace the national products of the currently industrialized nations;

➤ All advanced economies will struggle to adapt to a proportion of old- to working-age people that will be much greater than historic norms. This problem will appear sooner and be felt more sharply in Japan and the other advanced industrial economies. It may present somewhat less of a constraint on the public finances of China and other nations that are moving toward industrialized economies.

What of the rest of the world? It would not be surprising to see much or even all of Latin America develop significantly in economic terms, and some regions in Central Asia and elsewhere seem likely to benefit a good deal from oil production. South Asia is also showing signs of economic growth, although high rates of population growth there act as a brake. There are some signs of economic progress in the very poor countries of Africa and elsewhere, after two exceptionally bleak decades, but it will be a very long time before the desperate poor will see any significant amelioration of their miseries. And the numbers of the wretched will continue to climb for several decades at very least.

Oil Shocks?

While continued burning of oil may bring climate problems in the long run, cessation of oil burning would trigger catastrophe in the near term. By current estimates, we have consumed something like one-quarter to one-third of all the petroleum deposits in the world during the course of the twentieth century. At current rates of consumption, all the oil so far discovered but not yet consumed, plus all that estimated yet to be discovered, would not last out the next century.[15] But, in fact, consumption is rising in order to fuel economic growth. Long before the oil is all gone, a point will be reached at which production cannot keep pace with rising consumption—as early as 2010, by some estimates.[16]

This does not mean that liquid fuel stocks will be gone altogether: there are very substantial supplies of heavy oil, tar sands, shale oil, coal, and natural gas, all of which can be used as sources for liquid fuels—at a price. Or liquid fuels could be derived from agricultural products. Moreover, it might be possible to employ pure hydrogen as a fuel, if better means of storing it can be developed. It may be that good fortune or good management will result in a smooth rise in the price of petroleum to levels that will encourage the production of fuels from these petroleum substitutes by the time they are needed, thus minimizing economic disruption and distortion. But it seems more likely that there will be some fairly sharp price movements along the way, and that those who find themselves in control of critical and scarce supplies will be tempted to use their monopoly power for economic or political gain.

The United States, with large reserves of alternative sources and good technological resources, may well resume its long-time position as the world's greatest producer of liquid fuels, once petroleum stocks are significantly depleted, later in the twenty-first century. But in the meantime, we are bound to join the rest of the industrialized world in becoming progressively more dependent on imported oil, and protection of its supply is bound to be a significant security concern for us and for many allies.

Climate Catastrophe?

There are a few more relatively predictable factors. One is climate change. Except among the self-interested and self-deluded, the uncertainties about whether the world's climate will change are over: the evidence is akin to that linking smoking to cancer. Nor is there much more doubt that humankind's activities—especially the burning of hydrocarbons for heating and power generation—are among the principal driving factors.[17] To do anything about this will take virtually universal consensus on measures whose costs will be significant and immediate and whose benefits—the extent of which is unclear—will be experienced only by our descendants. But even if strong action were somehow to be taken very quickly, the consequences of anthropogenic climate change would continue to evolve throughout the twenty-first century and beyond. And even if conditions were somehow to be miraculously restored to those prevailing before humankind's advent, there would still be change in the climate, for research has shown that change is much more "normal" than the stability we have taken for granted. [18]

Not everyone will be affected equally. Indeed, it is thought that some areas will benefit, particularly in the earlier phases. But others will probably be harmed by reduced crop yields, droughts, floods, and other effects. Those who gain are likely to see it as a natural reward for their virtues, while those who lose will be tempted to believe they have been unjustly wronged. If the change is slow, as it is thought most likely to be, adjustment will be gradual enough to make serious tensions from this source seem unlikely.

But it could be worse, possibly a great deal worse. It is now known with considerable certainty from geological evidence that the Earth has experienced sudden major perturbations in global or regional climate at various times in the past. These can happen as a result of nonlinear "avalanche" effects, in which a gradual and steady change in one or more parameters (such as average temperature) can trigger a dramatic change in others once a critical threshold has been passed. There are, no doubt, many such mechanisms we remain happily unaware of, but one in particular has received some recent attention, with disturbing results.

This concerns the North Atlantic Ocean's "heat conveyor," the flow of warm water from the tropics northward, which keeps Europe much more temperate than other regions at similar latitudes. This flow is driven by the sinking of cold and salty—and hence quite dense—seawater to great depths near the polar icepack, thus drawing the warmer waters from the south to take its place. But this flow could stop if the water at the northern margins of the Atlantic were just a bit warmer or a bit less salty—as it could become, for instance, if the northern glaciers and icecaps were to start melting, or if rainfall in northerly regions were to intensify. Such a shutdown could come quite suddenly, and it could quickly plunge Europe into Siberia-like conditions.

In fact, the geologic record shows clearly that Europe has gone through abrupt cooling cycles in the past, and there is evidence to link these changes to just such kinds of shifts in ocean circulation. The pattern seems often to have been one of a warming trend interrupted by a sudden sharp cooling. Moreover, in at least some cases, these mini ice ages (lasting a few centuries each, typically) have been global and not confined to Europe—a fact more difficult to link clearly to the changes in ocean circulation, which do not seem capable of spreading to distant areas fast enough to account for the synchronism apparent in the paleoclimatic records. [19]

Some calculations suggest that continuation of present trends in CO_2 emissions could trigger an abrupt shutdown of the Atlantic heat conveyor at some point in the twenty-first century.[20] There are many uncertainties in these models, which could prove quite unduly pessimistic—or optimistic. Nevertheless, it is clear that we cannot altogether rule out the possibility of a dramatic shift in climate over a large region or even the entire world, within the space of a decade or two at some point over the next century. Even if we knew the timing and extent of such a shift well in advance, there would be no predicting the social and economic consequences. But it seems very likely that it would wreak wide-scale havoc.

Is this the business of the naval services? Clearly, if it becomes reasonably certain that humanity's activities are leading humankind to an environmental cataclysm, the sensible response is to avert or reverse the damaging actions, rather than make military preparations for the conflicts that the catastrophe might engender. If a clear chain of causation can be established between anthropogenic CO_2 and a prospective shutdown of the Atlantic thermohaline circulation, there is no doubt that an agreement on decisive action will be forged, for instance, regardless of the political and economic obstacles. But that works only for those catastrophes that can be seen clearly enough and soon enough to admit alleviation. What about those that are not foreseen? This, it seems to me, is indeed part of what nations like ours maintain armed forces for: to deal with improbable but unavoidable severe contingencies. One reason why public support for military budgets often seems to be higher than that expressed by the policy elites, who nominally concern themselves more deeply with such matters, may be that the public does not maintain so strong an illusion of omniscience.

A Century of Wealth—But Also Perhaps of Instability

To sum up, we can probably look forward to a twenty-first century in which wealth will be created at incredible, unprecedented rates, leading to vast improvements in conditions for large segments of our planet's growing population. We can also anticipate substantial shifts in the distribution of relative economic power among nations and regions, gains in some areas and losses in others from climate change and the gradual exhaustion of petroleum supplies.

All of these things are reasonably certain: they are based in good scientific evidence rather than on the speculative philosophizing that informs much prognostication. We can be much less sure about their impact on human affairs, which will depend critically on the economic and political choices made by people and their institutions. There is no necessary reason for these things to cause severe political strains, if adjustments are made progressively. But our experience with how people and institutions have responded to comparable changes and stresses in the past suggests that there could well be risks to U.S. security objectives, and very possibly some armed conflicts.

Additionally, there are potentials for sudden dislocations, driven perhaps by climatic factors, which could occur too rapidly for any really orderly adjustment.

Technology

I have argued above that the evidence for significant recent productivity benefits from technology is not strong. Yet there is an all-but-universal sense among all of us that technological advance is transforming our work and lives at a remarkable rate, even if the benefits are not measurable in added quantity of output. The form of technological advance that is receiving most attention is the computing revolution, now entering its sixth decade of explosive exponential growth in computing power. By one significant measure, computing power has grown about 35 percent a year for the past forty years.[21]

The technical and economic virtuous circle that has fed this growth cannot continue at this pace for very much longer, at least not in its present form. The computing revolution will be greatly transformed, if not sharply slowed, within three decades, according to present knowledge.[22] That is, we are now more than halfway through at least this phase of the computing revolution. To a considerable extent, the communications revolution has been an appanage of the computing revolution, and slowing of computing progress will probably slow progress in communications as well.

To a great extent, current advances in other technological areas appear to be products of computer application or in the nature of incremental refinements rather than soaring leaps. The principal exception is genetic biotechnology, of which more below.

Because major technological advances are almost always very dependent on scientific information for impetus and guidance, and because it generally takes decades to move from basic research to significant technological application, we can have at least moderate confidence about at least some of the general directions of technological change over the first half of the next century. These include:

➤ Genetic biotechnology, which may well be in the early stages of a sustained advance that will rival that of computation in importance. Medical applications receive the greatest attention, but industrial and agricultural uses will also be of great importance.[23]

➤ Molecular computation, in which DNA is used as the computing element. Molecular computers may prove useful for some large, well-structured batch processing problems, but seem unlikely to compete with conventional electronic computers for most applications. Crude proof-of-principle demonstrations have been achieved.[24]

➤ Quantum computation, in which quantum indeterminacy would be exploited for multistate computation. If such systems could be fully realized, their potential is all but unimaginable—they would literally allow real-time simulation of absolutely any physical system with perfect accuracy. Whether such performance can be achieved, or even whether *any* useful level of performance can be achieved, is still not certain, although the odds favoring at least limited eventual applications seem to be growing.[25]

➤ Photovoltaic solar cells, which are growing in efficiency and declining in price as a result of continuing process engineering advances somewhat akin to those in microprocessors for computers. It is beginning to seem likely that solar arrays will become a practical source of bulk electrical power generation, at least in areas where generating costs are now relatively high.[26] In the long run, it may be that photovoltaics will bring down electricity costs at a time when liquid fuel costs are rising and will serve to cut the costs of substitute liquid fuels. The United States with its generally high insolation (particularly in the Southwest) could be a major beneficiary.

➤ So-called "high temperature" superconducting materials, which retain their superconducting properties at the temperature of liquid nitrogen, well above absolute zero. These materials are difficult to work with, but are now starting to show promise for some applications.[27] It is possible that they will eventually markedly improve the efficiency of many electrical and electronic systems.

➤ Micro electromechanical systems (MEMS), in which the photolithographic production technology of microelectronics is employed to create microscopic electromechanical devices for sensing or actuation. MEMS sensors are in commercial use, and it seems likely that more applications will be found. Actuation systems involve difficult problems and progress has been slower.

➤ "Nanotechnology," but perhaps not of the sort often suggested. A widely publicized vision has everything from microscopic bearings to your kitchen table assembled an atom at a time by molecular-scale self-replicating machines. There are serious problems with this approach, which no one has any clear idea of how to resolve.[28] However, the basic notion of manipulating the structure of materials and devices at the molecular level is clearly extremely powerful. It is, of course, the fundamental basis for the microcomputer, although this is a relatively coarse, crude structure compared to what nature achieves. Efforts to learn from, adapt, and apply techniques from nature could ultimately prove to be productive of materials with remarkable new properties and devices with novel capabilities.[29]

➤ The much-deferred promise of controlled thermonuclear fusion still glimmers just beyond the horizon. Whether its prospects will command continued development of this expensive technology remains to be seen.[30]

This list is certainly not comprehensive, but it is representative. It is notable that most of the items concern manipulation of materials at very small scales. These are process technologies, and they tend to have large fixed capital costs but relatively low variable costs of production, thus favoring production in large batches or runs. In this they are like microelectronics, and they are likely to follow the same kind of economic cycle, in which each stage of technological improvement increases fixed research and capital costs, but results in new products that also increase the market by more than enough to pay for another cycle of improvements. The question is how great the gain is at each stage, and how rapidly that will push the technological development.[31] In areas where this sort of virtuous cycle operates, defense users can only step back and make use of whatever the market produces, as the costs and benefits sooner or later come to dwarf the sums available for defense purposes. (It is notable, however, that the initial stages in the case of microelectronics were largely paid for by the Department of Defense, at a point at which few commercially viable products had emerged.)

Ships, Aircraft, and Armor

What we do not see here is anything with prospects of very direct effects on the kinds of large vehicle systems that dominate Navy (and defense) acquisition expenditure: ships, aircraft, and armored vehicles. It can be shown from basic physics considerations that to first order the weight and power of a vehicle capable of carrying a specified payload (or warload) for a certain distance at a defined speed will depend on the following:[32]

➤ the efficiencies with which the propulsion, lift, and auxiliary systems convert stored energy from fuel into output
➤ the power density—output levels of the propulsion, lift, and auxiliary systems relative to their mass
➤ the energy density of the fuel—energy per unit mass
➤ the strength and weight ratio of the vehicle's structure
➤ the vehicle's drag or other retarding force relative to its weight

It is a well-established empirical fact that the cost of vehicles depends very strongly on weight and power, so these are also very important determinants of cost.

Many ways are known for improving all of these factors for most kinds of vehicles, but most of them involve steep cost increases. While some of the technology prospects listed earlier are likely to yield products that will be of value in improving one or more factors, these improvements will be secondary and incremental. It is revealing that, by contrast with fields such as computers and communications, the technology prospects for vehicles are sufficiently limited as to have largely dampened commercial investment, notwithstanding the great economic importance of vehicles for transportation.

The result is that, viewed purely as vehicles (that is, leaving aside the crew, and the weapon and sensor systems they carry) the ships, aircraft, and armored vehicles of 2050, say, are likely to differ only incrementally from their counterparts of 2000 in size, cost, and efficiency. Improvements will be relatively slow, and the Navy (or at least the Department of Defense) will have to pay most of the cost of developing them and putting them into production.

At the level of the whole system, the picture is slightly less bleak. There is some reason to hope for significant reductions in crew sizes through automation and work-saving measures (although the engineering effort to accomplish this will be considerable and there will be some resulting increase in development and acquisition costs), which will allow vehicle sizes and operating expenses to shrink a bit. And some of the systems carried by vehicles will become lighter and more compact as a result of various miniaturization trends—although there will be offsetting pressures to incorporate more systems or systems of greater capability or power.

In the absence of much technological "magic," incremental improvements in vehicle weight, cost, and capabilities have been attained to a considerable extent through vastly intensified engineering efforts, permitting far deeper exploration of alternatives, optimization of systems, and general refinement than has been possible in the past. The productivity of engineering design and technology work has benefited a great deal from the computing revolution, but the intensified development effort has nonetheless resulted in rising engineering costs. There is no obvious escape from this cycle, making it seem likely that engineering costs will continue to rise.

Unmanned Vehicles

There has long been considerable interest in remotely operated or autonomous unmanned vehicles and some types of UAVs (unmanned aerial vehicles) have seen limited service over the past forty years or so. There are many proposals for advanced unmanned vehicles of various sorts, and high hopes for them. Unfortunately, there are also some significant obstacles, largely unrecognized or willfully ignored.

With no crew to correct or compensate for defects or departures from expected behavior, unmanned vehicles have proven to be highly liable to loss. Most types of UAVs have averaged no more than ten flights or so between loss or serious damage. This, of course, results in very high costs per mission and makes them too costly for any but extraordinary needs, despite relatively low costs per vehicle. The only apparent solution is intensification of engineering and test efforts in developing unmanned vehicles. But there is an all-but-universal expectation that "unmanned" must equal "cheap," resulting in political demands for low development and acquisition costs. Unfortunately, it seems likely that this will continue to stymie effective wide-scale application of unmanned vehicles for some time to come.

Weapons

Weapons are increasingly becoming autonomous guided systems. In this, of course, they benefit from rapid advances in electronics. Not so long ago it was a given that more than half of the cost of any guided weapon would be accounted for by its electronic components. But this is fading even as seeker and control systems become more capable. Moreover, the reduced size of electronic components allows some gains in weapon performance or decreases in size.

There has been enthusiasm recently for advanced explosives and rocket propellants, yielding higher energies per unit of weight or volume. This is chemically possible, and prototype systems have been demonstrated at small scale. But the costs of scaling up the processes to production volumes are sure to be immense, and production costs will be high unless significant commercial applications can be found. Moreover, the benefits in terms of weapon size and cost are much less than is often naïvely supposed.

Sensors and Transparent Battlefields

Sensors also have been great beneficiaries of the microelectronics revolution. In many kinds of sensor systems, however, gains from signal processing and integration are running into steeply diminishing returns, as the limits of what is physically possible are approached ever more closely. No major fundamentally new sensors for military purposes have been developed in more than forty years, and in physics there is no reason to expect any to emerge for many decades to come. The prospect is for continued incremental improvement, at reasonably rapid rates, as microelectronics technology continues to improve. Moving to commercial subsystems or components as the system building blocks will bring significant economic benefits, resulting from the lower prices associated with larger volumes, where feasible.

The attractions of the "transparent battlefield," in which sensor networks will tell our forces of everything that is going on over a large area, are clear enough. But in technical terms we are a very long way from being able to realize them. Indeed, it is not clear how far we can get toward this goal, given that every sensor we know about is inherently vulnerable to concealment, deception, jamming, or other countermeasures to hinder its operation. Unless very considerable care is taken in their design and operation, very sophisticated sensors and networks can easily prove to be even more vulnerable than their simpler predecessors.

Cyberwar

With limited prospects for improvements in cost-effectiveness of traditional categories of naval and military systems, it is, of course, attractive to look for at least partial substitutes using technology more amenable to advancement. Information technology is a very natural place to begin. This is true not only because of the rapid progress of technology in this area but because many people believe very firmly that we live in an "information age," in which information (most generally in electronic form) has displaced all else in economic, political, and military significance. This gives rise to visions of "Cyberwar" or "infowar," in which attacks on an enemy's information systems will have devastating effects.[33]

As we have already seen, evidence for information technology's critical role in long-term economic well-being is not overwhelming. But there is little doubt that disruption of telecommunications, or widespread crippling of computers, would have very unpleasant effects. (Whether it is easier or more effective to achieve this through electronic or physical means is another question, however.) Certainly, the activities of Internet "hackers" should serve to alert us to the need to provide protection for our communications and computing systems proportionate to their importance and vulnerability.[34]

But our reasonable disinclination to accept such damage is not necessarily a good guide to gauging its effectiveness as an offensive weapon. In the Gulf War, information systems were a prime strategic target, and intensive efforts were devoted to identifying the nodes that were critical to isolating the Iraqi high command.[35] In technical terms, considerable success was achieved, but careful analysis suggests that the strategic results were negligible.[36] The fundamental problem was that communications and information were far less crucial than planners had supposed. Indeed, a remarkable recent study shows a systematic tendency over many decades to seriously overestimate the effects of infrastructure destruction on enemy ability and willingness to fight on.[37]

Technological Revolution?

As we have seen, there are a number of current technological developments that, if they bear fruit, could have major effects on the economy and society. It appears, however, that prospects for major changes in military technology are less clear, at least over the next few decades, because the technologies showing the greatest promise and those most likely to make it to the initial step of a self-sustaining virtuous circle of development and production are not well focused on military needs. There may be reasons to expect these trends to continue.

There appears to be a strong overall trend toward less support for basic scientific research and an emphasis on research directed toward meeting identified needs of particular companies and industries. This is a result of a combination of reduced federal funding for basic research and a redirection of industry-funded research efforts.[38] Moreover, the military services in general and the Navy in particular are being restrained from shifting more of their R&D funding from basic research to more focused efforts because of concerns about still further eroding basic research. Thus the Navy can look forward to a relatively restricted flow of innovations suited to its needs, except where these happen to coincide with those of industry.

Does this endanger our security? It is unlikely to expose us to risks of technologically superior threats, but it may raise the price of buying needed forces. While there are widely expressed concerns about U.S. R&D spending relative to that of other economies, our funding for military-related R&D remains at least an order of magnitude ahead of that of any conceivable enemy. There are also those who worry about asymmetric advantages gained by an opponent who targets technology specifically against particular critical weaknesses of our systems or forces. While this clearly remains a possibility to be very watchful of, it is difficult to make a case for systematic vulnerability. Specific scenarios that are offered usually appear to assume that the opponent enjoys far higher R&D productivity than we do (contrary to all historical trends), and that we do not respond with any effort to avoid or counter the threat. If we allow this to happen to any significant extent, we will indeed deserve a drubbing.

Perhaps of greater concern is the possibility that lack of R&D will cause our military forces to fall behind the civil economy in rate of productivity growth, making defense seem increasingly burdensome in economic terms.

Military Revolution?

There has been a great deal of discussion of revolution(s) in military affairs (RMA) in recent years. The term has been variously defined, or more often, discussed without definition.

The *fons et origo* of RMA thought has been the director of net assessment, Dr. Andrew W. Marshall, in the Office of the Secretary of Defense.[39] According to him, "Technology makes possible the revolution, but the revolution itself takes place only when new concepts of operation develop and, in many cases, new military organizations are created." The way we talk about the RMA, he goes on to say, could convey that, "It is already here, already completed. I do not feel that this is the case. Probably we are just at the beginning, in which case the full nature of the changes in the character of warfare has not yet fully emerged. The referent of the phrase 'the military revolution,' is therefore unclear and indeed should remain to some extent undefined for now. It would be better to speak about the **emerging** military revolution, or the **potential** military revolution. What we should be talking about is a hypothesis about major change taking place in the period ahead, the next couple of decades."[40]

Clearly, this emphasis on operational innovation is crucial if major improvements are to be achieved in an era of moderate change in military technology.

Innovating for the Twenty-First Century

Prompted in good part, I think, by Dr. Marshall's observations, the Navy and Marine Corps have launched daring and far-sighted efforts to develop, test, refine, and institute a wide range of advanced operational concepts to meet the diverse and unpredictable challenges that lie ahead. The processes are fluid and rapidly evolving, so it is by no means possible to give a definitive account of them, let alone of their outputs, but I will endeavor to provide a sketch.[41]

The two services have separate but closely interlinked processes for concept development. For the Marines, the Marine Corps Combat Development Command (MCCDC) at Quantico, Virginia, plays the central role, together with the collocated Marine Corps Warfighting Laboratory (MCWL, formerly the Commandant's Warfighting Laboratory, or CWL). The Navy's process has been somewhat looser, although a more formalized structure is now under consideration. In any case, both services draw conceptual inputs from a broad range of sources.[42]

Generally, in my experience, these concepts evolve through extended interchanges, in response to a variety of influences. They embody a range of views, primarily those of military officers, and derive from ideas concerning technology and sociopolitical trends as well as the study of military history and experience in recent operations. Any analysis at the conceptual stage is likely to be of a fairly general and philosophical nature, perhaps supplemented by narrow technical calculations regarding some particulars. By the time a concept is committed to paper (or briefing slides), there is usually a core of enthusiasts who believe in it implicitly and who are impatient to implement it at once, and a wider circle of those who are interested but not convinced—as well as people who are skeptical or even flatly opposed. The problem then is one of amassing sufficient evidence to engender a working consensus in favor of implementing, rejecting, or modifying the concept. When the concept has major implications for service capabilities and resources, this is inevitably a complex process.

It is natural in such circumstances to want to "try out" the concept, but this is rarely as straightforward as it sounds. Enthusiasts, already convinced, may favor a colorful "demonstration" intended (and possibly rigged) to advertise what they are sure is so. Hardened skeptics will scoff at the notion of spending precious resources on any dabbling with concepts they already "know" to be vacuous. Others must weigh sufficiency of evidence against cost. This is generally the point at which analysts are brought in.

It is rarely possible to "try out" a military concept in literal terms. Concepts that involve warlike force or very large-scale action are impractical of employment outside of war, and even if experimented within the context of a conflict, they almost never yield clear-cut and unambiguous results. Thus tests of concepts almost always involve simulation and sampling, to one degree and in one way or another.

In a certain sense, this is like verification of scientific hypotheses, but there are important differences. First, the concepts are generally not presented in readily testable or implementable form. And since those who must be drawn into the consensus are rarely scientifically trained and generally come from diverse professional and cultural backgrounds, the standards of evidence and argument are not clear-cut and may diverge widely from scientific norms. Considerations of expense, time, and impact on other military needs and operations generally prohibit anything like a comprehensive experimentation scheme.[43] Because many of those who must be convinced lack deep knowledge of the relevant technical issues, verisimilitude may take on an exaggerated importance in experiments, even to the point of naïveté, on occasion. In any event, some sort of "live" simulation in the field is generally necessary, regardless of the quality and extent of prior analysis and simulation. Planning, gathering meaningful data, and establishing soundly based conclusions from such field tests involve great difficulties and complexities.

It is in these activities that my organization, the Center for Naval Analyses (CNA) makes its most distinctive contributions to Navy and Marine Corps advanced concepts.[44] CNA, a nonprofit institute that has been associated closely with the Navy since 1942 and the Marine Corps since shortly after World War II, is the only research organization with a large pool of scientists who have extensive experience in supporting, observing, and analyzing military operations in the field, in war as well as in peace.[45]

The Navy conducted two fleet battle experiments (FBEs), while the Marines began a series of advanced warfighting experiments (AWEs). The two are similar in broad principle, and indeed FBE Alfa was conducted in conjunction with the Hunter Warrior AWE in March of 1997.[46] These have by no means settled all of the matters at issue, but they have provided very highly valuable data and insights and have certainly stimulated a great deal of productive and innovative thought.

To date, the focus in both AWE and FBE efforts has been on operations from the sea against enemies or objectives ashore—what has come to be called "operational maneuver from the sea" (OMFTS). This is a natural and appropriate emphasis in an era when threats at sea are minimal and the principal U.S. interests lie ashore in littoral regions. It is by no means the sum of the concerns that the Naval services must meet, however, and many further issues remain to be addressed.

Particularly important, in my view, is the economic challenge faced by the Marine Corps and Navy as our society looks forward to an era of sharply rising demands on public finances, brought on by the aging of our population. The services will undoubtedly be called on to make better and more efficient use of both manpower and capital to meet expanding needs in times of stringency. The apparatus of innovation that they have been developing will soon need to be turned to this problem if they are to be ready for the twenty-first century.

Notes

1. U. S. Bureau of the Census, International Data Base, 10 October 1997 edition.

2. U.S. Congressional Budget Office, "Long-Term Budgetary Pressures and Policy Options," March 1997.

3. Deborah Roseveare, and others, "Aging Populations, Pension Systems, and Government Budgets: Simulations for 20 OECD Countries," Economics Department Working Papers No. 168, Paris: OECD, 1996.

4. Data are from U.S. Bureau of the Census, International Data Base, edition of 10 October 1997. In these figures, I have included Hong Kong and Taiwan with China, and Belarus with Russia. The category of Southeast Asia includes all the nations in the region, including Indonesia—admittedly a very mixed group.

5. There is some dispute about future population trends. Some believe that the most likely scenario is that represented by the UN's low-variant projection, in which rapidly falling fertility results in a significant decline in world population before very long. See Ben J. Wattenberg, "The Population Explosion Is Over," *New York Times Magazine*, November 23, 1997, as well as his, "The Population Implosion," *Wall Street Journal*, October 16, 1997. Others argue that such dramatic declines in fertility are unlikely, making the medium-variant projection (which is very close to that presented in the Census Bureau's International Data Base that I use here) more likely. See G. K. Hellig, *World Population Prospects*, International Institute for Applied Systems Analysis, July 1997. In any event, the effects of these differing assumptions on the data shown in my charts would be slight, as I focus largely on people either already alive or born relatively early in the century. The major impact on the aged and the workforce will be seen after 2050—which is one major reason why I do not attempt to project beyond this date.

6. See also, "Asia's Population Advantage," *Economist*, September 13, 1997.

7. Paul R. Krugman, "The Myth of Asia's Miracle," *Foreign Affairs*, vol. 73, no. 6 (November–December 1994): 62–78.

8. World Bank, *China 2020: Development Challenges in the New Century*, Washington, D.C., 1997: 105–08.

9. "Is it Over?" *Economist*, March 1, 1997. World Bank, *China 2020*: 17–22.

10. Erik Brynjolfsson and Shinkyu Yang, "Information Technology and Productivity: A Review of the Literature," *Advances in Computers*, vol. 43 (1996), Academic P.: 179–214. Brynjolfsson has been a notable academic exponent of the productivity benefits of information technology and is not likely to have overlooked or downplayed any intellectually sound evidence for it.

11. Paul Kurgman, *The Age of Diminished Expectations*, 3d ed., MIT U.P., 1997 (esp. pp. 11–20). Jeffrey D. Sachs and Felipe Larrain B., *Macroeconomics in the Global Economy*, Prentice Hall, 1993 (esp. pp. 554–60).

12. Leonard Nakamura, "Is the U.S. Economy Really Growing Too Slowly? Maybe We're Measuring Growth Wrong," *Business Review*, Federal Reserve Bank of Philadelphia, March/April 1997.

13. Paul A. David, "Computer and Dynamo: The Modern Productivity Paradox in a Not-Too-Distant Mirror," *Technology and Productivity: The Challenge for Economic Policy*, OECD, 1991.

14. During the "golden age" of productivity gains, 1950 to 1973, a number of developing "catch-up" nations averaged more than 5 percent annual growth in labor productivity, but very few have been able to sustain 5 percent over longer periods. See Angus Maddison, *Monitoring the World Economy: 1820–1992*, Paris: OECD, 1995: appendix J.

15. U.S. Energy Information Administration, *International Energy Outlook 1997*.

16. Craig Bond Hatfield, "The Oil We Won't Have," *Washington Post*, October 22, 1997: A21. Craig Bond Hatfield, "Oil Back on the Global Agenda," *Nature*, vol. 387 (May 8, 1997) p. 121. The specifics of Hatfield's projections are disputed by oil industry representatives, but it is difficult to frame a plausible scenario under which production does not fall short at some time in the first half of the twenty-first century.

17. J. D. Mahlman, "Uncertainties in Projections of Human-Caused Climate Warming," *Science*, vol. 278 (November 21, 1997): 1416–17.

18. Jonathan Adams, "Sudden (Decade-Timescale) Transitions and Short-Lived Cold and Warm Phases in the Global Climate Record," Oak Ridge National Laboratory, <http://www.esd.ornl.gov/ern/qen/transit.html>. Mark Maslin, "Sultry Last Interglacial Gets a Sudden Chill," *Earth in Space*, vol. 9, no. 7 (March 1997): 12–14.

19. Wallace S. Broecker, "Thermohaline Circulation, The Achilles Heel of Our Climate System: Will Man-Made CO_2 Upset the Current Balance?" *Science*, vol. 278 (November 28, 1997): 1582–88. Delia Oppo, "Millennial Climate Oscillations," *Science*, vol. 278 (November 14, 1997): 1244–46. Gerard Bond, and others, "A Pervasive Millennial-Scale Cycle in North Atlantic Holocene and Glacial Climates," *Science*, vol. 278 (November 14, 1997): 1257–66. Scott Lehman, "Sudden End of an Interglacial," *Nature*, vol. 390 (November 13, 1997): 117–19. Jess F. Adkins and others "Variability of the North Atlantic Thermohaline Circulation during the Last Interglacial Period," *Nature*, vol. 390 (November 13, 1997): 154–56.

20. Stefan Rahmstorf, "Risk of Sea-Change in the Atlantic," *Nature*, vol. 388 (August 28, 1997): 825–26. Thomas F. Stocker and Andreas Schmittner, "Influence of CO_2 Emission Rates on the Stability of the Thermohaline Circulation," *Nature*, vol. 388 (August 28, 1997): 862–65.

21. Alfred E. Brenner, "The Computing Revolution and the Physics Community," *Physics Today*, October 1996: 24–30.

22. Gary Stix, "Toward 'Point One'," *Scientific American: The Solid-State Century*, 1997: 74–79.

23. Desmond S. T. Nicholl, *An Introduction to Genetic Engineering*, Cambridge U. P., 1994.

24. William P. C. Stemmer, "The Evolution of Molecular Computation," *Science*, vol. 270 (December 1, 1995), p. 1510.

25. Timothy P. Spiller, "Quantum Information Processing: Cryptography, Computation, and Teleportation," *Proc. IEEE*, vol. 84, no. 12 (December 1996)

1719–46. Seth Lloyd, "Quantum-Mechanical Computers," *Scientific American: The Solid-State Century,* 1997: 98–104.

26. Jack L. Stone, "Photovoltaics: Unlimited Electrical Energy from the Sun," *Physics Today,* September 1993: 22–29.

27. "Superconductivity in Electric Power: A Special Report, *IEEE Spectrum,* July 1997: 18–49.

28. Gary Stix, "Trends in Nanotechnology: Waiting for Breakthroughs," *Scientific American,* April 1996: 94–99.

29. George M. Whitesides, "Self-Assembling Materials," *Scientific American,* September 1995: 146–49.

30. Colin Macilwain, "Is Magnetic Fusion Headed for Ignition or Meltdown?" *Nature,* vol. 388 (July 10, 1997): 115–18. William Sweet, "Nuclear Fusion Advances," *IEEE Spectrum,* February 1994: 31–36.

31. G. Dan Hutcheson and Jerry D. Hutcheson, "Technology and Economics in the Semiconductor Industry," *Scientific American: The Solid-State Century,* 1997: 66–73.

32. George Gerard, "Structural Guidelines for Materials Development: Some Vehicle Performance and Design Generalizations," AIAA-68-331.

33. John Arquilla and David Ronfeldt, eds., *In Athena's Camp: Preparing for Conflict in the Information Age,* RAND, 1997. Provides a particularly breathless perspective.

34. Martin C. Libicki, "Information Warfare: A Brief Guide to Defense Preparedness," *Physics Today,* September 1997: 40–45.

35. Thomas A. Keaney and Eliot A. Cohen, *Gulf War Air Power Survey, Summary Report,* Washington, D.C.: GPO, 1993.

36. Robert A. Pape, *Bombing to Win: Air Power and Coercion in War,* Ithaca: Cornell U. P., 1996: 211–53.

37. Ibid.

38. Malcolm W. Browne, "Prized Lab Shifts to More Mundane Tasks, *New York Times,* June 20, 1995; Gina Kolata, "High-Tech Labs Say Times Justify Narrowing Focus," *New York Times,* September 26, 1995; Louis Uchitelle, "Basic Research Is Losing Out as Companies Stress Results, *New York Times,* October 8, 1996; William B. Scott, "U. S. Coming to Grips with R&D Crisis," *Aviation Week and Space Technology,* February 17, 1997; Bart Ziegler, "Gerstner Slashed R&D By $1 Billion: For IBM, It May Be a Good Thing," *Wall Street Journal,* October 6, 1997.

39. Thomas E. Ricks, "How Wars Are Fought Will Change Radically, Pentagon Planner Says," *Wall Street Journal,* July 13, 1994.

40. Director of Net Assessment, memorandum for the record, subject: "Some Thoughts on Military Revolutions—Second Version," August 23, 1993. Emphasis in original.

41. Because of the fluidity of the processes, they tend not to be very formally documented. Many of the references in this section will be to Internet World Wide Web sites rather than to specific documents.

42. See <http://138.156.112.14/CDCHome.nsf/?OpenDatabase> for MCCDC and <http://mcwl-www.cwlmain.org/> for MCWL. Navy sites of interest include <http://ndcweb.navy.mil/>, <http://copernicus.hq.navy.mil/>, and <http://www.usnwc.edu/nwc/cnws.htm>. Several Marine Corps concept papers have been published as inserts to *Marine Corps Gazette*, including "Operational Maneuver from the Sea," (June 1996), "Future Military Operations on Urbanized Terrain," (October 1997), and "Ship-to-Objective Maneuver," (November 1997).

43. "Army, Navy Juggle Experimentation with Need for Force Readiness," *Inside the Pentagon*, vol. 13, no. 48 (November 27, 1997): 1–2.

44. While this paper focuses on Navy and Marine Corps aspects, CNA also plays a like role in many joint test and demonstration programs.

45. As one example, more than two dozen CNA analysts deployed to support naval forces in the Gulf War, and CNA analysts have been on-scene for every major naval crisis or conflict operation since then. For CNA's earlier history see Keith R. Tidman, *The Operations Evaluation Group: A History of Naval Operations Analysis*, Annapolis: U.S. Naval Institute P., 1984.

46. In addition to the material on the web sites cited above, see James A. Lasswell, "Assessing Hunter Warrior," *Armed Forces Journal International*, May, 1997; "Equipping the Man," *Marines*, July 1997; "Hunter Warrior Proves Concept but Feeds Both Critics and Champions," *Inside the Navy*, vol. 10, no. 32 (August 11, 1997); "Marines Look Anew at Role of Attrition in Maneuver Warfare," *Inside the Pentagon*, vol. 13, no. 32 (August 7, 1997); Jon R. Anderson, "Praise and Contempt," *Navy Times*, August 18, 1997; Marine Corps Warfighting Laboratory, *Exploiting Hunter Warrior*, August, 1997. Additionally, the web site of the command that conducts the FBEs, the Third Fleet, contains material relevant to them—see <http://www.comthirdflt.navy.mil/>.

CASUALTIES, CNN, AND MODERN AMERICAN WARS

Harvey M. Sapolsky

No one should want to fight the United States.[1] We are the world's richest, most technologically capable nation. We can mobilize more combat power, move it farther and faster, and sustain it longer than any other nation. Sufficiently provoked we are very dangerous indeed.

Our vulnerabilities lie not in the quantity or quality of our weapons, but rather within ourselves and our society. On the one hand, we cannot be outspent, outresearched, outproduced, or outgunned. Our troops are superbly equipped, well led, extensively trained, and very brave. No one's forces see more or communicate better in the fog of war than do our own. We have great redundancies in our armed services that can serve to our benefit. Opponents never know which one of our four air forces, three missile forces, two armies, and a navy and a half they will encounter. Information warfare, unconventional warfare, nuclear warfare, symmetric or asymmetric warfare—pick the type and the United States will still be superior.

However, on the other hand, our strength is complicated by our own good fortune. We live in the quiet part of the world, surrounded by oceans and weak, friendly neighbors. Geography, a big population, and wealth help protect us. As we have come to recognize our strengths, we have imposed constraints on ourselves. In particular, we have grown ever more sensitive about casualties. We are concerned about our own military casualties, casualties among the civilian populations of opponents, and even the killing and wounding of enemy soldiers.[2]

Being sensitive to our own casualties is not unique among nations. All nations love their children, but only Americans have the hubris to think that they can protect them completely while they are in combat. One way we try to do this is to seek improvements in battlefield medical care. Thus we have been the innovators for air search and rescue, emergency medicine, the combat use of plasma and other blood products, and helicopter medical evacuations. One tenth of the five hundred thousand plus troops we sent to the Persian Gulf War were medical personnel.[3] But the main effort to protect our soldiers has been to increase their lethality by increasing their firepower. Throughout this century, we have substituted material for manpower, capital for labor in fighting wars.[4] The total tonnage of explosives expended per deployed soldier climbs in each of our wars and so does the accuracy of our weapons.[5] The goal has been to increase our ability to detect and kill the enemy at a distance. We want to destroy our opponents before they can engage us.

This desire to avoid our own casualties is at the root of our undeniable infatuation with air power. As Eliot Cohen pointed out in his insightful essay "The Mystique of U.S. Air Power," we want to be able to fly over potential battlefields and destroy the targets that hold the key to an opponent's ability to resist.[6] Although we have never quite found the formula—the target set that assures us a quick and cost-free victory—we keep trying to make air power work the way we want it to work. Air power advocates promise that the answer will be there for the next war, and we cannot help but believe them.[7] The human destruction we wrought in the process of continually rediscovering the limits of air power, however, has come to wear on us. In World War II, we intentionally bombed civilian populations, but with some regrets and not as much as did our British allies. In Korea and Vietnam, we sought to avoid what we unhappily call "collateral damage," at times at the risk of suffering additional military casualties of our own.[8]

Our sensitivities about civilian casualties have increased over the years. The Vietnam War taught us that even defeat did not matter in faraway wars. The dominos did not fall in Southeast Asia. The United States remained the strongest, most powerful nation on Earth even though we abandoned our South Vietnamese allies. Our position of leadership was unquestioned in Asia as well as in Europe. We were still safe, still prosperous. What mattered, it turned out, was the domestic interpretations of the fighting—the cost to families and to public life of the casualties we both suffered and inflicted. These political effects of war constrain American leaders far more than any comparative assessment of military forces when intervention is contemplated.

I have no doubt that if an enemy were coming over the Canadian border, killing Americans and threatening our national survival, even most of my good friends in Cambridge would join the rest of Americans in wanting them all dead and would gladly reap vengeance on their cities and civilian populations. But nearly all of our military engagements these days are far from our borders and debatably do not involve serious national interests let alone national survival. Mostly, we choose whether or not we will fight and, thus, whether or not we want to kill or risk being killed. Not surprisingly, our military deployments tend to focus on force protection above all other operational goals. The decisions to intervene gains public consent only on the promise of no or hardly any casualties. Vietnam made us aware of how costly wars of choice can be. The Gulf War seemed to indicate that, carefully executed war, for us at least, could be nearly bloodless.

We want wars to be nearly bloodless for our opponents as well. In the Vietnam War we used enemy body counts as a measure of success, an indicator of progress. In the Gulf War, official counts or estimates of Iraqi military deaths were unavailable, such tallies having become in the years since Vietnam very politically sensitive. In fact, one of the key reasons why the ground war came to a halt after only a hundred hours and before some major objectives were achieved was that there were strong indications from Washington that images of Iraqi dead, which were being shown on television, were giving the appearance that the fighting was quickly turning into a massacre.[9] The preferred images were those of precision guided weapons slamming through the airshafts of apparently unmanned command and control facilities in the middle of the night. But with the drive into Kuwait, reporters were able to observe and film the realities of unleashing the power of American armor and tactical air units. President George Bush later justified the decision to end the war early by saying we were not in the business of killing.[10] If wars are no longer about killing, then one might ask what are they about.

The constraints that are part of modern American warfighting are truly impressive. American military commanders must be prepared to explain every American casualty. There should be no friendly fire incidents, even though they have always been a risk of war. Innocent civilians cannot be hurt, except when lives of American soldiers are in immediate jeopardy. There should be no environmental damage as a consequence of our actions.[11] We cannot lose anything expensive or big such as a C-17 or warship. We must not kill many of their young soldiers who are, after all, draftees or who know no better than to oppose us. Instead, we must find specific bad guys, people with names, the instigators—the Noriegas, Aideeds, Saddams, or Karadzics of the conflict—and bring them to justice, but only if not many people will get hurt in the process.[12] It is no wonder that our troops in Bosnia, where all the precautions learned from past deployments are in place, call themselves the "prisoners of peace," guarding each other and doing little else. The phrase used increasingly by military personnel assigned to our Saudi Arabian compounds is that they are "serving time in a medium-security prison."

Our enemies are learning our politics. They know now or will know soon that they have to hide in the cities among the population of innocents to avoid our attack; that they must cultivate, not kill reporters; that they must show TV crews the devastation, contrived or not, that modern American weapons like cluster bombs can inflict on civilians caught in the wrong place at the wrong time; and that they must be aware of the grim arithmetic of modern American war: kill a few American soldiers and our forces might withdraw; kill too many of our soldiers and you will likely have World War III on your hands. Our enemies must make us wonder whether or not the effort is worth the price in American lives and dead civilians. They must make us wonder why it is not our allies that are doing the bleeding and how much democratic theory anyone is absorbing while being subject to one of our bombing campaigns.

When Americans learn about disaster abroad—failing states, famine, ethnic strife, refugees—they want to help. That is why we founded CARE and Project Hope and give to the Red Cross and Catholic Charities. But in the post–cold war years, several of these disasters have become major deployments for the American military. Some commentators like to cite the so-called CNN effect—television coverage of the disasters—as the main cause for the United

States taking the crucial steps beyond providing charitable relief for foreign disasters toward making a military-backed commitment to influence circumstances in particular affected nations.[13] The process by which this occurs appears to be more complicated. CNN and the other television networks do, in fact, have an impact by showing us the human horrors of these disasters. But by themselves the awful images do not drag us into missions of mercy and reform. Rather, there is usually a coalition of dedicated advocates from international humanitarian and religious agencies, sympathetic federal bureaucrats, and eager officials aspiring to leadership, sometimes from Congress and sometimes from the executive branch, that devises an action plan for American intervention in a particular country and campaigns hard, if not always visibly, for its adoption. Getting sympathetic television coverage is but one of the objectives to involve the United States in such missions. It is the vagaries of politics and the skill of coalition leaders that determine which disaster wins the commitment and which gets the limited aid package and the get-well wish.[14] To most of the coalitions, however, the American military is the instrument of choice to do the work because of its obvious combat and logistics capabilities and because of its apparent wealth and ready availability. Once started, the missions can and do easily shift from relief and pacification to governmental reconstruction, and from governmental reconstruction to creating an economically viable and democratic society. It matters not that the military, ours or anyone else's, is rarely successful in such nation-saving, nation-building undertakings. Worse still, these ventures require the American military to punch softly and to impose order without incurring or inflicting many casualties.[15]

For the "can-do" American military, all problems have solutions (or at least viewgraphs that portray solutions), including the problem of intervening militarily in other countries without incurring or inflicting many casualties. Their approach has been first to limit American presence where possible so as to reduce exposure to possible casualties. Accommodating and competent allies would help accomplish this goal, but there are too few of either in most situations. Instead, we have been increasingly substituting contractors for support troops.

Rather than deploying active or reserve quartermasters and engineers, cooks or mail sorters we use Brown&Root and DynCorp employees, a few of whom may be ex-U.S. military, but most of whom are local or third-country citizens who make distinctly less useful targets for publicity-seeking opponents than do U.S. troops.[16] In addition, the military has been seeking technological solutions, the silver bullets that will allow us to dominate any fighting that might occur, bloodlessly or nearly bloodlessly. Thus there is a desire to acquire for our forces such equipment as sensors to locate the bad guys, robots to enter dangerous places, and nonlethal weapons to persuade civilians to separate themselves from the enemy so that the latter can be seized.[17]

Some thought that the All Volunteer Force, created at the end of the Vietnam War, would give the United States a military that would be immune from casualty concerns, deployable, and largely forgettable as were the Marines that enforced our will in Latin America and Asia during the first half of this century. But no one is expendable these days, not even the unrepresentative few in America who choose a military career when there is a thriving economy and no draft. The Rangers and other special operations soldiers who were killed in Mogadishu were three-time volunteers, having selected the Army, paratrooper training, and their special operations career specialization in order to be involved in the mission. None had an elite education or came from a famous family. And yet their deaths caused great public anguish and had political consequences. But unless some of our troops are expendable, it will be difficult indeed to carry our writ far. As the Army and the Marine Corps have increasing occasion to remind us, it usually takes a rifleman with boots on the ground to enforce our will.[18] Neither logistics contractors nor technological magic can do it. Policing the world takes policemen, now often in the camouflage fatigues and flak jackets of American forces.

In a wonderful 1938 movie titled *Things To Come*, H. G. Wells foresaw World War II, the cold war, the space program, the atriums in Hyatt Regency hotels (his atrium was in the equivalent of NASA headquarters), and our current dilemma. Fascism would be defeated, he told us, but World War II would be followed by chaos and competing centers of power. After a long struggle, the good guys win and impose an era of peace on the world. The good guys are airmen who, through an organization, "Wings Over The World," conquer bloodlessly and rule benevolently. Unfortunately, the mechanism the airmen use to subdue those who resist is the Gas of Peace, no doubt environmentally unacceptable these days and probably banned under the recently ratified Chemical Weapons Treaty.

The Gas of Peace does not exist. Our overseas policing requires soldiers as well as airmen for these difficult and unpleasant ventures. More important, these ventures will likely demand more fighting and killing than our civil libertarian values will permit. Some will certainly tire of our direction and seek to contest our self-appointed authority. They can never win by direct assault, but they will learn to test our desire to be brutal. When national survival and other vital interests are not at stake, America's reluctance to expend lives will overwhelm the humanitarian urge to fix the world.

We should not regret the considerable political constraints we place on the use of our troops. We should instead take seriously the lesson offered by the military on how to avoid another Vietnam, apply decisive force, and have the public's full support when military force is used. If we have to fight, inflict, and suffer the human and physical destruction of war, then it should be for a cause for which we are willing to pay the costs. Given our inherent security and significant prosperity, the threshold for violence ought to and will be very high. We should fear enough and hate enough to want to kill. We should be able to see clearly the connection between that place on Earth where our soldiers or Marines will fall and our streets at home.

Notes

1. This paper is based on Harvey M. Sapolsky and Jeremy Shapiro, "Casualties, Technology, and America's Future Wars," *Parameters*, vol. 26, no. 2, (Summer 1996), but I hasten to exonerate Jeremy of any responsibility for this version.

2. Harvey M. Sapolsky, "War without Killing," in Sam C. Sarkesian and John Mead Flanagin, eds., *U.S. Domestic and National Security Agendas* (Westport, Conn.: Greenwood Press, 1994), pp. 27-80.

3. "Another War . . . and More Lessons for Medicine to Ponder in Aftermath," *Journal of the American Medical Association*, vol. 266 (7 August 1991), pp. 619–21.

4. Capital substitution is a major theme in the excellent paper by Alex Roland, "Technology, Ground Warfare, and Strategy: The Paradox of the American Experience," *Journal of Military History* (October 1994), pp. 447–67.

5. William D. White, *U. S. Tactical Air Power* (Washington, D. C.: Brookings Institution, 1975), tables 2.1 and 2.2, pp. 5–7.

6. Eliot A. Cohen, "The Mystique of U. S. Air Power," *Foreign Affairs*, vol. 73 (January–February 1994), pp. 109–24. Note also Michael Howard, "The Concept of Air Power: An Historical Appraisal," *Air Power History*, vol. 42 (Winter 1995), pp. 4–11.

7. One of the most visible advocates in recent years has been John A. Warden III. See his "The Enemy as a System," *Air power*, vol. 9 (Spring 1995).

8. See Marshall L. Michel III, *Clashes: Air Combat over North Vietnam 1965–1972* (Annapolis Md: Naval Institute Press, 1997).

9. MG. Steven L. Arnold, Special Seminar, MIT Security Studies Program, May 24, 1993, Cambridge, Massachusetts.

10. President George Bush, "Address to the Veterans of Foreign Wars Convention," Indianapolis Indiana, August 17, 1992.

11. Contemplate conducting today an all-out campaign against oil tankers as we did during World War II, when we sank nearly every Japanese cargo or fuel-carrying vessel.

12. For an assessment of current U.S. foreign policy where some of these constraints are discussed, see Robert A. Manning and Patrick Clawson, "The Clinton Doctrine," *Wall Street Journal*, December 29, 1997.

13. For a discussion of the CNN effect and its value, see Andrew Natsios, "Illusions of Influence: The CNN Effect in Complex Emergencies," in Robert Rotberg and Thomas Weiss, eds., *From Massacres to Genocide: The Media, Public Policy, and Humanitarian Crises* (Washington, D.C.: Brookings Institution, 1996), pp. 149–68; see also Johanna Newuman, *Lights, Camera, War* (New York: St. Martin's Press, 1996). More typical is Jessica Mathews, "Policy vs. TV," *Washington Post*, March 8, 1995, p. A19.

14. Steven Livingston and Todd Eachus, "Humanitarian Crises and U.S. Foreign Policy: Somalia and the CNN Effect Reconsidered," *Political Communica-*

tions, vol. 12, no. 4 (1995). Note also that David Burbach is doing a dissertation on the subject at MIT with the tentative title: "Marketing Intervention."

15. See Mark Walsh, "NATO Targets Collateral Damage," *Defense News*, August 11–17, 1997, p. 6. The UN apparently insisted that any air attacks conducted at its request in Bosnia by NATO forces not involve collateral damage. NATO commanders thought the demands absurd but now seek to fulfill such requirements.

16. Jeremy Shapiro, "The Limits of Privatization," *Breakthroughs*, Spring 1998.

17. Sandra I. Meadows, "Weapons to Control Crowds Now Needed in U. S. Arsenal," *National Defense* (December 1997), pp. 16–17; Edward G. Liska and Col. Dennis B. Herbert, "Non-Lethal Capabilities Are a Viable Option in a Fast Changing Landscape," *National Defense* (December 1997), pp. 17–18; Mark Walsh, "Hurdles Remain for Deployment of U. S. Nonlethal Arms," *Defense News*, September 15–21, 1997; Col. Frederick M. Lorenz, "Less-Lethal Force in Operation United Shield," *Marine Corps Gazette* (September 1997), pp. 69–76.

18. Others hold a somewhat similar view. Note Robert D. Kaplan, "Idealism Won't Stop Mass Murder," *Wall Street Journal*, November 14, 1997, p. 18A.

WOMEN IN THE MILITARY AND THE WARRIOR ETHIC

Rosemary Bryant Mariner

In Dave Palmer's book *1794*, he describes the difficult situation of armed aggression on the frontiers and at home facing President George Washington that same year. The framers of the Constitution, including Washington, had been moved to action by the Shay Rebellion. The Whiskey Rebellion, where roughly fifteen thousand insurgents occupied Pittsburgh, hijacked the mail, and otherwise terrorized four counties, was a direct challenge to the new republic that could not be ignored. With the legion committed in the Northwest Territory, Washington's only option was to use his constitutional powers to mobilize a national force, using "the militia of several States." [1]

Washington was fully aware that the use of this option would be a direct test of the Constitution's viability. In the attempt to ensure domestic tranquillity, the armed forces could not subvert the very integrity of the document they were defending. In recognition of this point, Washington called the nationalized force the "Army of the Constitution." In addressing the assembled force before the expedition took place, the president told the federal soldiers they must campaign with "a conduct scrupulously regardful of the rights of their fellow citizens" and to comport themselves with "exemplary decorum, regularity and moderation."[2]

Contrast these words with those predominately civilian commentators who attempt to excuse the criminal behavior of Tailhook and Aberdeen—misconduct directed toward fellow uniformed members—with an emotional appeal that the "warrior spirit" demands such excesses. These situations raise some interesting questions that I will examine further in this chapter. What does it mean to be a warrior? Specifically, what does it mean to be an *American* warrior? What is the operative "warrior ethic" of our armed forces and how is it taught? Are American military women "warriors" in the same sense as fellow military men? Or as some would have it, are women and warriors mutually exclusive terms? And finally, what does all of this have to do with the common defense of the United States of America?

Given the emotionally charged nature of anything to do with military women, I will preface my comments by making it clear that I am not interested in destroying the warrior spirit or emasculating male warriors. I not only respect and admire true warriors, including the strong macho type, but I also have had the privilege to serve with many of these men throughout my naval career. I even married one. Based on that overwhelming positive experience, I firmly believe that strong female warriors who share the same values, professional and ethical standards, and common purpose in no way diminish or otherwise threaten strong men. We must never overlook the vast majority of dedicated male and female service members who are serving together as professionals and warriors in harm's way.

In answering these questions, I will start with the father of political philosophy, Plato. Four hundred years before the birth of Christ, the *Republic* described a notional Just City defended by an elite Guardian Class, whose defining characteristic was *thymos*, loosely translated as "spiritedness."[3] Because this trait was not a function of gender, but found in select individuals of both sexes, Plato argued that "what has to [do] with war, must be ascribed to women also, and they must be used in the same ways."

> Plato contended that man's distinguishing characteristic was the ability to reason, an ability shared equally by women. If properly trained and freed of child rearing responsibilities, women could be educated to serve as leaders and warriors. The concept of men and women marching alongside in battle had nothing to do with equal opportunity or radical feminism, concepts notably absent in Greek philosophy, but rather was considered Just and provided for the city's best defense. However, Plato concluded that such a state could not exist until "philosophers became kings and kings became philosophers." The *Republic* is a fascinating series of discourses on educating the "co-ed" guardian class, including all the hot button "bedroom and bathroom" issues of today, from public nudity in the gymnasiums to collective child rearing. Referring to the spirited dog who bites his master, Plato also spends six books in the *Republic* describing how to cultivate and tame *thymos*, for it can also be the source of tyranny.[4]

Of course, Plato's views on women were very much in the minority through most of history. The pervasive view reflected the Aristotelian position that women, as "unfinished men," were not their equals in any sphere. However, both philosophers agreed that membership in the Guardian Class was a perquisite of full citizenship. Twenty-five hundred years later, debates about warriors, women, and citizenship are still argued along the same lines outlined in the *Republic*. They are as emotional as they are esoteric, for what is really being argued is not the nature of war, but human nature.

A reading of *The History of the Peloponnesian War* today can be found to be as relevant as ever, because Thucydides was ultimately talking about human nature, not warfare. The familiar traits used to describe the warrior ethos—personal courage, fighting spirit, sacrifice, camaraderie, service, and a host of others—are qualities derived from that aspect of human nature we call character. They are not gender specific.

Nor are great warriors all cut from the same mold. Joan of Arc arguably had as much impact on France's destiny as did Napoleon. In American history alone, we admire Sherman, Pickett, and Patton as well as Chamberlain, Lee, and Bradley. Our Medal of Honor awardees included the unassuming Sergeant York and little Audie Murphy—very different from popular media images of John Wayne and Rambo. The reality is that the term "great warrior" covers a broad territory.

In answering the specific question of what it means to be an American warrior, we must go back to the founders and their fear of domestic tyranny, be it of the one, the few, or the many. The framers were well educated in the Greek and Roman classics.[5] To these men, Julius Caesar and Alexander the Great were history's greatest villains.[6] The mixed government of the Roman Republic rather than the Roman Empire was the desired model. They were also very much aware of the lessons of the English Civil War between the King and Parliament in the mid-seventeenth century.

In its cause against the monarchy, Parliament found in Oliver Cromwell a military leader of outstanding ability to lead its armies and win the war. Having been defeated, Charles I was taken prisoner and, after a decision was taken by a tribunal of 135 judges, he was sentenced to execution. After the Glorious (Bloodless) Revolution of 1688, an agreement was made between William and Mary to assume the throne, provided they agree to a Declaration of Rights, which became a Bill of Rights passed by an act of Parliament in 1689. This document severely limited the size of a standing army during peacetime without the consent of Parliament. As a result of these events, a precedent, followed to this day, was set of retaining civilian control of the army, which is always subject to approval by Parliament. As Dave Palmer, in his book *1794*, describes it: "The concepts embedded in those measures also provided precedent for men sitting in Philadelphia a century later. Fear of a standing army . . . no concern over a Navy . . . funding centered in the legislative body . . . command of forces entrusted to the executive . . . prohibitions against military involvement in internal affairs . . . short term authorizations for the use of force. It was not by coincidence that the emerging Constitution would reflect many of the concepts developed at such terrible cost in the mother country."[7]

George Washington was one of the men sitting in Philadelphia. To him and fellow framers, the model warrior was the legendary Roman Republic general, Cincinnatus, who twice refused dictatorship of Rome to return to his farm.[8] With this background, it is easier to picture what must have been going on in Washington's mind when contemplating how he would handle the Whiskey Rebellion as president, commander in chief, and retired general officer. His resulting actions and personal example, including the decision not to lead the force into battle, have been a primary source of the American warrior ethic. Crucial to this American warrior ethic is the principle of absolute primacy of civilian control over the military.

This constitutionally embedded heritage is why being an *American* warrior is profoundly different from just being a warrior. To this day, members of the American armed forces take an oath to uphold and defend the Constitution against all enemies, foreign and domestic. The American military is a Guardian class of citizen-defenders. Our allegiance is not to state or emperor, but to a set of principles establishing a mixed government and Bill of Rights, designed to prevent tyranny.

In answering the question of how this operative warrior ethic is instilled in our armed forces today, I will describe an incident in my own naval career. Ten years ago, when I was a young lieutenant commander jet pilot, I had a heated discussion with a female Air Force colonel from the Strategic Air Command (SAC) whom I had just met during a professional conference.

What struck me was her insistence that, as military officers, "peace was our profession," the official motto of SAC at the time. I thought that was the dumbest, most "peacenik" statement I had ever heard out of the mouth of a uniformed officer. As military aviators, our job was to break things and kill people, or support those who did. War, not peace, was our profession! I proclaimed this not only with indignant passion, but with a great sense of superiority. While I did not know it at the time, I was affirming how Hegel defined the warrior ethos—"the sense of innate superiority based on the willingness to risk death."[9]

My reaction was predictable for a naval aviator who had spent all of her adult life in that most macho of worlds, tactical aviation (TACAIR). I had the honor of learning to fly jets, including bombing and strafing, taught by young lieutenants and seasoned commanders fresh out of the Vietnam War. Every flight was briefed, flown, and debriefed with this invaluable perspective, emphasizing how to get bombs on target, keep the wingman alive, and still get back aboard "the boat." While I was not a frontline combat pilot, my bosses, peers, mentors, and, yes, heroes were invariably seasoned combat aviators.

What I knew about the warrior ethic had not been gained through any formal education—I learned by example and heard numerous sea stories. Few of these men had ever read the ancients, let alone Hegel, Clausewitz, Mahan, or Samuel Huntington. Their knowledge was empirical. And I, like all good students, was echoing what my elders had taught me.

But this version of warrior ethos had more than a little added baggage. While naval aviators had played the largest role (and highest price in terms of KIAs and POWs) of their service in the Vietnam War, there was little talk of glory. Their lessons always included the paradox of fighting a foreign enemy (including female Vietcong) unwilling to accept defeat, while American leadership seemed uncommitted to victory. Like fellow airmen, soldiers, and Marines, their accounts had an undercurrent of being cannon fodder in a war the nation did not support and of personal betrayal by civilian authorities.

The theme of unappreciated sacrifice, so different from tales of World War II veterans, always reminded me of Michener's classic book, *The Bridges of Toko-Ri*. But unlike this Korean War novel, there was a thread of cynicism and open defiance that would not have fit with the admiral's famous "where do we get such men" passage. Among a certain segment of naval aviators, there was a world in which rules were made to be broken, because civilian leadership had broken faith with the military. Which rules could be broken was never clear—it could be little ones, like drinking aboard ship, or large ones, like lying about enemy actions to cover up various rules of engagement violations. But if the country no longer seemed loyal to its warriors, loyalty between shipmates was honored. So maybe it was acceptable to lie to protect a buddy against clueless McNamara types and spineless generals—maybe it was actually the right thing to do. It was vintage situational ethics.

I tell this story for several reasons. First, my internalization of this version of the warrior ethic is probably reflective of my generation of officers who entered military service on the tail end of the Vietnam War. We are also the same generation that had the privilege of serving in the Gulf War under a commander in chief who allowed us to fight to win. Like many of my fellow naval officers, I did not really start thinking about the larger issues of being an American warrior until I was a post command O-5 student at the National War College.

Second, my strong reaction of superiority in articulating warrior values to a peace-promoting Air Force colonel represents the dark side of the warrior ethic. As the ancient philosophers and historians warned, and Oliver Cromwell demonstrated, too much *thymos* can overcome all the high ideals, cause Guardians to turn weapons on civilian masters, and lead to tyranny. Service and sacrifice are replaced by privilege and power. On the individual level, it can cause otherwise decent human beings to rationalize unethical behavior toward those they deem their inferior, using their warrior status as an excuse.

Third, any discussion of women in the armed forces today must address the impact of the Vietnam War. Women serve in large numbers in the armed forces today because the American people no longer supported peacetime conscription to man the "large standing army" required to "fight the cold war." In previous wars, women had freed men for combat duty. In the post-Vietnam All Volunteer Force, women replaced men who wanted to remain civilians. (The fact that the Equal Rights Amendment was three states short of ratification no doubt influenced the decision to recruit female high school graduates in numbers and roles not filled by women since World War II. However, it must also be remembered that the women's movement had a strong pacifist background. The "bra burners" did not support anyone wearing a uniform, including women.)

Fourth, whatever crisis in civil-military relations we may have today, its seeds were sown in the Vietnam War. Unlike the Korean War case, President Lyndon Johnson did not mobilize the reserves. Outside the eve of World War II (1940–41), the twenty-year period between the Korean War and Vietnam was the only time this nation had evoked peacetime conscription. It was conscription in an undeclared war that enabled Johnson to deploy large numbers of foot soldiers to engage in what the founders may have thought of as unwise foreign adventure. In my opinion (certainly not original), this was the beginning of what journalist Bob Timberg calls a fault line between those who served in Vietnam and those who did not, especially those who were able to avoid the draft. The military's sense of betrayal by the civilian sector festered for several years, erupting in occasional outbursts such as overt animosity toward the press.

Yet through determined leadership and committed service, the men and women who stayed in uniform after the Vietnam War were able to turn their respective services into the most combat-capable force in our history. The success of a professional All Volunteer Force was demonstrated beyond a doubt in the Gulf War.[10] In a defining moment for the nation, the American people watched on television as forty-one thousand female troops deployed to the Gulf War theater.

Which brings me to the question of American women serving as warriors. First, a reality check. Women have always "been in combat." Anyone selling the notion that women are somehow protected from the horror of war need only read the newspaper accounts of Bosnia or Rwanda, let alone the Bible. While women are invariably among war's many innocent victims, some have always refused to be the passive spoils of war, and have taken up arms and fought back. From Margaret Corbin to the pioneer women on the American frontier, Deborah in the Old Testament to Joan of Arc, the Vietcong to the Gulf War, women have fought and killed. The consternation over women warriors is a peacetime one, for in wartime, necessity drives policy toward inclusion. The tougher the fighting gets, the greater the need to expand the pool of potential combatants.

There is also a need to set the record straight on the repeal of the combat aviation exclusion laws for the Air Force and the Navy (the Army has never had a statutory restriction on the assignment of female members). Contrary to revisionist history, these laws were repealed as a result of women's service in the Gulf War, not the Tailhook scandal. In the House, even Representative Bob Dornan (former R-Calif.) supported opening combat aviation to female pilots. In the Senate, Senator William Roth (R-Del.) sponsored an amendment with Senator Ted Kennedy (D-Mass.) to the FY 92 Defense Authorization Bill supporting the House version, which called for repeal of the 1948 laws. Voting against a motion to table the Roth-Kennedy Amendment, the Senate repealed the laws by a 69-30 roll call vote on July 31, 1991— months before the infamous Tailhook Convention even took place.

Known "radical feminists" voting for repeal included Republican Senators Bob Dole, Alan Simpson, and Dan Coats. The overwhelming bipartisan vote ensured that it was only a question of time before repeal would be implemented. President George Bush could have vetoed the Defense Authorization Bill carrying the amendment, but declined. In April 1993, Secretary of Defense Les Aspin announced the opening of most combat aviation positions to women.

The common approach to the topic of women in combat is to cover all the old chestnuts of pregnancy, cohesion, social experimentation, double standards, physical strength, POWs, sex in the barracks, and female-nazi conspiracies and end with a sweeping statement that the military's purpose is to win wars. Proponents refute negative examples with positive examples. Opponents, citing the traditional myths of male protectors and manly warriors, conclude that women and war do not mix. If women do well, it is because they are getting special treatment; if they do poorly, it is because they are women. Combat-experienced military men who support women in uniform, or who simply behave like professionals, are castigated as "politically correct" wimps scared to death of "radical feminists," all of which is very interesting, but ultimately irrelevant.

The fundamental issue is a classic existentialist "either or" proposition. Are men and women equal human beings first and thus participate in society as *individuals*, or does gender override individual accountability and thus participation is predicated by *group* membership? Are American women full citizens under the Constitution, as the Fourteenth and Nineteenth Amendments indicate, or are they some lesser citizen whose rights are proscribed by class, to be "protected" like children? Either we make our way in this world as individuals first, or the accident of birth determines our place in society, the very thing many of our ancestors left Europe and other societies to get away from. Which brings me to the final question of how all of this relates to the common defense.

It is my contention that, with the ratification of the United States Constitution and Bill of Rights, philosophers became kings and ensured that future kings would have to honor philosophy. While our society is far from perfect, we have enjoyed unprecedented liberty and prosperity, always progressing toward the principle that all men are created equal. Illustrating the ancient connection between membership in the Guardian Class and citizenship, after every American war there has been an expansion of suffrage.[11]

The acknowledgment of women as full citizens is an affirmation that men and women are equal human beings first, with the same individual rights. Therefore, the participation of citizens in the armed forces should be predicated on individual ability and aptitude for women, just as it is for men. We do not take men into the military or make them warriors simply because they are male, but because of what they bring to the table as individuals. Not only is this consistent with the principles embodied in the Constitution and our tradition of citizen-armies, but it enhances the common defense by increasing the pool of eligible citizens from which to draw the best qualified guardians.

As a retired guardian, but most of all as an American, I will also comment on the nature of the current debate surrounding women in the military, because it gets to the heart of civil-military relations. When I joined the Navy in the final days of the Vietnam War, serving members of the armed forces were openly defamed by the radical left. Today, these orchestrated attacks on military men and women come from the radical right.

From fancy subsidized think tanks to grassroots organizations, we see the same old tactics of labeling, scapegoating and demagoguery that pit soldier against soldier. Only now we have the fax machine, so that every pejorative article in the *Current News Early Bird*, no matter where it comes from, appears on unit bulletin boards around the world. Few of these critics have ever served in the military, and those who have typically did not serve with women in operational roles. While some commentators debate real issues in a sincere manner, others advocate what is close to sedition. Sounding more like the radical left than the right, an implicit premise throughout the rhetoric is that individual rights (at least those of women) must be subjugated for the "good of society," which, of course, the critics get to define.

I have a straightforward, classical American response: do not tell me how to live my life. If some women are unable or unwilling to defend their country, then they should not join the All Volunteer Force. Gender should not be used as an excuse for what is an individual matter. If some men feel they are unable or unwilling to serve with women (or African-Americans, or Jews, or Muslims, or whatever group they do not want to be around), then they should not join, because America's armed forces belong to all of us, not just an elite few. And now, as in George Washington's time, the military cannot violate the very principles they exist to defend.

I will close by referring to that great American warrior, General Douglas MacArthur, whose memorable "duty, honor, country" address at West Point probably comes closest to articulating the American military ethos of this century. I do not know if he would have supported women in combat—probably not—but he did force the Japanese to give women the vote and divorce rights. He is quoted as saying "Women, like men, have souls. Therefore they should be treated equally."[12]

MacArthur is a fascinating figure, sometimes called the American Caesar (some said that if he did not cross the Rubicon, his horse's hoofs got wet), a general who wanted to be president.

Yet, in 1962, when MacArthur addressed the corps, he reasserted the primacy of civilian authority.

Most military officers are familiar with MacArthur's edict that "Your mission remains fixed, determined, inviolable. It is to win our wars." But fewer recall another passage in the same speech where he told them:

> Let civilian voices argue the merits or demerits of our processes of government: whether our strength is being sapped by deficit financing indulged in too long, a federal paternalism grown too corrupt, by crime grown too rampant, by morals grown too low, by taxes grown too high, extremists grown too violent; whether our personal liberties are as firm and complete as they should be. These great national problems are not for your professional participation or military solution. Your guidepost stands out like a tenfold beacon in the night: duty, honor, country.

MacArthur also repeated Plato's words that "Only the dead have seen the end of war." In America, it is a fact that in our next war, men and women will serve side by side as warriors. As MacArthur voiced so eloquently, being an American warrior is a noble calling. And what is noble in men is noble in women.

Notes

1. Dave Palmer, *1794: America, Its Army and the Birth of the Nation* (Navato, Calif.: Presidio Press, 1994), p. 263.

2. Palmer (1994), p. 276.

3. Francis Fukuyama, *The End of History and the Last Man* (New York: The Free Press, 1992) p. 162.

4. Fukuyama (1992), p. 183.

5. Carl Richard, *The Founders and the Classics* (Cambridge: Harvard University Press, 1994), pp. 12–38

6. Richard (1994), p. 93.

7. Palmer (1994), pp. 99–100.

8. Richard (1994), pp. 70–72.

9. Fukuyama (1992), p. 148.

10. While it may be popular for various pundits to pooh-pooh the Gulf War as not a real war, one wonders in comparison to what? Maybe we should have drawn it out for six or seven years and killed thousands of more soldiers to qualify?

11. Bruce Porter, *War and the Rise of the State: The Military Foundations of Modern Politics* (New York: The Free Press, 1994), p. 247.

12. William Manchester, *American Caesar* (Boston: Little Brown and Company, 1978), p. 594.

THE CHANGING NATURE OF THE U.S. MILITARY PROFESSION IN THE POST-COLD WAR ERA

Thomas E. Ricks

U.S. military professionalism appears to be undergoing rapid change, but this has not really been examined much. There is some talk of a decline in American military professionalism. I am not willing to go that far—yet—but it does strike me that the nature of the profession is changing in ways that have not been understood or even really noticed. Let me say emphatically that I am not talking about a coup d'état, or any other hint of military takeover of civilian powers. But I do agree with academics, such as Harvard political scientist Michael Desch, that we may be seeing less-certain civilian control of the military in the exercise of military functions.

What do I see changing?

First, I see a separation between the military and American society. This is not a thought that is original to me. I think retired Admiral Stanley Arthur put it best in his essay, published by the Army War College, in which he worried that the U.S. military thinks it has become better than the society it protects. In the same vein, I see a tendency in some military commentary to dwell on the weaknesses of American society without offering a commensurate appreciation of the powerful strengths of this society.

For example, over the last thirty years, this society has made a dynamic leap from being an industrial-based economy to an information-based economy. The rest of the world is struggling to keep pace with the United States. We now have the healthiest economy in twenty-five years, since the oil shocks of the early 1970s began to force us to begin that change. I sometimes wonder if we now have a maneuver-warfare society, but a largely attrition-oriented, industrial-era military. The military commentator Ralph Peters once said that our military talks Sherman, but acts McClellan. I agree. Who knows more about maneuver warfare—the information warriors at Microsoft, or the military officers who talk expeditionary warfare yet want to upgrade a seventy-ton tank?

I am an admirer of the Marine Corps culture. It is flexible, adaptive, and more intellectually supple than the other services. Even so, every other Marine Corps captain I meet seems to believe that American society is troubled, even collapsing. Yes, this society does face major problems. In particular, we need to do a better job of educating our youths, intellectually and morally.

But I do not think, as some have argued in the *Marine Corps Gazette*, that the next war the U.S. military fights will be on American soil.

The second trend I want to point to is the politicization of the military. Until recently, this was purely anecdotal—sensed frequently, erupting occasionally in news stories, but lacking broad statistical evidence. Professor Ole Holsti, a political scientist at Duke University, released data confirming that not only has the American military grown more conservative, but it also has become more partisan. Every four years since 1976, Professor Holsti, a specialist in foreign policy and public opinion, has polled four thousand Americans listed in "Who's Who in America" and similar publications. Until he conducted the research for his latest project, he had never separated out the opinions of service members who were included. When he did, the results were startling.

In 1976, *one-third* of senior military officers interviewed said they were Republicans. By 1996, that share had doubled to *two-thirds*. The ratio of conservatives to liberals in the military went from about four to one in 1976, (about where I would expect an inherently hierarchical institution such as the U.S. military to be), to twenty-three to one in 1996. This came even as there were more women and minorities in the ranks of senior officers and there was a much smaller rightward shift in the civilians polled by Professor Holsti: from 25 percent Republican in 1976 to 34 percent in 1996, and from 30 percent conservative in 1976 to 36 percent in 1996.

When I first saw Professor Holsti's numbers, I felt a twinge of sympathy for Bill Clinton. When he appears in front of military audiences, he is speaking to probably the most Republican group he ever will address. I am sure he is a good enough politician to pick this up through some political sixth sense. No wonder he appears so uneasy when he stands up before military personnel.

But the most worrisome trend Professor Holsti detected had to do with the decline in nonpartisanship. This used to be the single largest category—independent, or nonpolitical. In 1976 more than half the officers polled said they were independent or nonpartisan. Now only a quarter say they are.

Evidence from the field suggests these numbers are accurate. When I was in California in December, a Marine told me that the commander of his unit plays the right-wing commentaries of Rush Limbaugh over loudspeakers, so, the commander supposedly said, that "everyone can enjoy it while they work."

What all this indicates, I think, is a major change in the nature of the U.S. military professional. In *The Soldier and the State*, the classic text on U.S. civil-military relations, Professor Samuel Huntington pointed toward that nonpartisanship as a pillar of the American military tradition. It appears that over the last twenty years that pillar has fallen.

There are historical reasons for that to occur. It can be explained. The Vietnam War destroyed the hawkish wing of the Democratic Party associated with Senator Henry "Scoop" Jackson, leaving many military officers with the feeling that they no longer had a home in that party. Also, at the same time, white Southerners as a class moved toward open identification with the Republican Party. But explainable is not the same thing as excusable.

Why should this trend be worrisome? For a simple reason: historically, in this country and in others, politicization of the officer corps leads to military ineffectiveness. When people are promoted for their politics rather than their combat leadership or management skills, military effectiveness inevitably suffers. Take it far enough and the result is a banana republic military, one by definition better at politics than at fighting.

Combine these two overarching trends—a separation from society, and a politicization—and you have what Professor Desch describes as a "semiautonomous" U.S. military. It is, I think, a military that is not always responsive to civilian control, one that in some ways is beginning to act as its own interest group. The model I see increasingly in Washington is traditional interservice rivalry extended to other branches of government. Where the Navy, Air Force, and Army used to have a confrontation over budget matters, we now see that jousting extended to the White House and Congress.

The policy from 1992 to 1995 on Bosnia may serve as a good example. First, the former chairman of the Joint Chiefs, General Colin Powell, ran an op-ed piece in October 1992, in the middle of the presidential campaign, opposing candidate Bill Clinton's views on Bosnia, which was the single largest foreign policy issue in the campaign. Later, a variety of actions by the U.S. military took place in Europe as it split with explicit national U.S. policy that the Bosnians were the victims of Serb aggression. Even as late as the U.S. air campaign in Bosnia in September 1995, according to Richard Holbrooke, senior U.S. military officers maintained that they "didn't have a dog in this fight." (Ambassador Holbrooke also believes that senior U.S. military officers lied to him during that air campaign.)

I am not saying there should not be military dissent. It is clearly the obligation of the military professional to give his or her best opinion, most especially when he or she thinks his or her superiors are moving in the wrong direction. But I think more thought should be given to the proper modes and styles of dissent. As Eliot Cohen, the Johns Hopkins University strategist and historian, has observed, during World War II, when President Franklin Roosevelt overruled the considered advice of his senior military leadership and decided to invade North Africa, think of how difficult it would have been for him if, in addition, he had had to worry about how their differing opinions would play a few days later on the front pages of the *Washington Post*, the *New York Times*, and the *Wall Street Journal*.

I want to leave you with three broad questions.

First, what are the proper channels of military dissent? Why is it permissible for Air Force General Charles Boyd, while still on active duty as deputy commander of the U.S. military in Europe, to have his staff draft a piece for *Foreign Affairs* magazine that explicitly opposes the Clinton administration's policy in Bosnia? It is possible that the U.S. European Command's position on

Bosnia interfered with proper planning for the eventual intervention in December 1995. I remember asking an engineer from the 1st Armored Division, as we stood on the banks of the Sava River, why they did not have better plans, and he replied, "Until six weeks ago, we never thought we were coming here."

Conversely, why is it not permissible for commanders to tell the tactical truth about events on the ground—twenty-five years after the Vietnam War supposedly taught the U.S. military that such truth telling is essential? I am thinking here of Colonel Gregory Fontenot, who commanded the lead element of the U.S. military intervention, the 1st Brigade of the 1st Armored Division. He said two things that got him into trouble: that the Croats were prone to act like racists (this is a warning to some of his African-American NCOs), and that the U.S. military would be in Bosnia more than one year (a message that needed to be conveyed to local factions, especially to Serb militia leaders). History indicates that not only was Colonel Fontenot speaking honestly, but that he was correct on both counts.

The second question I want to pose has to do with a kind of puritanical swing I see going on in parts of the U.S. military.

There is an open religiosity in some quarters—wearing one's religion on one's sleeve—that could have unintended side effects. An officer at the Air Force Academy, for example, told me recently that if you do not attend the Monday-morning Bible meeting in his department, then you are out of the loop for the week. In the Marine Corps, there is fear among some that if you are not properly religious, you damage your chances for promotion. I have heard some younger Marine officers express suspicion that some of their colonels are "finding" religion to boost their chances of making general.

Is it appropriate to begin a lunch meeting at the Pentagon with an open prayer to Jesus Christ? Is it appropriate for the Army to ask for a judgment of the morality of the officer in question? What will happen if the person making that judgment believes that abortion is immoral—and the officer being rated just had an abortion, maybe to ensure that she could deploy to fly her attack helicopter in the Persian Gulf?

My last question may prove the most significant. What happens to a politicized, conservative-oriented U.S. military when it finds out that congressional conservatives are not necessarily promilitary?

This question was first posed by Professor Andrew Bacevich, former professor at Johns Hopkins University. We first got an indication of what the answer might be in the spring of 1997, when Senate Majority Leader Trent Lott told the Air Force to "get real" about Kelly Flynn, the insubordinate, Air Force officer who lied. I remember that across the military, Senator Lott's comment was taken as a slap in the face.

I think Senator Lott's attitude may indicate the wave of the future. It will not be the Democrats who take down the defense budget. They are too vulnerable in that area. Like the child nervously whistling past the school bully who takes his lunch money, they are only too happy to give the Pentagon two hundred and fifty billion dollars a year just as long as the military does not beat up the White House. Republicans do not have that vulnerability. If a Republican "deficit hawk" wins the White House in 2000, 2004, or 2008, he or she, looking at the Social Security problem, may be inclined to take the defense budget down by twenty billion dollars annually. This would be the domestic equivalent of Nixon going to China.

What would happen then to a politicized military? Would it become depoliticized? Or would it become more alienated, more bitter, and shot through with distrust of the American political system?

INDEX

ABOUT THE CONTRIBUTORS

Dr. Alberto R. Coll is professor of strategy and policy at the U.S. Naval War College, a position he has held since 1993. Currently, he serves also as dean. Between 1990 and 1993, Dr. Coll served as principal deputy assistant secretary of defense for special operations and low intensity conflict, where he was principal adviser and deputy to the assistant secretary of defense for special operations and low-intensity conflict. Dr. Coll joined the U.S. Naval War College in 1986 as secretary of the navy senior research fellow and subsequently served as professor of strategy. In 1989 he was asked to occupy the Charles H. Stockton Chair of International Law, the oldest chair in the college. Before that he was a member of the faculty in the Department of Government at Georgetown University, where he taught international relations, law, and organization. He is the author of a number of books and articles, including *The Wisdom of Statecraft*.

Colonel Charles J. Dunlap Jr., USAF, is staff judge advocate (SJA), for the Ninth Air Force/United States Central Command Air Forces (USCENTAF), Shaw Air Force Base, South Carolina, a position he assumed in July 1998. He was SJA at the U.S. Strategic Command in Omaha, Nebraska, from 1995 to 1998. In 1994, following Iraqi troop movements near the Kuwait border, he deployed to Saudi Arabia in support of Operation Vigilant Warrior as SJA for U.S. Central Command. This followed a position with USCENTCOM in 1992 as deputy SJA, where he was later deployed in support of relief operations in Somalia. In this assignment, he served as both the SJA and the plans and policy officer (J-5) for Joint Task Force Provide Relief. A recipient of several writing awards, Colonel Dunlap has written many articles on national security affairs, including "Technology and the Twenty-first-Century Battlefield" (*USASSI, 1999*), "The Law of Cyberwar" (*Cyberwar 2.0, 1998*), "21st Century Land Warfare: Four Dangerous Myths" (*Parameters*, 1997) and "What Kind of Marine Corps Is This?" (*Proceedings*, 1997). Currently, he is working with the BBC on a series about future conflicts.

Lieutenant Colonel Ronald V. Dutil, USMC, is U.S. Marine Corps attaché at the U.S. embassy in Paris (France). He assumed this position on May 4, 1999. Previously, from September 1996 to November 1998, he was NATO/Europe desk officer, strategy and plans division, plans, policies, and operations department at headquarters, U.S. Marine Corps. From July 1990 to June 1993, Lieutenant Colonel Dutil was assigned as an action officer, with the emerging issues branch (later renamed the strategic concepts branch), plans division, plans, policies, and operations department, U.S. Marine Corps headquarters.

He was also selected for the commandant of the Marine Corps fellowship program. In 1990, he obtained the degree of master of arts in international relations at The Fletcher School of Law and Diplomacy.

Admiral James O. Ellis Jr. is the commander in chief of U.S. Naval Forces in Europe and commander in chief of Allied Forces in Southern Europe. In 1991, he assumed command of USS *Abraham Lincoln* (*CVN 72*) and participated in Operation Desert Storm. In the past, he served as director for operations, plans, and policy on the staff of the commander in chief, U.S. Atlantic Fleet. In June 1995, Admiral Ellis assumed command of Carrier Group FIVE / Battle Force Seventh Fleet. In this capacity he led contingency response operations to both the Arabian Gulf and Taiwan Straits. In November 1996, he assumed duties as deputy chief of naval operations (plans, policy, and operations). From January to July 1999, Admiral Ellis served as NATO Joint Force commander for Operation Allied Force and commander of U.S. joint task force Noble Anvil, exercising command of U.S. and allied forces in Kosovo combat and humanitarian operations.

Lieutenant General Carlton W. Fulford, Jr. USMC is currently the director of the Joint Staff of the U.S. Marine Corps. From 1998 until 1999 he was commander, U.S. Marine Corps Forces Pacific, commanding general, Fleet Marine Force, Pacific, and commander, U.S. Marine Corps Bases, Pacific headquartered at Camp H. M. Smith, Hawaii. His most recent FMF assignments include commanding officer, Task Force Ripper during Operations Desert Shield and Desert Storms; commanding general, III MEF; and commanding general, 1 MEF. Lieutenant General Fulford completed several non-FMF assignments and served in Vietnam.

Brigadier General Wallace C. Gregson, USMC, currently serves as the director for Asian and Pacific Affairs in the Office of the Secretary of Defense for international security affairs. He was assistant deputy chief of staff for plans, policies, and operations, (strategy & plans), at Headquarters, USMC in Washington, D.C. Promoted to brigadier general in July 1996, he previously served as executive / military assistant to the director of intelligence, Washington, D.C. Brigadier General Gregson's Fleet Marine Force operational assignments include assistant operations officer (J-3A) of Unified Task Force Somalia during Operation Restore Hope and operations officer (G-3) of 1 Marine Expeditionary Force.

Major General Edward Hanlon Jr., USMC, is currently serving as the commanding general, Marine Corps Base, Camp Pendleton, California a position he assumed on 21 August 1998. From July 1996 until August 1998, he was director, Expeditionary Warfare Division (N85), Office of the Chief of Naval Operations, the Pentagon. He assumed this position following his promotion to major general in July 1996. His several assignments include deputy commander, Naval Striking and Support Forces, Southern Europe, Naples, Italy;

commanding officer of the 10th Marines, 2d Marine Division; fleet Marine officer, U.S. Atlantic Fleet; and assistant chief of staff for plans (G-5) and operations (G-3) at Headquarters Fleet Marine Force Europe in London, United Kingdom.

Senator John F. Kerry is currently in his third consecutive term (since his initial election in 1984) as United States senator from Massachusetts. He has been a leading voice in the Senate on a number of issues, including education, safety, environment, jobs, and health care and has sponsored important bills in these and other areas. In 1997 Senator Kerry authored his second book, *The New War: The Web of Crime That Threatens America's Security*, in which he discusses the threat of global crime organizations and the need for international collaboration to fight this new international threat. He is also the author of *The New Soldier*. Senator Kerry served in the Navy, becoming an officer on a gunboat in the Mekong Delta in Vietnam. He received a Silver Star, a Bronze Star, and three Purple Hearts for his service. Upon his return home, he became an active leader of the Vietnam Veterans against the War and a cofounder of the Vietnam Veterans of America. Before his election to the Senate, Senator Kerry served as lieutenant governor in Massachusetts (1982–84) and before that was assistant district attorney in Middlesex County (1976–82).

Dr. Andrew F. Krepinevich Jr. is executive director of the Center for Strategic and Budgetary Assessments (CSBA), an independent policy research institute established to promote innovative thinking about defense planning and investment strategies for the twenty-first century. Dr. Krepinevich also served as a member of the Department of Defense's National Defense Panel. He gained extensive planning experience in national security and technology policy through his work in the Department of Defense's Office of Net Assessment and by serving on the personal staff of three secretaries of defense. He has taught a wide variety of national security and defense policy-making courses while on the faculties of West Point, George Mason University, the Johns Hopkins University of Advanced International Studies, and Georgetown University. In 1993, following an Army career that spanned twenty-one years, Dr. Krepinevich retired from military service to assume the directorship of what is now CSBA.

General Charles C. Krulak, USMC (Ret.) served as the thirty-first commandant of the Marine Corps from 30 June 1995 until 30 June 1999. General Krulak has held a variety of command and staff positions, including commander of Marine Forces Pacific/commanding general, Fleet Marine Forces Pacific (1994–95); commanding general, Marine Corps Combat Development Command, Quantico (1992–94); and assistant deputy chief of staff for manpower and reserve affairs (Personnel Management/Personnel Procurement), Headquarters Marine Corps (1991–92). His experience includes commanding a platoon and two rifle companies during two tours of duty in Vietnam.

Vice Admiral Conrad C. Lautenbacher Jr., USN, is deputy chief of naval operations (resources, warfare, requirement, and assessments), a position he assumed in November 1997. From November 1996 until November 1997 he was director at the Office of Program Appraisal on the staff of the secretary of the navy. Vice Admiral Lautenbacher has served in a broad range of staff, command and operational billets. He served as special assistant secretary of the navy (Financial Management) and director of force structure, resources, and assessment (J-8) on the Joint Staff, where he contributed to the development of the Base Force and Bottom-Up Review. Vice Admiral Lautenbacher was also commander, Third Fleet, where he introduced integrated, joint and combined training concepts to the Pacific Fleet, prepared the Third Fleet to function as the core of a sea-based Joint Task Force, and developed the sea-based Battle Laboratory Initiative.

Rear Admiral Thomas F. Marfiak, USN, is the CEO/publisher of the U.S. Naval Institute, a position he assumed in August 1999. From 1997 to 1999, he was commandant of the National War College, National Defense University, located at Fort McNair, Washington, D.C. He served as director for plans and policy (J-5), U.S. Central Command. Before that he was director for plans, programs, and budgets for the Surface Warfare Division on the staff of the Chief of Naval Operations (1992–95). Previously, he served on the staff of the Chief of Naval Operations in strategy and plans and on the CNO's Executive Panel, where he was deputy director. He was also assigned as special assistant to the secretary on the immediate staff of the secretary of the navy and secretary of defense. Rear Admiral Marfiak has served at sea in both the Atlantic and Pacific theaters.

Captain Rosemary Bryant Mariner, USN (Ret.) is a research fellow at the University of Tennessee's Center for Study of War and Society and serves on the executive group of the secretary of the navy's personnel task-force. She was the chairman of the Joint Chiefs of Staff (CJCS) professor of Military Strategy for the National War College. Previously, she served on the Joint Staff where she conducted independent field assessments of the combatant commanders' preparedness to carry out their assigned missions. Captain Mariner was the first military woman to command an operational aviation squadron and to be selected for major aviation shore command. A nationally recognized expert on military women and gender integration, she is the author of several articles and commentaries, as well as of books and publications, including *Crossed Currents: Navy Women from WW1 to Tailhook, Women in the Military: An Unfinished Revolution, Tailspin,* and *Ground Zero: The Gender Wars in the Military.*

Mr. David Ochmanek is a senior defense analyst at the RAND Corporation, an association held from 1985 until 1993, and again since 1995. While at RAND, he has worked on assessments of the capabilities of U.S. conventional and strategic nuclear forces, arms control, defense planning, regional security, and national security strategy. From 1989 through 1992, he headed the National Security Strategies Program of RAND's project Air Force. From 1993 to 1995, he served as deputy assistant secretary of defense for strategy. Before joining RAND, Mr. Ochmanek was a member of the Foreign Service of the United States, serving from 1980 to 1985 in the Bureau of Politico-Military Affairs, U.S. Embassy Bonn, and the Bureau of European and Canadian Affairs. From 1973 to 1978, he was an officer in the USAF.

Mr. William D. O'Neil is vice president of the Center for Naval Analyses, where he directs a research division dealing with issues of requirements and technology for the entire range of systems for naval operations. He joined the government in 1969, serving as a technical adviser on the staff of the secretary of the navy. From 1973 to 1984, he worked in the Office of the Under Secretary of Defense for research and engineering, where he became head of the office dealing with naval systems of all kinds. In 1984 he joined Lockheed and for the next seven years worked in a variety of capacities, including chief of systems engineering for the F-22 advanced tactical fighter program and corporate director of strategic planning. He has occupied his current position at CNA since 1991.

Lieutenant Colonel Ralph Peters, USA, (Ret.) is an officer with over two decades of service. He was engaged in an examination of the future of warfare for the Army Staff. He served as a special assistant for strategic planning in the White House drug policy office, where he was able to continue his research into cultures in conflict. Previous positions include being commissioned into Military Intelligence and serving as a foreign area officer for Eurasia. He has spent many years overseas in numerous countries. Lieutenant Colonel Peters has published a book on strategy, *Fighting for the Future: Will America Triumph?* and dozens of articles on military theory, strategy, and the changing nature of conflict, which have helped shape military doctrine. Lieutenant Colonel Peters is also a novelist, several of whose ten books have been bestsellers.

Dr. Robert L. Pfaltzgraff Jr. is president of the Institute for Foreign Policy Analysis (IFPA) and Shelby Cullom Davis Professor of International Security Studies, The Fletcher School of Law and Diplomacy, Tufts University. Dr. Pfaltzgraff has taught at the University of Pennsylvania, at the College of Europe in Belgium, at the Foreign Service Institute, and at the National Defense College in Japan. He has served as a consultant to the National Security Council, the Department of Defense, the Department of State, and the U.S. Information Agency. His professional interests include U.S. foreign and national security policy; alliance policies and strategies; the interrelationships of political, economic, and defense policies; the implications of trends and projections of change in the emerging security environment; crisis management; and international relations theory. Dr. Pfaltzgraff writes and lectures widely in the United States and abroad. Some of his most recent publications include: *War in the Information Age* (coeditor) (1997); *Security in Southeastern Europe and the U.S.-Greek Relationship* (coeditor) (1997); *Contending Theories of International Relations* (coauthor) (1997).

Brigadier General Richard J. Quirk III, USA, is currently deputy commanding general, United States Army Intelligence Center and Fort Huachuca, Fort Huachuca, Azizona, a position he assumed in September 1999. From January 1997 until August 1999, he was director, Intelligence Directorate (J-2) at the United States Southern Command (USSOUTHCOM) in Miami, Florida. From 1995 to 1997, he served as chief, Command Support Group, Office of Military Affairs, Central Intelligence Agency, Washington, D.C. Previously, he served as commander, 525th Military Intelligence Brigade (Airborne) and before that deputy G-2 (Intelligence) for the 18th Airborne Corps at Fort Bragg, North Carolina. During Operations Desert Storm and Desert Shield in Saudi Arabia, he served as G-2 for the 24th Infantry Division (Mechanized).

Vice Admiral John Scott Redd, USN (Ret.) is the president and CEO of the NETSchool Corporation, a high technology education company headquartered in Atlanta, Georgia. He retired from active duty on 1 September 1998. He was director for strategic plans and policy (DJ-5) on the Joint Staff, a position he assumed in August 1996. He has served three tours on the staff of the Chief of Naval Operations, as well as two joint tours on the staff of the secretary of defense, as the assistant to the under secretary of defense for policy. He was the assistant and later the acting deputy chief of naval operations for plans, policy, and operations (N3/5). Vice Admiral Redd has had five operational commands. From 1994 to 1996 he commanded all U.S. Naval Forces in the Central Command theater of operations. In 1995, he became also commander of the Fifth Fleet.

Mr. Thomas Ricks covers the military for the *Washington Post*. Until the end of 1999 he covered the same subject for the *Wall Street Journal*. He has reported on U.S. military activities in Somalia, Haiti, Korea, Bosnia, Macedonia, Kuwait, the Persian Gulf, and elsewhere. His major articles have looked at the changed nature of peacekeeping (1992), nonlethal weapons (1993), the breakup of the old military-industrial complex (1993), the revolution in military affairs (1994), and the U.S. Army's preparation for and entry into Bosnia (1995). He is author of the book *Making the Corps*, which won the Washington Monthly's "Political Book of the Year" award. He also has written on defense matters for the *Atlantic Monthly* and other publications. Mr. Ricks was the editor for national security in the *Wall Street Journal*'s Washington bureau. Before that, he reported for the *Wall Street Journal* from Miami, covering a range of security issues, including the invasion of Grenada.

Professor Harvey M. Sapolsky is professor of public policy and director of the security studies program at the Massachusetts Institute of Technology (MIT). He has worked in a number of public policy areas, notably health, science, and defense, where he examines the effects of technical change, institutional structures, and bureaucratic politics on policy outcomes. In defense he has served as a consultant to the Commission on Government Procurement, the Office of the Secretary of Defense, the Naval War College, the Office of Naval Research, the RAND Corporation, and the Applied Physics Laboratory at Johns Hopkins. He is currently focusing his research on military innovation, the constraints on U.S. foreign interventions, the politics of advice, and the restructuring of defense industries in the US and Europe. Professor Sapolsky's books include *Science and the Navy, Consuming Fears,* and *The American Blood Supply.*

Professor Richard H. Shultz Jr. has been since 1988 director of the International Security Studies Program and since 1983 associate professor of international politics at The Fletcher School of Law and Diplomacy, Tufts University. Professor Shultz was formerly Olin Distinguished Professor of National Security Studies, U.S. Military Academy, Secretary of the Navy Senior Research Fellow at the U.S. Naval War College, and research fellow, Hoover Institution on War, Revolution, and Peace, Stanford University. During the period of 1998 to 1999, he was the recipient of the Brigadier General H. L. Oppenheimer Chair of Warfighting Strategy, U.S. Marine Corps University. Professor Shultz has authored, co-authored, edited, and co-edited numerous books, articles, monographs, and reports. His most recent book *The Secret War Against Hanoi: Kennedy and Johnson's Use of Spies, Saboteurs, and Covert Warriors in North Vietnam* was published in November 1999.

Mr. Frederick C. Smith was nominated, for the year August 1999–July 2000, visiting professor at the United States Naval Academy. From May 1994 until July 1999, he served as principal deputy assistant secretary of defense for international security affairs. Before this appointment, Mr. Smith served as director of the Bosnia Task Force, where he helped formulate U.S. policy and coordinate military actions. Between 1982 and 1988, he was the director for policy analysis and responsible for analyzing international political, military, and economic issues; reviewing U.S. strategy and military planning; making recommendations for U.S. force structure; and providing guidance on U.S. force movements and military operations. At the Pentagon, as Director for Near Eastern and South Asian Affairs (1988–1994), Mr. Smith was responsible for U.S. defense policy in Northern Africa, the Middle East, Persian Gulf, and South Asia. He was one of the key players at the Department of Defense during Operations Desert Shield and Desert Storm.

Lieutenant General Martin R. Steele, USMC (Ret.) is the President and CEO of the Intrepid Sea-Air-Space Museum in New York City. He retired from active duty in the Marine Corps on 1 August 1999 from the position of deputy chief of staff for plans, policies, and operations, Headquarters Marine Corps, Washington, D.C., which he had assumed in February 1997. Previously, he served as the director for strategic planning and policy, J-5, USCINCPAC, Camp H. M. Smith in Hawaii. He has served in various command positions, including commanding general, Marine Corps Base, and director, Warfighting Development Integration Division, both in Quantico, Virginia. During Operation Desert Shield and Desert Storm, he served as G-3 Marcent (FWD) aboard the USS *Blue Ridge*. He also served in combat in Vietnam.

Dr. Susan L. Woodward is a senior research fellow at the Conflict, Security, and Development Group at the Center for Defense Studies, King's College, London. She worked in the Foreign Policy Studies Program at the Brookings Institution, from 1990 until 1999. Before joining Brookings, Dr. Woodward was a national fellow at the Hoover Institution; associate professor of political science at Yale University; and instructor at Williams College, Mount Holyoke College, and Northwestern University. She has also been an adjunct professor at George Washington University, Georgetown University, and the Johns Hopkins University School of Advanced International Studies. She has held fellowships at Harvard, Stanford, and Princeton Universities, and is a member of the Council on Foreign Relations. In addition, she serves on the board of directors of the National Council for Eurasian and East European Research and of Women in International Security. She was chair of the Committee on the Status of Women of the American Political Science Association and has testified frequently before congressional committees on policy toward war and peace in Bosnia. She has written on a variety of subjects, most recently on the Balkans. She is the author of *The Balkan Tragedy: Chaos and Dissolution after the Cold War* and *Socialist Unemployment: The Political Economy of Yugoslavia, 1945–1990*.

Colonel Stephen E. Wright, USAF, is currently chief for capabilities and development division, at the Air Combat Command Headquarters in Langley, Virginia. He was national defense fellow in the International Security Studies Program at The Fletcher School of Law and Diplomacy, Tufts University, during the academic year 1997–98. Previously, Colonel Wright completed back-to-back command tours at Dyess Air Force Base, Texas, as commander of, first, the 9th Bomb Squadron, and then the 28th Bomb Squadron. He also completed a staff tour at Headquarters, Eighth Air Force, serving as the air operations strategist responsible for regional operational planning and air operations center functions.

responses and experimentation. Because the timing of such interventions is late in the process of a state's disintegration, it occurs only after the local means to enable a brief external intervention and to allow outsiders to leave no longer exist. And even when the mission is only disaster relief, to provide food and shelter temporarily, and when this can be handled largely by non-governmental organizations, *soldiers are needed* because one of the two characteristics of these conflicts is the state's loss of a monopoly over the use of force and the uncontrolled proliferation of weapons and people willing to use them without authority.

The problem of a nonfunctioning state, for both citizens and intervenors, is first and foremost physical security and lawlessness. In the absence of a standing United Nations force or of rapid reaction forces assigned to regional organizations, the need for soldiers and the accompanying logistics and communications sends the crisis directly to the door of the very states—the major powers, and above all the United States—who earlier declined action on the grounds that troops should only be sent when there is a vital national interest.

Disproportion Number Three: Characteristics of Failed States versus Our Current Preparation

There is a great disparity between the characteristics of these cases and what we are organized and prepared (and even preparing) to do. The key characteristic of these cases is the decay and collapse of state authority, but to act, actors in the international community (whether states, diplomats, international organizations, or militaries) need counterparts—people who are organized as they are, as sovereign powers, with authority and capacity to implement agreements made, and operating within a law-bound state apparatus. We look for them by habit, by bureaucratic and statutory rules, and by the wish to preserve consent and minimize the need for coercion. Without such accountable counterparts, intervention risks becoming occupation, assistance gives way to domination, and relief becomes nation building.

The disparity between threat and interest thus translates into a serious operational problem. With insufficient national or collective interest to dictate a result, we intervene only when the conditions on the ground permit nothing else. But the political conditions at home that led to intervention do not adjust. The counterparts we seek are scarce or nonexistent, while the reluctance to be interventionist remains.

The implementation of the Dayton accords in Bosnia in 1996–97 is an excellent example. The struggle for implementation in the first two years focused on getting the parties to "cooperate" with the agreements they signed, accusing them of "lack of political will" when they did otherwise. Although many politicians had no intention of implementing those parts of the accords with which they did not agree (and Bosnian Serb leaders had not even been permitted to sign the accords and thus felt freer to ignore provisions they contested), officials in the military and civilian operations on the ground were more often faced with the problem of finding someone in authority to vation, and gross violations of human rights; refugees flooding onto the shores of rich countries or threatening to destabilize surrounding countries. It is these external consequences that attract our attention, not the facts of internal turmoil alone. They begin to affect us directly only as violations of our moral conscience, of international law and conventions, of the stability needed for trade and investment, or of risks to the stability of countries that do fall within our strategic purview.

Thus, we only begin to contemplate action when the state has already failed and when internal conflicts have reached the point of no return. That is, we consider intervention in a context that has two characteristics: (1) where there is no sovereign authority, or there is a raging contest over who is sovereign, and (2) where the state's legitimate monopoly over the use of force and its ability to enforce its authority and laws are gone, challenged by or abandoned to rival armies, paramilitaries, criminal networks, bandits, and armed street gangs.

Nonetheless, our response has *not* been to the problem of state disintegration or to its causes, but to the external consequences that affect us. We respond in humanitarian, not political terms; as an emergency to be ended quickly, not a political collapse to be reversed and aided, let alone prevented; and as a problem to be contained, not to be solved. Our lack of perceived strategic interest reinforces the inclination to respond in terms of disaster relief and the rules governing such relief—yielding to public pressure to provide charity and save lives, protected by international norms that permit legitimate intervention, such as violations of humanitarian law.

The lack of sufficient national interest to intervene early thus continues with intervention itself, in a reluctance to violate norms of sovereignty and take responsibility for the problem. This caution often contributes further delay because the obligatory request to intervene, when addressed to nominal rulers who do not want to undermine their authority further by acknowledging their need for assistance, is often rejected several times over. Then, if intervention occurs, it is also structured as much as possible in terms of *consent*, to reduce the risk of casualties, ensure ease of access, identify legal responsibility for costs and damages, and add an ounce of safe measure. Even when Chapter 7 legitimation is invoked by the United Nations Security Council, declaring the interests of global security to override sovereignty, intervening powers do their best to limit intervention, to work with persons they recognize as sovereign authorities, and to operate under *rules* developed for peacekeeping operations.

In contrast to peacekeeping operations or disaster relief, however, the immediate cause of the crisis is a collapse of authority or a contest among rival factions in which none is likely to prevail. Rules of intervention aimed at protecting sovereignty under such political conditions have the opposite effect, making the intervenors participants in the political contest without the resources or mandate to be strategic and to influence the outcome. With rules designed for other situations, the intervention tends to be driven by ad hoc